V&R Academic

Reformed Historical Theology

Edited by
Herman J. Selderhuis

in Co-operation with
Emidio Campi, Irene Dingel, Elsie Anne McKee,
Richard Muller, Risto Saarinen, and Carl Trueman

Volume 43

Jon Balserak / Jim West (eds.)

From Zwingli to Amyraut

Exploring the Growth
of European Reformed Traditions

Vandenhoeck & Ruprecht

Bibliographic information published by the Deutsche Nationalbibliothek
The Deutsche Nationalbibliothek lists this publication in the Deutsche Nationalbibliografie;
detailed bibliographic data available online: http://dnb.d-nb.de.

ISSN 2198-8226
ISBN 978-3-525-55279-7

You can find alternative editions of this book and additional material on our Website: www.v-r.de

Typesetting by Konrad Triltsch GmbH, Ochsenfurt
Printed and bound by Hubert & Co GmbH & Co. KG, Robert-Bosch-Breite 6, D-37079 Göttingen

Printed on aging-resistant paper.

Contents

Jon Balserak / Jim West

Editorial Preface

Zwingli to Amyraut:
Exploring the Growth of European Reformed Traditions

As we approach 2017, the editors of this volume sought to collect essays which explored a wide range of subjects. In particular, we wanted to take the opportunity provided by the occasion of this year, which marks the 500th anniversary of the German monk and reformer, Martin Luther, posting his 95 theses on October 31 1517, to probe less-explored corners of the Reformation. To be sure, Martin Luther himself receives attention in this volume. But our aim here is really to take the occasion provided by the increased attention paid to the Reformation during this year to explore other theologians, movements, and ideas. The expanding of the scholarly mind and opening up of new vistas often overshadowed by larger figures, like Luther, can only be good for the study of the Reformation and Early Modern era.

This volume explores a number of themes. On the Bible, exegesis, translation, and the Republic of Letters, one finds in the chapters below essays such as Emidio Campi's which examines Giovanni Diodati (1576–1649), translator of the Bible into Italian. Hywel Clifford has also contributed an essay that looks at the "'Ancient Jewish Church': the anti-Unitarian exegetical polemics of Peter Allix." Both of these chapters examine the cutting-edge work done in the Early Modern era on sacred texts. Pushing the boundaries of this theme, two contributions look at the relationships that formed around texts. Jim West's "Zwingli and Bullinger Through the Lens of Letters" looks at the interaction between Zwingli and his protégé as seen through previously-untranslated letters. Likewise, Rebecca A. Giselbrecht's "Cliché or Piety: Heinrich Bullinger and Women in Alsace" explores correspondence between Heinrich Bullinger and a number of women, most notably Anna Alexandria zu Rappoltstein and Elisabeth von Heideck.

Various aspects of Christian soteriology also receive attention. Stefan Lindholm works carefully and quite meticulously through the scholastic element of Christology in Reformed thought in his "Reformed Scholastics Christology: A Preliminary Sketch." Alan C. Clifford explores the rise and development of Amyraldian soteriology in the Continent and the British Isles in "Amyraldian Soteriology And Reformed–Lutheran rapprochement." And Joe Mock considers

Bullinger's understanding of the Lord's Supper and compares it to that of many of Bullinger's own contemporaries.

Finally a number of broad, sweeping themes that emerge during the Reformation receive the notice they merit in this collection of essays. Jordan Ballor has written on the "Reformation's Constantinian Moment," examining "Luther's Futile Appeal to Imperial Authority" in his efforts to reform the Christian church. Pierrick Hildebrand examines the covenant in a chapter entitled, "Zwingli's Covenantal Turn." And Jon Balserak looks, in "Inventing The Prophet; Vermigli, Melanchthon, and Calvin on The Extraordinary Reformer," at the category of prophecy and the development, by some thinkers, of a new type or class of prophet.

Though only so much can be accomplished in a small volume such as this, it is the hope of the editors that the contributions we have collected together here will contribute to the ever-growing interest in a wider-range of Reformation-oriented topics.

We certainly wish to thank our colleagues for their excellent and informative work and we also wish to thank Herman Selderhuis for including this collection in the present series of very highly regarded books. Naturally, we are also happy to thank our publisher, Vandenhoeck and Ruprecht.

We dedicate this work to the named and unnamed, known and unknown, remembered and forgotten Reformers whose efforts were and remain as significant to the course of the Reformation's development as Luther's and Calvin's and Zwingli's.

Jon Balserak
Jim West

Jordan J. Ballor

The Reformation's Constantinian Moment: The Significance of Luther's Futile Appeal to Imperial Authority

When it became clear to Martin Luther that the prospects for reform within the clerical hierarchy were unlikely, Luther appealed to civil authorities, and particularly the emperor, to reestablish their sacred authority and work for the reform of the church. When viewed within the context of the centuries-long developments preceding his action, it becomes apparent that Luther was advocating for a reversal of what Harold J. Berman has called "the Papal Revolution," in which "the emperor's constitutional role within the church was greatly reduced; he became a mere layman" (1983, 484).

The significance of a "Constantinian moment" in the early years of the Reformation, specifically between Luther's publication of the 95 Theses in 1517 and the Diet of Worms in 1521, is not only that an appeal to the emperor to reassert a long-departed authority in the sacred sphere was plausible, or even possible. The failure of such an appeal illustrates decisively that coinciding with the evaporation of imperial authority in the church was a diffusion of power in the civil sphere as well. The Holy Roman Emperor was increasingly constrained by legal, political, and economic realities in the wake of the Papal Revolution. Otto von Gierke describes the decline of imperial prestige through the early modern period: "It was as but a lifeless phantom that the 'imperium mundi' was dragged along by the imperialistic publicists" (1966, 262; see also Kuyper: 2016, 377).

Even by the dawn of the sixteenth century, princely power was gaining ground against imperial authority as well as feudal sovereignty:

> Everywhere in Europe, however, royal power over the feudal nobility was increasing, secular authority was asserting itself against ecclesiastical authority, and territorial loyalties were intensifying. Everywhere in Europe strong voices were advocating reduction of ecclesiastical power and reformation of both church and state. Everywhere the cities were seeking greater autonomy. (Berman: 2003, 38)

The dynamics of Luther's appeals between 1517 and 1521 evince this new situation. In these years Luther shifts between the established authorities of pope and emperor, seeking a solution to the religious and economic oppression of the

German people. These appeals were to be futile, not only because of recalcitrant religious and theological sensibilities (accompanied by economic incentives), but also because of developments within the political and legal landscape over the previous five hundred years.

The failure of Luther's appeals only became apparent in 1521 with the clear decision of Emperor Charles V at the Diet of Worms to support the papacy and declare Luther to be a heretical outlaw. Luther had appealed to Charles V to act as Constantine had done, to convene a free council and to reform the church. The result of Luther's failure was something new, however. After 1521 there was an increasing rise to prominence of the "lesser" magistrate, territorial sovereignty, and the role of Christian conscience in spurring individual acts of responsibility. Luther's appeal to the emperor, because it was grounded in the realities of the legal environment of his time rather than being a principled argument from divine ideals about the particular form of civil order, inherently allowed for adaptation and development under new circumstances. When stymied by both pope and emperor, Luther's new targets as agents for religious reform were Christian princes and magistrates, as well as other laypersons more broadly. Where the medieval struggles between church and state had largely been fought between popes and emperors (and their proxies), Luther's reform became a legal revolution in its own right by expanding the field of players to include princes as well as university administrators, abbots, city councils, burgomasters, parents, and, in the end, individual Christians and their consciences.

This essay will examine in closer detail the dynamics of the period between 1517 and 1521 and the corresponding "Constantinian moment," as it might be called, in which Luther held out real hope for religious reform led by the Holy Roman Emperor. Historiography often tends to skip over this revealing period, in part because the futility of such appeals is readily apparent after the fact. What is really significant for many is the new situation that arises after 1521. But it is also revealing that the conditions for the legal and religious revolution that would take greater shape after 1521 were already in place beforehand. As Berman describes Luther during this period:

> At first he hoped that the Roman Catholic hierarchy itself would accept his new teaching. His first appeal was, in effect, to the pope himself. When he found no support from Rome, he turned to the emperor and to the imperial nobility for help. In this, too, he was unsuccessful. When the emperor outlawed him, his own prince protected him but did not endorse his views. (2003, 48)

John Witte Jr. observes that:

> Luther had, at first, hoped that the emperor would endorse the Reformation, and accordingly included in his early writings some lofty panegyrics on the imperial au-

thorities of the Holy Roman Empire of his day and of the Christian Roman Empire of a millennium before. (2002, 110)

Likewise James M. Estes writes that even before Luther:

church reformers, having lost their hope for a general reform of the church by pope and council, and knowing that the emperor could not deliver a national reform, devoted themselves instead to efforts to local reforms carried out under the authority of the princes, whom they encouraged in the belief that they were responsible for the spiritual as well as the temporal welfare of their subjects. (2005, 3)

When seen in this light, Luther's appeal to the emperor is the last and ultimately futile attempt to employ older institutions (the papacy, councils, the empire) to address the new challenges of religious reform. As Estes puts it:

Any assessment of Luther's thought on the role of secular rulers in ecclesiastical reform has to begin with the observation that it was only after more than two years of public effort on behalf of reform that Luther made his decision to invoke the aid of princes and nobles. (2005, 7)

Berman, Witte, and Estes cover what I have called the "Constantinian moment" in these brief sentences; other surveys often skip over this pivotal period and emphasize the novelty of later developments in Lutheran political thought. Luise Schorn-Schütte, for instance, locates the origins of Lutheran political thought within the context of conflict between Charles V and the imperial princes, but identifies the "early phase" of this development with the period 1529–1550 (2016, 108).

After briefly sketching the larger context of the strife between pope and emperor leading up to Luther's early work, I will examine two pivotal works from 1520 in turn. The first of these, *On the Papacy in Rome* (1520a), is a broadside by Luther against the corruptions of the papacy and its pretensions to temporal as well as spiritual supremacy (1970, 55–104). The second, Luther's address *To the Christian Nobility* (1520b), is Luther's substantive appeal to the emperor as well as the rest of the German nobility on the basis of these concerns about the papacy (1966, 123–217). Luther's efforts in this period, culminating in the finding against him by the emperor at Worms in 1521, form the basis of transition from an older model of pope against emperor to a new dynamic in the modern relationship between church and state.

The Emperor and the Papal Revolution

For Harold J. Berman, the Papal Revolution of 1075–1120 represents the inauguration of the first truly Western system of law: canon law. Berman's conception of revolution is "total," in the sense that such revolutions

> involved not only the creation of new forms of government but also new structures of social and economic relations, new structures of relations between church and state, and new structures of law, as well as new visions of the community, new perspectives on history, and new sets of universal beliefs and values. (1983, 20)

The Gregorian Reform, or the Papal Revolution, is the first legal revolution in the West (Berman identifies five others: the German [Lutheran] Revolution of the sixteenth century; the English Revolution of the seventeenth century; in the eighteenth century, the American Revolution and the French Revolution; and the Russian Revolution of the early twentieth century). Canon law was developed under Gregory VII as a response to the ecclesiastical and political challenges of his time. Thus Gregory

> denounced the imperial and royal law by which the Church had been governed—laws which permitted bishops and priests to be appointed to their posts by the secular authorities, church offices to be bought and sold, and the clergy to marry. (Berman: 1983, 21)

The Papal Revolution was, in this sense, a revolution against the prevailing authority of secular figures, including emperors, kings, and princes. The Papal Revolution displaced secular authorities from the church, creating a binary between sacred and secular realms. After the conversion of Constantine and the subsequent Christianization of the empire under Theodosius in the fourth century, the split between the Western and Eastern portions of the Roman empire limited the territory of Western emperors until the decline of the Western empire in the fifth century.

Afterwards, the preeminent ruler in the Christian West eventually came again to be known as the emperor, but the geographic jurisdiction of this authority was limited to the Latin West, and the kind of authority enjoyed by this figure was also different from his ancient counterparts. The Western empire

> was not a territorial entity but was the sphere of authority—the *imperium*—of the person of the emperor, who represented the religious unity of Western Christendom and its military resistance to Norse, Arab, Slavic, and Magyar attacks. (Berman: 1983, 483)

As Berman describes it:

> In the twelfth century, the empire itself came to be called, for the first time, the Roman Empire; by then, however, papal supremacy over the church had been established, and

the word 'Roman' in the title of the empire symbolized its political and legal unity and authority in the secular sphere. (Only in the thirteenth century did it come to be called the Holy Roman Empire and, finally, in the fifteenth century, the Holy Roman Empire of the German Nation.) (1983, 483)

Two features of the imperial office after the Papal Revolution are particularly noteworthy. First, the emperor's authority was essentially secularized. Thus, writes Berman:

> The Papal Revolution significantly altered the nature of the imperial office, and with it the scope and character of imperial law. On the one hand, the emperor's constitutional role within the church was greatly reduced; he became a mere layman, albeit a powerful one since bishops and abbots, though no longer invested by him with their ecclesiastical powers, remained his feudal vassals. (1983, 484)

Second, although Berman traces the origin of secular statecraft to this limitation of the emperor's authority to the civil realm, it is also the case that as the centuries passed the imperial office became more constrained even within the context of civil authority. As popes and emperors vied for supremacy, princes and other nobles mediated between the two and became increasingly independent (Berman: 1983, 485). James M. Estes observes that during the developments of the fifteenth century as conciliarism was on the retreat,

> the popes joined hands with the crowned heads of Europe to consolidate its victory over the conciliar movement. In Germany this meant that, in return for declarations of support for papal supremacy in the church, the popes formally conceded to many German territorial rulers, starting with the emperor himself in his Austrian hereditary lands, those rights in ecclesiastical affairs that they had already assumed or were attempting to assume for themselves. (2005, 3)

So the emperor did enjoy some ecclesiastical authority, but it was not primarily due to his imperial office but rather connected to his territorial holdings.

Berman notes at the dawn of the sixteenth century:

> Everywhere in Europe, however, royal power over the feudal nobility was increasing, secular authority was asserting itself against ecclesiastical authority, and territorial loyalties were intensifying. Everywhere in Europe strong voices were advocating reduction of ecclesiastical power and reformation of both church and state. Everywhere the cities were seeking greater autonomy. (2003, 38).

The emperor was not determined by genealogical succession, but was rather elected by a select group of nobles. Thus, "the emperor became wholly dependent on the dukes and other princes of the empire for his election" (Berman: 1983, 485).[1] It was to this group, the emperor as well as his increasingly powerful

---

1 See also Witte, "The law of the Holy Roman Emperor was increasingly subject to the local control of the German princes, cities, and estates.... But in circa 1500 neither the Holy Roman

imperial electors and broader nobility, that Luther would address his appeal in 1520: "To His Most Illustrious, Most Mighty, and Imperial Majesty, and to the Christian Nobility of the German Nation" (1966, 124). But earlier that same year, Luther would lay out his complaint against the papacy in a scathing tract, *On the Papacy in Rome.*

On the Papacy in Rome

Luther's publication of his theses against indulgences in 1517 inaugurated a flurry of publishing activity. Defenders of the papacy would oppose Luther with treatises, and Luther would take up the pen to answer. 1520 was a particularly active year in which Luther, "published five books that offered a platform for reforming Christendom" (Hendrix: 2015, 85). Luther wrote treatises on good works, the papacy, the civil authorities, the "Babylonian captivity" of the church, and Christian liberty. Although these works share common concerns, *On the Papacy in Rome* and the address *To the Christian Nobility* deal more directly with church and civil political realities, and thus are worth close attention in dealing with the question of the relationship between pope and emperor.

On the Papacy in Rome is Luther's response to an attack by Augustin von Alveldt (1480–c. 1535), a Franciscan at Leipzig, who had written both a Latin (1520a) and later a vernacular (1520b) defense of the divine institution of the papacy (see also Hendrix: 2015, 87). Luther took up the question, "*Whether the papacy in Rome, possessing the actual power over all of Christendom, as they say, is derived from divine or from human order*" and the corresponding issue, "whether it would be a Christian statement to say that all other Christians in the whole world are heretics and schismatics" who, despite unity in sacramental practice and confession of faith, "honor the pope without spending money for the confirmation of their bishops and priests" (1970, 57–58).

Among the arguments that Luther takes on and rejects is what he calls an argument from "natural reason," which posits that any social body must have a single head (1970, 62). It was this logic that led to the conflict between the pope and emperor as each strove for primacy, to be the only head of Christendom to which all others must be subjected.

Luther makes both a theological and an empirical argument against this view. Theologically, Luther asserts that Christ is the single head of his body, and that his lordship over all the earth must be distinguished from his headship over those to whom he is bound organically and spiritually. Luther thus distinguishes be-

---

Emperor nor any of these local princes or city councils could match the power or the prestige of the Church and its canon law" (2002, 34).

tween "spiritual" and "material" unity, finding that in the former case, such unity as it exists is found in Christ as head of the church. But this church is not understood as institutionally or externally unified. Rather:

> This community or assembly means all those who live in true faith, hope, and love. Thus the essence, life, and nature of Christendom is not a physical assembly, but an assembly of hearts in one faith. (Luther: 1970, 65)

In terms of material or temporal unity, however, Luther asks:

> How many principalities, castles, cities, and families can be found where two brothers or lords rule with equal power? Even the Roman Empire and many other empires in the world for a long time governed themselves very well without a single head! (1970, 64).

Luther may be referring here to the Roman polity as divided between eastern and western empires, or the even more distant time of the Roman republic, which indeed was not politically unified under a single political ruler. He also points positively to contemporary examples and in reference to the Swiss confederacy he wonders, "How do the Swiss govern themselves in our own time?" (Luther: 1970, 64). The conclusion from all this is that

> there is no single overlord in worldly regiment since we are all one human race and have come from one father, Adam. The kingdom of France has its king; Hungary, Poland, Denmark each have their own. But they all are still one people of the worldly estate within Christendom, even though they do not have a single head; nor does this cause these kingdoms to disintegrate. (Luther: 1970, 64)

Luther likewise makes the case for the diversity of church political forms by appealing to churches outside of Roman influence that must still be considered churches.

In this way Luther contradicts the claim of natural reason that all bodies, whether civil or ecclesiastical, must be united under a single head. The significance of this is that while Luther accepts the office of Holy Roman Emperor, he does not view it as a divinely mandated office. Neither does he grant the papacy an ontic status superior to that of civil authority.[2] While it may be politically appropriate and expedient in a particular time and place to have an emperor, as it might also theoretically be possible to have a pope if understood rightly, it is not a divinely ordained or required institution. Different times and places require different forms of government: "Many countries have many customs" (Luther: 1970, 75).

---

2 In this way Luther's argument upsets the medieval "Dionysian" account of reality that holds the spiritual authority as a necessary mediator between God and temporal sovereigns. Here Luther anticipates significant later developments in Protestant political thought (see Kirby: 2007, 68; and Kirby: 2004, 291–304).

In Luther's distinction between the spiritual and material aspects of human existence, we have an early expression of Luther's *zwei Reiche lehre*, his doctrine of the two kingdoms, articulated within the context of his ecclesiology:

> Therefore, for the sake of better understanding and brevity, we shall call the two churches by two distinct names. The first, which is natural, basic, essential, and true, we shall call 'spiritual, internal Christendom.' The second, which is man-made and external, we shall call 'physical, external Christendom.' Not that we want to separate them from each other; rather, it is just as if I were talking about a man and called him 'spiritual' according to his soul, and 'physical' according to his body, or as the Apostle is accustomed to speak of an 'internal' and 'external' man. (1970, 70)

The two kingdoms relate to the spiritual and material aspects of human beings, respectively.

A key feature of the papacy's corruption, for Luther, is its pretentions to rule not only in the spiritual but also in the temporal, material realm. Speaking spiritually, "The head must instill life. That is why it is clear that on earth there is no head of spiritual Christendom other than Christ alone" (Luther: 1970, 72). But not only has the papacy arrogated spiritual supremacy to itself; it has also aimed at temporal dominion and, in particular, economic advantage:

> Why then does the Roman see so furiously desire the whole world? Why did it steal and rob country, city, indeed, principalities and kingdoms, and now dares to produce, ordain, dismiss, and change as it pleases all kings and princes, as if it were the Antichrist? (Luther: 1970, 84)

Neither pope nor emperor rule as a single head over Christendom by divine right: "all of Christendom has no other head than Christ, even on earth, because it has no other name than the one derived from Christ" (Luther: 1970, 68). The offices of pope and emperor must be understood, then, as providential ordinations, either of judgment or mercy, which have particular responsibilities and duties defined by human convention. The natural conclusion for Luther is that where ecclesiastical authorities, and the papacy in particular, have proven unable to reform, the civil authorities would take up the responsibility for reform. The spiritual and economic oppression of the German people is such that, "if the German princes and the nobles do not do something about it soon, and with decisive courage, Germany will be desolated or forced to devour itself" (Luther: 1970, 60). Luther concludes with a call for "kings, princes, and all the nobles" to expel Roman influence from Germany, and cease to, "let such a horrible disgrace of Christendom gain the upper hand. Yet they see that the people in Rome think of nothing but becoming more and more senseless and increasing all misery, so that there is no more hope on earth except with worldly power" (1970, 103). These concerns presage those developed in Luther's subsequent appeal to Charles V and the German nobility.

To the Christian Nobility

To say that the legal situation in Germany at this time was complex would be something of an understatement. As Berman summarizes the context:

> In the year 1521, the Holy Roman Empire of the German Nation consisted, in hierarchical order, of the emperor, the seven prince-electors, 50 archbishops and bishops, 83 ecclesiastical prelates (chiefly abbots and abbesses), 31 secular princes, 138 counts and lords, and representatives of 85 imperial free cities—almost 400 political jurisdictions in all. (2003, 36)

Charles V had acceded to the imperial throne in June of 1519, and Luther's appeal indicates a measure of hopefulness that the new emperor would be willing to take on the difficult demands of religious reform. "God has given us a young man of noble birth as head of state, and in him has awakened great hopes of good in many hearts," writes Luther, "Presented with such an opportunity we ought to apply ourselves and use this time of grace profitably" (1966, 125). Luther goes on to note the example of previous emperors who had valiantly attempted, but ultimately failed, to undo papal tyranny. Recognizing that the practical prospects for reform seemed dim, Luther encourages Charles to be faithful according to faith in God rather than relying on human reason:

> I fear that this is why the good emperors Frederick I and Frederick II and many other German emperors were in former times shamefully oppressed and trodden underfoot by the popes, although all the world feared the emperors. It may be that they relied on their own might more than on God, and therefore had to fall. (1966, 125)

Luther locates the responsibility of the Christian nobility, including the emperor, to reform religion in the common calling of Christians to defend and promote the gospel. Thus, says Luther, "it is the duty of every Christian to espouse the cause of the faith, to understand and defend it, and to denounce every error" (1966, 131). Because the princes and emperor bear the sword of temporal justice, they are to use their power in service of Christ and his kingdom:

> everyone must benefit and serve every other by means of his own work or office so that in this way many kinds of work may be done for the bodily and spiritual welfare of the community, just as all the members of the body serve one another. (Luther: 1966, 130)

This is as true for the cobbler as it is for the emperor.

By virtue of the Christian emperor's spiritual membership in the church, the temporal power has been given a spiritual significance and responsibility. In this way:

> Inasmuch as the temporal power has become a member of the Christian body it is a spiritual estate, even though its work is physical. Therefore, its work should extend without hindrance to all the members of the whole body to punish and use force

> whenever guilt deserves or necessity demands, without regard to whether the culprit is pope, bishop, or priest. (Luther: 1966, 131)

In this treatise, Luther expresses hope not only that the emperor will act, with the support of the rest of the Christian nobility, but that he will do so in accordance with the precedents set by previous Christian emperors. Constantine is held up as a model for Charles V, as Luther observes

> the Council of Nicaea, the most famous of all councils, was neither called nor confirmed by the bishop of Rome, but by the emperor Constantine. Many other emperors after him have done the same, and yet these councils were the most Christian of all. (1966, 137)

On this basis the new emperor should act in his own time, as

> when necessity demands it, and the pope is an offense to Christendom, the first man who is able should, as a true member of the whole body, do what he can to bring about a truly free council. No one can do this so well as the temporal authorities, especially since they are also fellow-Christians, fellow-priests, fellow-members of the spiritual estate, fellow-lords over all things. (Luther: 1966, 137)

Echoing the complaints of economic injustice and spiritual abuse he had described in *On the Papacy in Rome*, Luther wonders:

> How is it that we Germans must put up with such robbery and extortion of our goods at the hands of the pope? If the kingdom of France has prevented it, why do we Germans let them make such fools and apes of us? We could put up with all this if they stole only our property, but they lay waste to the churches in so doing, rob Christ's sheep of their true shepherds, and debase the worship and word of God. (1966, 142)

This is an outrage that the emperor and princes should neither tolerate nor allow to continue.

Thus, urges Luther:

> the German nation, bishops and princes, should consider that they, too, are Christians. They should rule the people entrusted to them in temporal and spiritual matters and protect them from these rapacious wolves in sheep's clothing who pretend to be their shepherds and rulers. (1966, 144–145)

Although he is not optimistic about the worldly prospects for success, Luther is committed to remaining true to what he sees as his primary responsibility as a theologian: faithful exposition and application of the Word of God (Hendrix: 2015, 48, 66). Luther vows, "I shall sing my fool's song through to the end and say, so far as I am able, what could and should be done, either by the temporal authority or by a general council" (1966, 156).

In the second half of the treatise, Luther moves from general complaints and appeals for religious reform to specific issues and proposals. In each case the remedy is clear: the temporal authorities, and above all the emperor, need to act:

Every prince, every noble, every city should henceforth forbid their subjects to pay annates to Rome and should abolish them entirely. (Luther: 1966, 156–157)

The Christian nobility should set itself against the pope as against a common enemy and destroyer of Christendom for the salvation of the poor souls who perish because of this tyranny. (Luther: 1966, 158)

An imperial law should be issued that no bishop's cloak and no confirmation of any dignity whatsoever shall henceforth be secured from Rome, but that the ordinance of the most holy and famous Council of Nicaea be restored. (Luther: 1966, 158)

The temporal authorities, therefore, should not permit sentences of excommunication and exile to be passed where faith and morality are not involved. (Luther: 1966, 160)

In the end, concludes Luther, "the emperor and his nobles are duty-bound to prevent and punish such tyranny" (1966, 164).

Although Luther addresses his appeal to the emperor as well as the nobility, he does allow for the possibility that, just as the pope had failed to do his duty to reform the church, the emperor and princes might fail to act as well. Luther thus carries through the logic of relying on the nearest responsible authority to its conclusion:

Every town, council, or governing authority not only has the right, without the knowledge and consent of the pope or bishop, to abolish what is opposed to God and injurious to men's bodies and souls, but indeed is bound at the risk of the salvation of its souls to fight it even though popes and bishop, who ought to be the first to do so, do not consent. (1966, 183)

Should the emperor, the princes, and the nobility fail to act, lesser authorities ought to act. And if even these ordained authorities should fail, other authorities, notably those of the universities, and even individual Christians, must act out of faithful obedience to God.

Luther's radical relativizing of the offices of pope and emperor allow him to move quickly and prudentially to address other sources of authority and reform. As Witte writes, "Luther had no firm theory of the forms of political office. He did not systematically sort out the relative virtues and vices of monarchy, aristocracy, or democracy" (2002, 111). Luther's immediate and plaintive appeal in 1520, however, is to the emperor:

Let the German emperor be really and truly emperor. Let neither his authority nor his power be suppressed by such sham pretensions of these papist deceivers as though they were to be excepted from his authority and were themselves to rule in all things. (1966, 211–212)

Conclusion:
The Christian Prince, Conscience, and the Care of Religion

In his 1520 appeal to Charles V to embrace his historical role as emperor to reform the church, Luther is essentially asking for a return to the situation before the Papal Revolution nearly five hundred years before. As Berman puts it,

> Prior to the Papal Revolution, of course, the emperors appointed abbots and bishops (including the Bishop of Rome), called and presided over church synods, and even occasionally promulgated ecclesiastical canons of both a theological and a legal character. (1983, 484)

Given the political, economic, and social developments in the intervening centuries, however, there was no going back to a time of imperial supremacy over the church. The office had declined in its influence and, in fact, no civil power would be capable of maintaining a unified Christendom in the face of religious upheaval and external danger.

What began as a movement for reform within the church thus became a revolution only when all other measures of recourse had been exhausted.[3] The pope proved unwilling or unable to address the corruptions and decadence of the papacy. Likewise, the Holy Roman Emperor decided "to reestablish the concept of the Christian unity of Europe under papal and imperial leadership" (Berman: 2003, 37). Neither pope nor emperor would be capable of making changes necessary to maintain a united Christendom, and this is the immediate context for the futility of Luther's efforts at reform between 1517 and 1521. Thus, writes Berman,

> This, indeed, was the revolutionary situation: that the apocalyptic vision of the Papal Revolution had failed, and that the political legal order, whose inner tensions had produced an overwhelming pressure for fundamental reform, was inherently incapable of accomplishing that reform. (2003, 39)

Practically speaking, then, the temporal unity of Western Christendom was in such decline that even if Luther's appeal to Charles had been successful, the end result would have likely been the same: a confessionally divided continent presaging the rise of nation-states.[4] Something like a Roman Catholic Schmalkaldic League would undoubtedly have been formed, and as was evidenced in the later defeat of the Lutheran alliance and the subsequent and unstable Peace of Augsburg in 1555, the problem of the Reformation was not to be solved by the temporal sword.

---

3 Berman, "Thus when one speaks of the German Revolution, one must have in mind a total upheaval, a 'turning around' of a whole people and a whole culture. The Revolution constituted a lasting transformation of the very nature of the German people, both collectively and individually, and not only of the German people but also eventually of Western society as a whole" (2003, 32).

4 On the later possibility of a Lutheran emperor, see Berman: 2003, 52.

The Reformation's "Constantinian moment" passed with the Diet of Worms in 1521. And despite other reformers' interest in the models of the godly magistrate, and even the Christian emperor, a reassertion of imperial supremacy appears to have been only a passing and fleeting possibility.[5] Luther's futile appeal to imperial authority set the stage for a thoroughgoing reformation of not only the church but indeed all of society, one that would in fact be a revolution, in which new legal and social institutions would come to prominence. The care of religion would devolve to the "lesser" magistrate, and as the power of the papacy and the emperor declined, the confessional territory and eventually nation-state would appear.

As the Christian prince became more powerful, the role of individual conscience also was asserted. Luther's appeal was not only to the German nobility in support or in lieu of imperial action. It was, in the end, an appeal for responsible action to protect and promote true religion that devolved to every individual Christian, first to the emperor and if necessary to the cobbler. Luther's appeal to everyone, no matter his or her station, to defend and promote the gospel as was possible, is in accord with sentiments expressed throughout the works of 1520. Estes, quoting Luther's treatise on good works, writes,

> In these circumstances, 'anyone who is able to do so' should help in whatever way he can. There are doubtless 'bishops and spiritual prelates' who would like to combat the infamy of Rome, but they are paralyzed by fear. It is thus the solemn duty of everyone else to offer whatever resistance they can. (2005, 10)

As Luther appealed to his conscience in his appearance before Charles V at Worms, so too did he depend on the Christian prince Frederick III for temporal protection. The increasing prominence of these two realities, the Christian prince and the Christian conscience, thus marked the passing of the Reformation's "Constantinian Moment" and the decline of both papal and imperial power.

Bibliography

VON ALVELDT, AUGUSTIN (1520a), Eyn gar frucht bar vnd nutzbarlich buchleyn von den babstlichen stule, Leipzig.
— (1520b), Super apostolica Sede An Videlicet diuino sit iure nec ne, Leipzig.
BALLOR, JORDAN J. (2012), Covenant, Causality, and Law: A Study in the Theology of Wolfgang Musculus, Göttingen: Vandenhoeck & Ruprecht.

---

5 By the middle of the century, other reformers such as Wolfgang Musculus would redefine sovereignty and the corresponding care of religion to rest primarily not with imperial authority but rather with lesser, civil magistrates (see Ballor: 2012, 193–194). On the broader Reformation approaches to Christian magistracy and the model of Christian emperors within the context of excommunication, see Ballor: 2013, 106–107.

— (2013), Church Discipline and Excommunication: Peter Martyr Vermigli among the Disciplinarians and the Magistraticals, Reformation & Renaissance Review 15.1, 99–110.

BERMAN, HAROLD J. (1983), Law and Revolution: The Formation of the Western Legal Tradition, Cambridge: Harvard University Press.

— (2003), Law and Revolution, II: The Impact of the Protestant Reformations on the Western Legal Tradition, Cambridge: Belknap.

ESTES, JAMES M. (2005), Peace, Order and the Glory of God: Secular Authority and the Church in the Thought of Luther and Melanchthon, 1518–1559, Leiden: Brill.

VON GIERKE, OTTO (1902), Johannes Althusius und die Entwicklung der naturrechtlichen Staatstheorien, 2nd ed., Breslau: Marcus.

— (1966), The Development of Political Theory, trans. Bernard Freyd, New York: Howard Fertig.

HENDRIX, SCOTT H. (2015), Martin Luther: Visionary Reformer, New Haven: Yale University Press.

KIRBY, TORRANCE (2004), Peter Martyr Vermigli and Pope Boniface VIII: The Difference between Civil and Ecclesiastical Power, in: Frank A. James III (ed.), Peter Martyr Vermigli and the European Reformations: Semper Reformanda, Leiden: Brill, 291–304.

— (2007), The Zurich Connection and Tudor Political Theology, Leiden: Brill.

KUYPER, ABRAHAM (2016), State and Church, Ajren Vreugdenhill/Nelson D. Kloosterman (trans.), in: John Halsey Wood Jr./Andrew M. McGinnis (ed.), On the Church, Bellingham: Lexham Press, 373–437.

LUTHER, MARTIN (1520a), Von dem Bapstum zu Rome: wyder den hochberümpten Romanisten zu Leiptzck, Wittenberg.

— (1520b), An den christlichen Adel deutscher Nation von des christlichen Standes Besserung, Wittenberg.

— (1966), To the Christian Nobility of the German Nation Concerning the Reform of the Christian Estate, 1520, Charles M. Jacobs/James Atkinson (trans.), in: James Atkinson/Helmut T. Lehmann (ed.), Luther's Works, Vol. 44: The Christian in Society I, Philadelphia: Fortress Press, 123–217.

LUTHER, MARTIN (1970), On the Papacy in Rome, Against the Most Celebrated Romanist in Leipzig, 1520, Eric W. Gritsch/Ruth C. Gritsch (trans.) in: Eric W. Gritsch/Helmut T. Lehmann (ed.), Luther's Works, Vol. 39: Church and Ministry I, Philadelphia: Fortress Press, 55–104.

SCHORN-SCHÜTTE, LUISE (2016), Obrigkeitsverständnis im Luthertum des 16. und frühen 17. Jahrhunderts, in: Christopher Spehr/Michael Haspel/Wolfgang Holler (ed.), Weimar und die Reformation: Luthers Obrigkeitslehre und ihre Wirkungen, Leipzig: Evangelische Verlagsanstalt, 107–117.

WITTE JR., JOHN (2002), Law and Protestantism: The Legal Teachings of the Lutheran Reformation, New York: Cambridge University Press.

Pierrick Hildebrand

Zwingli's covenantal turn[1]

Past Research

Gottlob Schrenk, one of the earliest scholars of the historical-theological development of Reformed covenant theology[2] who acknowledged Huldrych Zwingli (1484–1531) to be the initiator of this theological tradition,[3] wrote in the first quarter of the 20th century that "the conflict with the Anabaptists and the will for a state church are the moving forces which lie behind these thoughts."[4] He went so far as postulating the very emergence of the covenant concept in Anabaptist circles, which Zwingli opportunely took over to polemicize against infant baptism. Schrenk based his thesis on only three writings of the Reformer dated not earlier than 1526.[5] The thesis, that Zwingli developed his theology of the covenant for the pragmatical purpose of justifying pedobaptism against the sectarianism of the Anabaptists, has been widely reasserted in the scholarly research of the last century.[6] It has an explanatory scope that definitely merits consideration.

1 This essay is the outworking of a short paper presented at the fifth annual RefoRC conference in Leuven (Belgium) in May 2015.
2 "Reformed covenant theology" does not precisely refer here to covenant theology in a generic sense which would be per se "Reformed", but to the theological outworking of the biblical motif of the covenant *within* the Reformed tradition beginning with Zwingli. As Horton justly points out, "the Reformed tradition hardly has a patent on this widely attested biblical motif." Horton: 2008, ix.
3 The first to recognize (or ever consider) Zwingli as standing at the very beginnings of Reformed covenant theology was von Korff in 1908. Cf. Von Korff: 1908, 10: "Suchen wir nun nach den Anfängen der Foederaltheologie, so ist zurückzugehen bis auf Zwingli."
4 Schrenk: 1923, 36: "Der Kampf gegen die Täufer und der Wille zur Volkskirche sind die treibenden Kräfte, die hinter diesen Gedanken stehen." See further Schrenk: 1923, 36–40.
5 The writings considered by Schrenk are *De peccato originali declaratio* of 1526 (Cf. Zwingli: 1935), *In catabaptistarum strophas elenchus* of 1527 (Cf. Zwingli: 1961) and *Fidei ratio* of 1530 (Cf. Zwingli: 1964). Cf. Schrenk: 1923, 37, footnote 4.
6 That even Gottfried W. Locher, probably the most influential Zwingli-scholar in the twentieth century, discussed covenant unity in chapter XIII called "Die Täufer" under "7. Aus Zwinglis Entgegegnungen" is symptomatical. Cf. Locher: 1979, 261–263. See also more recently McCoy,

Zwingli's denying of any ontological-transformative value to the sacraments *ex opere operato* left himself compelled to find another rationale for baptism – especially for infant baptism – which was, in western theology at least since Augustine (354–430), related to the removal of original sin.

From the first Anabaptist controversies in 1523 on, the sources show a continuing and struggling development in Zwingli's theological thinking on this matter.[7] However, it does not necessarily follow from the fact that Zwingli's use of the biblical idea of covenant became the key theological concept in arguing for pedobaptism, that covenant theology has been developed *ad hoc* for that purpose. Relying on insights from Jack W. Cottrell's unpublished yet unsurpassed dissertation on Zwingli's covenantal thinking, namely *Covenant and Baptism in the Theology of Huldreich Zwingli* (Cottrell: 1971),[8] this essay will actually challenge this predominant view, drawing upon a less known source: the *Subsidiary Essay on the Eucharist* (Zwingli: 1525) of August 1525.[9] In this polemical writing on the proper interpretation of the Lord's Supper, Zwingli challenges Roman Catholics in arguing for the very first time from covenantal continuity and lay thereby the ground for the subsequent development of covenant theology in the Reformed tradition.[10]

There actually exist, so far, only two monographs on Zwingli's covenant theology. The first one is Cottrell's (just mentionned above), which in its first and essential part consists of a historical-chronological account of its development starting from the primary sources. His focus on the relation between covenant and baptism has a heuristic end, and is indebted to Schrenk's legacy, with which Cottrell eventually disagrees. The second one is Scott A. Gillies' unpublished thesis "*Huldrych and the origins of the covenant: 1524–1527*" (Gillies: 1996), of which a summarizing article was published in 2001 (Gillies: 2001). His thesis is basically a variant of Schrenk's, in that he borrows some of Cottrell's insights, but reframed them after the former's pattern. He asserts that Zwingli's covenant theology is due to a reactionary and scholarly hermeneutic encompassing a new

---

Baker: 1991, 21: "[…] for Zwingli, the covenant motif remained essentially a basis for his reply to the Anabaptist teachings on baptism."

7 For a short overview on the development of Zwingli's thinking on baptism see Stephens: 1986, 194–217.

8 See also a sort of excerpt thereof in Cottrell: 1975, 75–83.

9 For the original Latin work of 1525 *Subsidium sive coronis de eucharistia*, see Zwingli: 1927, 458–504. We'll use in the main text Preble's English translation: Zwingli: 1984, 191–227. It will be referred to as the *Subsidiary* in the essay.

10 Against Hagen and Baker, who take Zwingli's *Antwort über Balthasar Hubmaiers Taufbüchlein* of November 5th to be the first source testifying covenantal thinking, cf. Hagen: 1972, 18–19: "Later in the year there is a noticeable shift in Zwingli's evaluation of the Old Testament and the New Testament's relationship to it ('Antwort über Balthasar Hubmaiers Taufbüchlein,' 5 Nov. 1525)."; Baker: 1980, 181: "The Zurich covenant notion founds ist earliest notion configuration in Zwingli's 'Reply to Hubmaier' of November 5, 1525".

appraisal of the Old Testament, for the sake of defending infant baptism against an Anabaptist democratic and New Testament-monistic hermeneutic, to which Zwingli as an Erasmian humanist would have previously adhered. In our view there are several weaknesses in Gillies' work, which cannot be discussed here at length. The main problem lies in his "reversed" methodological approach, which tends to be circular. He essentially starts from secondary sources, which he takes for granted and uses them as a framework for his interpretation of the development of Zwingli's theology of the covenant.[11] Another problem with Gillies' thesis is the misquoting and misinterpretations of Cottrell's work – especially in the thesis – although clearly indebted to it in respect to the historical-chronological outline.

Before we begin our argumentation there is a basic issue to begin with, namely the definition of Reformed covenant theology. We cannot determine Zwingli's move *from testamental discontinuity to covenantal continuity* – what we call here his *covenantal turn* – before defining what covenant theology actually is. And there is still disagreement among scholars on an appropriate definition.[12] I will propose here a cautious working definition ad hoc, which admittedly does not take every nuance into account, but gets to the core of our issue: *we can speak of Reformed covenant theology when the covenant of grace as the New Testament of Christ is said to already be effective back in the Old Testament.*

---

11 Drawing heavily on secondary literature Gilles has basically three assumptions. (1) He assumes, that Zwingli did not depart from Erasmus' hermeneutics, especially from his highly depreciative view of the Old Testament, before being in conflict with the Anabaptists. (2) He refers to the commonly called *Baker-thesis* in order to determine Zwingli's move from the theology of a unilateral testament to one of a bilateral covenant. Here, he seems to have miss Baker's very point, who never posited any genuine theology of a bilateral covenant by Zwingli (McCoy/Baker: 1991, 21), which he ascribes first to Bullinger. I can't see how Baker can be of any help to him here. (3) He assumes Zwingli's departure from a democratic reading of Scripture commonly shared with the Anabaptists to a scholarly (i. e. authoritative) reading of the Scriptures once the conflict had broken, giving rise to the Prophezei. Gillies does not, in our view, provides sufficient evidences from primary sources to backup this assertions. I will here only point out that Zwingli had learnt Hebrew (contrary to Erasmus) already in 1522, that the very depreciative claims found by Erasmus on the OT are missing in the zwinglian sources, and that Zwingli's emphasis on the theological education of pastors and the project of a theological seminary antedates (September 1523) the open conflict with the Anabaptists. Lastly, Gillies gives no explanation at all in light of his own thesis, why the very first evidences (with datable certainty) of a genuine covenant theology by Zwingli are to be found in a writing on the Eucharist addressed to Roman Catholics.

12 For an overview of the different definitions proposed so far, see Lillback: 2001, 26–28.

The *Subsidiary*

As the title of the *Subsidiary Essay on the Eucharist* suggests, this writing was meant as a further support to Zwingli's own view on the controversial discussion about the Lord's supper. The last time he had given his opinion on the subject in written form was in his *Commentary on true and false religion*[13] in March of 1525. A month later Zwingli could push the definitive abolition of the mass in Zurich by the council of the city-state – with a thin majority though – against his Roman Catholic opponents and the first evangelical Supper was celebrated on Easter 1525. The main speaker of the opponents was Joachim Am Grüt, to whom the *Subsidiary* was supposed to give an answer. Zwingli obviously felt obligated in spite of his victory to reinforce his set of arguments for his view on the Lord's supper.[14] It cannot be stressed enough that Zwingli has the "Old believers" in mind in this writing– as the Roman Catholics used to name themselves – and not the Anabaptists at all, although Zwingli was more and more in conflict with the latter at that time.[15]

As Zwingli explicitly writes in the *Subsidiary*, he does not only want to repeat what he had already said in his *Commentary*.[16] The main part of this writing deals firstly with points that escaped him during the writing of the Commentary; secondly with points that occured to him afterwards; and thirdly with answers to some objections he very probably had to face before the council.[17] It is this third part, where Zwingli addresses eight points of criticism from his counterpart that will be the focus of our attention, because in the answer to the last point Zwingli uses an argument from the covenant imbedded in a covenant theology as we defined it above for the very first time.

The last objection which Zwingli addresses is an argument raised by his opponents from the Pauline rendering of the words of institution in chapter eleven of the first epistle to the Corinthians, where the cup is called "the new testament in my blood."[18] The argument can be simplified as follows: As being the new

---

13 Cf. Zwingli: 1914, 773–820.
14 Cf. Köhler: 1927, 443.
15 The conflict with the Anabaptists broke out openly after the second disputation in October 1523, the latter becoming suspicious of Zwingli's obligation to a *magisterial* Reformation, see Locher: 1979, 240ff. In *Wer Ursache gebe zu Aufruhr* of December 1524 (Zwingli: 1914) Zwingli addresses the Anabaptists – among other groups threatening the forthgoing of the Reformation – for the first time in his writings. *Von der Taufe, von der Wiedertaufe und von der Kindertaufe* of May 1525 (Zwingli: 1927) is the first writing solely dedicated to the Anabaptists. The baptismal controversy with the Anabaptists began as a "side battle", which would take Zwingli's attention more and more, once the battle for the Supper against his Roman Catholic opponents in Zürich – the "main battle" – was definitely "won".
16 Cf. Zwingli: 1927, 466–467; Zwingli: 1984, 197.
17 Cf. Zwingli: 1927, 467; Zwingli: 1984: 197–198.
18 1 Cor 11:25.

testament itself, the cup must therefore contain the corporeal blood of Christ.[19] Zwingli begins his refutation with an explanation of the biblical use of the *word* "testament" and writes: "The testament, as far as the present case is concerned, is nothing other than an agreement promised by God, as when the Lord struck a compact or covenant with Abraham in Genesis 17."[20] Zwingli cites thereupon the relevant verses of the chapter to point out the covenant terms[21] and then adds: "But there are added to covenants signs, which though also called by the name of covenants yet are not covenants, as is plainly shown in the same passage."[22] Zwingli alludes here to the circumcision which is in verse 10 first called "covenant", and in the subsequent verse "sign of the covenant".

Up to this point Zwingli had argued from Genesis 17 in respect to the Abrahamic covenant only in one writing out of his entire work.[23] It was in his first polemical writing against the Anabaptists[24] in relation to baptism, *Von der Taufe, von der Wiedertaufe und von der Kindertaufe*[25] at the end of May 1525, which is not long before the *Subsidiary*. It is worth it here to shortly remind ourselves what Zwingli had previously said there. Zwingli's basic thesis was that circumcision "[…] was in the Old Testament alike to what baptism is in the new",[26] as he wrote in the letter of dedication. But when Zwingli came to the section on infant baptism, he then explained that God gave Abraham "circumcision as a pledge or covenant sign for the sake of his offsprings as it is stated in Genesis 17."[27] The question we have to ask here is the following one: Had Zwingli put Abraham's covenant on one and the same level as the New Testament? Our response is no! He

---

19 Cf. Zwingli: 1984, 223: "What is offered here is the new testament; but the new testament is not a symbol, it is the blood of Christ itself. Since, therefore, this cup is the new testament, it is necessarily the corporeal blood of Christ, for that is the new testament."; Zwingli: 1927, 499: "Quod hic praebetur, novum testamentum est. Sed novum testamentum non est symbolum aliquod, sed ipse sanguis Christi. Cum ergo poculum hoc sit novum testamentum, necesse est sanguinem Christi corporeum esse; is enim testamentum est."

20 Zwingli: 1984, 223. Cf. Zwingli: 1927, 499: "Testamentum, quod ad praesens adtinet, nihil aliud est quam conditio a deo promissa. Ut quum dominus cum Abraham ferit pactum sive foedus. Gen. 17."

21 Gen 17:1, 7–8, 10–11.

22 Zwingli: 1984, 223. Cf. Zwingli: 1927, 499: "Sed adduntur foederibus signa, quae, tametsi foederum quoque nominibus vocentur, non tamen foedera sunt, ut eodem loco manifeste patet."

23 There is but one allusion in the *Commentary*, cf. Zwingli: 1914, 823.

24 It is actually Zwingli's first polemical writing, which has *only* the Anabaptists in mind. In *Wer Ursache gebe zu Aufruhr usw.* of December 1524 Zwingli had already polemised against them, especially against Conrad Grebel (1498–1526), cf. Zwingli: 1914, 368–469.

25 Cf. Zwingli, Von der Taufe, 206–337.

26 Cf. Zwingli: 1927, 212: "[…] sunder imm alten testament glych das gewesen ist, das imm nüwen der touff ist."

27 Cf. Zwingli: 1927, 292: "Sunder er hat imm die bschnidung zuo eim pflicht- oder pundts-zeichen ggeben um siner nachkommen willen, als Genesis am 17."

had actually argued from analogy. It was even an argument *a fortiori*, from the lesser to the greater (if..., much more...), grounded in a law-grace-dialectic,[28] which definitely precludes any equalization. One quote will here suffice to make the point. Zwingli had namely written:

> For if physical descent from Abraham, Isaac and Jacob meant so much that the children in their childhood were to walk in the steps of their fathers, much more in the new families, who are **under grace and not law**, should the children be numbered with their fathers among the people of God, and should walk with them under one pledge no less thant those.[29] (Emphasis added)

Let's go back now to the *Subsidiary*, where we just stopped. After having shown from Genesis 17 that the covenant sign of circumcision can also just be called the covenant, though not being the covenant itself, Zwingli brings new support to this point with the meaning of baptism. He writes:

> [...] baptism is just as much the symbol of the Christian people that has received from God the covenant that his son should be ours, as circumcision was once the symbol of that covenant that the Lord should be their God and they should be his people.[30]

Up to that point, Zwingli seems to argue in a similar way from analogy (see the change of addressee ours – their).[31] But then he continues:

> I want now to pass over from the covenant or testament of Abraham to the testament of Christ. The covenant which was struck with Abraham is so strong and valid that unless you keep it always you will not be faithful. For unless the Lord is your God and you are worshipper of him only (for "you shall worship the Lord your God, and serve him only" [Dt. 6:13]), you have no reason to boast that you are faithful. But he whom you worship and adore thus is your God, that is, the supreme good, because he gives himself freely to you and casts himself into death for you by which he might reconcile you to himself.[32]

---

28 Not in the Lutheran intensity, as the law does still have a positive role in the Christian's life in Zwingli's theology, cf. Stephens: 1986, 164–167.

29 Translation from Cottrell, cf. Cottrell: 1971, 161. Cf. Zwingli: 1927, 326: "Denn galt von Abrahamen, Isaacken und Jacoben lyplich geborn sin so vil, das die kinder in der kintheit den vätteren nachgiengend; vil me imm nüwen gschlecht, das **under dem gnad** lebt, **nit under dem gsatzt**, söllend die kinder mit den vätteren under gottes volck gezellt werden, und nütz weniger mit inenn under einem pflichtszeichen wandlen weder yene." (Emphasis added)

30 Zwingli: 1984, 224. Cf. Zwingli: 1927, 500: "[...] est baptismus Christiani populi, qui foedus hoc a deo accepit, ut filius eius noster sit, aeque symbolum, atque olim circumcisio huius foederis erat symbolum, quod dominus esset eorum deus, et ipsi essent eius populus."

31 Although the promise is actually the same: God's promise to be the God of the covenanted.

32 Zwinglis: 1984, 224. Cf. Zwingli: 1927, 500: "Est foedus, quod cum Abraham percussum est, sic firmum ac minime abrogatum, ut ni perpetuo serves, non sis fidelis futurus; nisi enim dominus sit deus tuus, et tu eius unius cultor sis (dominum enim deum tuum adorabis, ac illi soli servies [cf. 5. Mos. 6. 13]), non est, ut te fidelem iactes. At ille, quem sic colis et adoras, sic est deus tuus, hoc est: summum bonum, quod se tibi gratuito impertit, ut pro te in mortem sese abiecerit, quo te sibi reconciliaret."

Zwingli admittedly speaks of a transition from one testament to another but it becomes clear from what follows that this transition relates not to some basic change of content, but to a time-related sequence. Interestingly, there is a change of addressee (you), that is, the Abrahamic covenant has been struck not only with "them", but with us. Abraham's covenant is "so strong and valid", that is, that it is not abrogated but fulfilled in or as Christ's testament. Then, when we look closer at the content, we see that the framework of the testament of Christ is given through the terms of the testament of Abraham given in Gen 17:1, which Zwingli earlier paraphrased as follows: "I will be your God. You will walk before me most uprightly."[33] God's promise to be Abraham's God is ultimately interpreted as God's gift of himself in the death of Christ for reconciling everyone's falling short of the required covenantal faithfulness. The Abrahamic covenant of Genesis 17 is substantially equalized with the New Testament. There is no hint of a law-grace-dialectic as it was expressed in *Von der Taufe* anymore. A shift from analogy to univocity has taken place in Zwingli's thinking on the biblical covenant motif.[34] *We call it a covenantal turn because it is as though we take part in the birth of Reformed covenant theology here.*

There are at least two further insights that Zwingli alludes to which are of critical relevance. In the subsequent sentence to the last quote Zwingli adds: "This grace had been promised by him who has given it, long ago, when our first parent transgressed his law, and he constantly renewed this promise to our fathers."[35]

The first insight is that the Abrahamic covenant, which we conclude to be the retrojected or anticipated New Testament of Christ, is actually only a renewal of an agreement that God had already promised earlier in the past "when our first parent transgressed his law". Zwingli is going further back to Adam's fall and to the so-called Protoevangelion, that is God's cursing the serpent in Genesis 3:15, which Zwingli interprets as a promise pointing to Christ,[36] as others have before

---

33 Zwingli: 1984: 223. Cf. Zwingli, 499: "Ego ero deus tuus. Tu ambulabis coram me integerrime." See also Zwingli's own translation of Gen 17:1, Zwingli, 499: "Ego deus omnipotens, [...] ambula coram me et sis integer!"

34 See also the writing addressing the Anabaptist controversy of November 1525, namely Zwingli's *Antwort über Balthasar Hubmaiers Taufbüchlein* which is in line with the *Subsidiary*: "Es ist offenbar by allen glöubigen, **das der christenlich pundt oder nüw testament eben der alt pundt Abrahams ist,** usgenommen, das wir Christum, der yenen nun verheissen was, bar habend." (Emphasis added) Zwingli: 1525, 634–635.

35 Zwingli, Subsidiary, 224; cf. Zwingli, Subsidium, 500: "Promiserat hanc gratiam ipse, qui praestitit, iam olim, cum parens noster legem eius praevaricaretur; ac deinde eam promissionem patribus semper refricuit."

36 See also Zwingli's interpretation of Gen 3: 15 in the Farrago annotationum in Genesim published in 1527 (Zwingli: 1963, 28): "Mysterium dixit hic latere altissimum; nam quid hoc magni erat, si inter mulierem et serpentem essent insidiae aut inimicitiae? Hic iam **ab initio promittitur liberatio et semen illud benedictum,** per quod benedicendae erant omnes gen-

him since the time of the ancient church.[37] What is only alluded to here, becomes afterwards more explicit:

> And the reason why he made the promise was none other than because blessedness could not come to us, however much we toiled and sweated, while the fall of the first parent had not been atoned for. But when Christ, slain for us, appeased the divine justice and became the only approach to God, God entered into a new covenant with the human race, not new in the sense that he had only just discovered this remedy, but because he applied it at the right moment, having prepared it long before.[38]

Zwingli is arguing here *heilsgeschichtlich* in a preparation-application pattern, or in other words, in a promise-fulfillment-pattern imbedded in one unique covenant. The distinction between the Abrahamic and the new covenant does not pertain to a different substance such as law and grace. It pertains to one's perspective depending on one's position on the timeline, that is a prospective or retrospective view on the one historical Christ's event. We can already speak here, as will the later Reformed tradition after Zwingli, of *the foedus gratiae or covenant of grace*, which redemptive-historically began just after the fall in Genesis 3:15 and will extend to eternity.[39]

The second insight is intimately related to the first one and relates to the prelapsarian state of relationship. If, after the fall, Adam was put by God under the terms of the covenant of grace, under what terms did Adam stand *coram Deo* before the fall? Zwingli is admittedly not interested at all in developing this question. After all, that would not add further arguments to his point of differentiating between covenant and covenant sign. There is one hint however, which could almost remain unnoticed but actually gives us and important clue. Zwingli defines the fall as "when our first parent transgressed his law". The logical inference out of this statement, is that the prelapsarian God-man-relationship was one essentially grounded in law. To assert more would be source misuse, but

---

tes." (Emphasis added) Zwingli obviously builds here a bridge between Gen 3:15 and the Abraham's narrative, especially Gen 12: 1–3 and Gen 17:4–8.

37 There are probably evidences of christogical interpretation already in the New Testament, see for example 1 Joh 3, 4–10 cf. http://www.bibelwissenschaft.de/wibilex/das-bibellexikon/lexikon/sachwort/anzeigen/details/protoevangelium/ch/0e57f4cfcc789d4291ff54fa0d84117f/.

38 Zwingli: 1984, 224; cf. Zwingli: 1927, 500: "Causa vero, cur promiserit, alia non fuit, quam quod beatitudo nobis contingere nequibat, quantumvis conantibus et sudantibus, cum lapsus primi parentis expiatus non esset. Cum autem Christus iam pro nobis mactatus divinam iustitiam placavit ita, ut per ipsum solum accedatur ad deum, iam novum foedus iniit deus cum humano genere, non sic novum, ut hanc medelam vix tandem invenerit, sed quod olim paratam, quum tempestivum esset, adhibuerit."

39 See for example Zacharias Ursinus' (1534–1583) *Summa Theologiae* or Larger Catechism probably written before the Heidelberg Catechism (1563) but published posthumously for the first time in 1584, especially Questions-Answers 30–33, cf. Ursinus: 1967, 155f. For an english translation, see Ursinus: 2005, 167f.

Zwingli, interestingly enough, stands in some continuity with the second generation of Reformed covenant theologians. In their development of Reformed covenant theology they would still hold to the covenant of grace first granted in Genesis 3:15 and renewed with Abraham in Genesis 17, and define it as Christ's fulfilling the *foedus naturale or covenant of creation*[40] in accomplishing precisely what the adamic couple failed to, namely God's law, but taking the condemnation upon himself of failing to do so.

The Genesis "commentary"

How is Zwingli's covenantal turn in mid 1525 to be explained? If it was the Anabaptist controversy, would we not expect the first writing testifiying to covenantal thinking to be an anti-Anabaptist writing on baptism? The contrary is actually the case, the *Subsidiary* being an anti-Roman-Catholic writing on the Eucharist. The Anabaptist controversy certainly played a role similar as a catalyst but it was not decisive, neither was it, in our view, the battle over the Supper. Cottrell's assumption, namely that Zwingli's intensive exegetical work on the book of Genesis lies at its core, seems more conclusive. We cannot get rid of the fact that Zwingli understood himself as a theologian committed to *sola (et tota!) scriptura* and this should be taken into account in any serious historical-theological survey. This is not to deny the fact that the question of baptism (and the supper) stood in the background of course. Mid 1525 coincides with the transformation of the "Grossmünsterstift" or canon of the minster into the *Prophezei*, which was chiefly intended to be a sort of biblico-theological seminary for the Zürich pastorate, though also open to laymen. This was the fulfillment of a project already planned with the city-council in September 1523 at the latest; that is, before the conflict with the Anabaptists broke out.[41] As Zwingli started to preach in Zürich the whole Scriptures after the *lectio-continua* method in 1519, so were the books of the Bible methodically interpreted by the different scholars at the new institution. The teaching program started on the morning of the 19th of June. It basically followed a four-step pattern.[42] First, a student began by reading the biblical text out of the Vulgate. Second, the same text was read in Hebrew by the competent *lector* – initially Jacob Ceporinus (1499–1525), followed by Conrad Pellican (1478–1556) from 1526 on – who also added some linguistic and factual comments in Latin. Zwingli presented in a third step the Greek *lectio* out of the Septuagint and closed with an interpretation of the text in Latin. Finally, Zwin-

---

40 Cf. Ursinus: 1967, 156; Ursinus: 2005, 168.
41 Cf. Egli: 1879, 169; Locher: 1979, 151.
42 Cf. Bullinger: 1838, 289 ff; Locher: 1979, 161 f.

gli's interpretation was translated into German by a pastor – usually Leo Jud (1482–1542) or Caspar Megander (1495–1545), sometimes even by Zwingli himself.

The first book they began with was the very first book of Scripture, although the *lectio-continua* method did not necessarily imply following the canonical order of the biblical books as the practice of the *Prophezei* afterwards also shows. So the book of Genesis began to be lectured on from the 19th of June – that is before the "Subsidium" – on up to the 5th of November. And the so-called *Farrago annotianum in Genesim ex ore Huldrychi Zuinglii per Leonem Iudae et Casparem Megandrum exceptarum*[43] goes back to Zwingli's business at the *Prophezei*. This source should potentially inform us on Zwingli's covenantal thinking in the mid of 1525, but we are confronted with a twofold problem: a chronological one and one of transmission. The work was not immediately published after the *lectiones* on the book of Genesis at the *Prophezei*, but only two years later in March 1527. And as the title openly attests, it was not written with Zwingli's own pen, but with those of Jud and Megander, who worked up their own notes *ex ore* of the master's lectures. It must however not be forgotten that they published the work under Zwingli's approbation, and the latter wrote the foreword. Nevertheless Künzli, as Farner before him, thought it probable "[…] that some comments from Zwingli's corresponding sermons has been processed later into it."[44] Zwingli had preached on the whole book of Genesis between the 8th of July 1526 and the 2nd of March 1527,[45] right before the publication of the *Farrago annotianum in Genesim*. Bolliger recently spoke of "an elementary consensus" in scholarship, that all *annotationes* are the redactional product relying on two sources, namely the lecture notes and Zwingli's related sermons, which cannot as such be reconstructed *a posteriori*. He shows "[…] in principle a threefold dating chronology with the sequence Annotations/lections – Sermons – Final editing/printing."[46] This makes the *Farrago annotianum in Genesim* not unconditionally reliable for determining Zwingli's covenantal turn, so that our earliest reliable source for determining the *terminus ante quem* remains the *Subsidium*. Nevertheless we must admit with Cottrell "the possibility if not the

---

43 Zwingli: 1963.

44 Künzli: 1959, 872: "[…] dass nachträglich auch einzelne Äusserungen aus den entsprechenden Predigten Zwinglis mit hineinverarbeitet worden sind." See also Künzli: 1950, 19; 290; Farner: 1954, 84–89; Farner: 1963, 290.

45 See Bolliger: 2013, 528; Künzli: 1959, 872 against Farner: 1963, 290 who includes not only the Genesis lections but all of the lections on the Pentateuch in this period of 20 weeks.

46 Bolliger: 2013, 526: "[…] eine im Prinzip dreiteilige Datierungschronologie mit der Abfolge Annotationen/Vorlesungen – Predigten – Endredaktion/Drucklegung."

probability that it does represent Zwingli's thinking at this time",[47] that is, at the time of his lectures.

Conclusion

I come now to the conclusion of the essay. We began with Schrenk's influential and persistent thesis that Zwingli developed his theology as a reaction against the Anabaptists in a quasi monocausal fashion. We already alluded to one weakness of his thesis, namely that it rested on Zwingli's writings from 1526 on.

Our investigation of Zwingli's *Subsidiary* led us to a more differentiated position that we will summarize as follow. 1) We have shown in the *Subsidiary* what we called a covenantal turn by Zwingli, that is, a hermeneutical move from an analogical to an univocal view upon the relation between the Abrahamic covenant and Christ's New Testament. Christ's New Testament is thereby considered as proleptically anticipated back in the Old Testament in Zwingli's thinking for the very first time. This covenantal turn must have taken place somewhere between *Von der Taufe* of May 1525 and the *Subsidiary* of August 1525. 2) The *Subsidiary*, being an anti-Roman-Catholic writing on the Eucharist and the first source testifying of Zwingli's covenantal turn with datable certainty, the eucharistic controversy and not the baptismal one in Zurich comes out to be the immediate context in which covenant theology is used for the first time for polemical aims. 3) The theological insights of Zwingli are theologically so foundational for the later Reformed tradition that they cannot be solely confined to an ad hoc-argument for Zwingli's sacramental and church policy. 4) Zwingli's exegetical work at the Prophezei on the book of Genesis seems to be the decisive factor for explaining his covenantal turn. While it can't be denied that the Anabaptist controversy has contributed to Zwingli's theological development on the covenant, the source evidence leads us to consider the Anabaptist factor not to be the only one nor the main one. Schrenk's thesis and all its manifold reassertions are too reductionistic to explain Zwingli's covenantal turn.

Bibliography

BAKER, J. WAYNE (1980), Heinrich Bullinger and the Covenant: the other Reformed Tradition, Athens Ohio: Ohio University Press.

BOLLIGER, DANIEL (2013), Nachwort, in: Max Lienhard and Daniel Bolliger, Huldreich Zwinglis sämtliche Werke, Vol. 21, Corpus Reformatorum 108, Zürich: TVZ, 503–566.

---

47 Cottrell: 1971, 180.

Bullinger, Heinrich (1838), Reformationsgeschichte, J.J. Hottinger und H. H. Vögeli (ed.), Vol. 1, Frauenfeld: Ch. Beyel.

Cottrell, Jack Warren (1971), Covenant and Baptism in the Theology of Huldreich Zwingli, Princeton theological Seminary, Princeton New Jersey: PhD Dissertation.

— (1975), Is Bullinger the source for Zwingli's doctrine of the covenant?, in: Ulrich Gäbler/ Erland Herkenrath (ed.), Heinrich Bullinger 1504–1575: Gesammelte Aufsätze zum 400. Todestag, Zürcher Beiträge zur Reformationsgeschichte 7, Zürich: TVZ, 75–83.

Egli, Emil (ed.) (1879), Actensammlung zur Geschichte der Zürcher Reformation in den Jahren 1519–1533, Zürich: J. Schabelitz.

Farner, Oskar (1954), Huldrych Zwingli: Seine Verkündigung und ihre ersten Früchte, Zürich: Zwingli-Verlag.

— (1963), Nachwort zu den Erläuterungen zur Genesis, in: Emil Egli et al. (ed.), Huldreich Zwinglis sämtliche Werke, Vol. 13, Corpus Reformatorum 100, Zürich: Verlag Berichthaus, 289–90.

Gillies, Scott A. (1996), Huldrych and the origins of the covenant: 1524–1527, Queen's University, Kingston Ontario Canada: M. A. thesis.

— (2001), Zwingli and the origin of the reformed convenant 1524–7, Scottish Journal of Theology 54.1, 21–50.

Köhler, Walther (1927), Einleitung zu 'Subsidium sive coronis de eucharistia', in: Emil Egli et al. (ed.), Huldreich Zwinglis sämtliche Werke, Vol. 4, Corpus reformatorum 91, Leipzig: Verlag von M. Heinsius Nachfolger, 440–455.

Künzli, Edwin (1950), Zwingli als Ausleger von Genesis und Exodus, Zürich: Buchdr. Berichthaus.

— (1959), Zwingli als Ausleger des Alten Testamentes," in: Emil Egli et al. (ed.), Huldreich Zwinglis sämtliche Werke, Vol. 14, Corpus Reformatorum 101, Zürich: Verlag Berichthaus, 869–899.

Hagen, Kenneth (1972), From Testament to Covenant in the Early Sixteenth Century, in: The Sixteenth Century Journal, Vol. 3, No.1, 1–24.

Horton, Michael S. (2008), People and place: A Covenant Ecclesiology, Louisville: Westminster John Knox Press.

Lillback, Peter A. (2001), The Binding of God: Calvin's role in the Development of Covenant Theology, Grand Rapids: Baker Academic.

Locher, G. Walter (1979), Die Zwinglische Reformation im Rahmen der europäischen Kirchengeschichte, Göttingen: Vandenhoeck & Ruprecht.

McCoy, Charles S. and Baker, J. Wayne (1991), Fountainhead of Federalism: Heinrich Bullinger and the Covenantal Tradition, Louisville: Westminster John Knox Press.

Schrenk, Gottlob (1923), Gottesreich und Bund im älteren Protestantismus vornehmlich bei Johannes Coccejus: zugleich ein Beitrag zur Geschichte des Pietismus und der heilsgeschichtlichen Theologie, Gütersloh: C. Bertelsmann.

Stephens, W. Peter (1986), The Theology of Huldrych Zwingli, Oxford: Clarendon Press.

Von Korff, Emanuel Graf (1908), Die Anfänge der Foederaltheologie und ihre erste Ausgestaltung in Zürich und Holland, Bonn: Eisele.

Ursinus, Zacharias (1967), Summa Theologiae, in: A. Lang (ed.), Der Heidelberger Katechismus und vier verwandte Katechismen (Leo Juds und Microns kleine Katechismen sowie die zwei Vorarbeiten Ursins), Darmstadt: Wissenschaftliche Buchgesellschaft, 152–199.

— (2005), The Larger Catechism, in: Lyle D. Bierma et al. (ed.), An Introduction to the Heidelberg Catechism: Sources, History, and Theology (With a Translation of the Smaller and Larger Catechisms of Zacharias Ursinus), 163–223.

ZWINGLI, HULDREICH (1914), De vera et falsa religione commentarius, in: Emil Egli et al. (ed.), Huldreich Zwinglis sämtliche Werke, Vol. 3, Corpus Reformatorum 90, Leipzig: Verlag von M. Heinsius Nachfolger, 628–911.

— (1914), Wer Ursach gebe zur Aufruhr, in: Emil Egli et al. (ed.), Huldreich Zwinglis sämtliche Werke, Vol. 3, Corpus Reformatorum 90, Leipzig: Verlag von M. Heinsius Nachfolger, 374–469.

— (1927), Subsidium sive coronis de eucharistia, in: Emil Egli et al. (ed.), Huldreich Zwinglis sämtliche Werke, Vol. 4, Corpus Reformatorum 91, Leipzig: Verlag von M. Heinsius Nachfolger, 458–504.

— (1927), Von der Taufe, von der Wiedertaufe und von der Kindertaufe, in: Emil Egli et al. (ed.), Huldreich Zwinglis sämtliche Werke, Vol. 4, Corpus Reformatorum 91, Leipzig: Verlag von M. Heinsius Nachfolger, 206–337.

— (1927), Antwort über Balthasar Hubmaiers Taufbüchlein, in: Emil Egli et al. (ed.), Huldreich Zwinglis sämtliche Werke, Vol. 4, Corpus Reformatorum 91, Leipzig: Verlag von M. Heinsius Nachfolger, 585–642.

— (1935), De peccato originali declaratio ad Urbanum Rhegium, in: Emil Egli et al. (ed.), Huldreich Zwinglis sämtliche Werke, Vol. 5, Corpus Reformatorum 92, Leipzig: Verlag von M. Heinsius Nachfolger, 369–396.

— (1961), In catabaptistarum strophas elenchus, in: Emil Egli et al. (ed.), Huldreich Zwinglis sämtliche Werke, Vol. 6.1, Corpus Reformatorum 93, Zürich: Verlag Berichthaus, 21–196.

— (1963), Farrago annotationum in Genesim: ex ore Hulryci Zuinglii per Leonem Iudae et Casparem Megandrum exceptarum, in: Emil Egli et al. (ed.), Huldreich Zwinglis sämtliche Werke, Vol. 13, Corpus Reformatorum 100, Zürich: Verlag Berichthaus, 5–288.

— (1964), Fidei ratio, in: Emil Egli et al. (ed.), Huldreich Zwinglis sämtliche Werke, Vol. 6.2, Corpus reformatorum 93.2, Zürich: Verlag Berichthaus, 790–817.

— (1984), Subsidary Essay on the Eucharist, translated by Henry Preble, revised and edited by H. Wayne Pipkin, in: H. Wayne Pipkin (ed.), Huldrych Zwingli: writings, Vol. 2, Allison Park, Pennsylvania: Pickwick publications.

Jim West

Zwingli and Bullinger Through the Lens of Letters

Huldrych Zwingli's successor in Zurich, Heinrich Bullinger, corresponded with Zwingli very few times. This fact in and of itself is remarkable given the influence Zwingli had on Bullinger's thought and Bullinger's theological development.

The letters we have preserved for us shared between the two number only three. Two of them are from Bullinger to Zwingli and these have no extant responses. Zwingli's singular letter to Bullinger seems to be a response to a now lost letter from the latter to the former.

In other words, we have letters from Bullinger to Zwingli for which we have no response and we have a response from Zwingli to Bullinger for which we have no question. This is a regrettable situation as it leaves us with serious gaps in our knowledge of the interactions between these two remarkable Reformers.

In what follows the letters are reproduced for the first time in English translation[1]. Explanations are kept to a bare minimum in hopes that the focus of readers will be on the thoughts which are expressed by our correspondents. It is hoped that English renditions of these letters will stir further interest in both the letters of Bullinger and the letters of Zwingli, for it is in these sorts of materials that we get the clearest idea of the minds at work in Zurich and vicinity in the heady days of the 16th century Swiss Reformation.

---

1 I have been unable to locate any translation of these three letters into English. If any exist, they are unknown to me. As to the method of translation, the rendering is dynamic rather than literal. My goal is to provide the sense and tone of the letters rather than a merely wooden rendition of Latin into English. Latin purists will be disgruntled but as they can manage Latin themselves, my translation is completely unnecessary for them and they are free to make their own should they wish.

Letter One – Bullinger To Zwingli:

> Grace and peace from the Lord.
>
> I pray you sincerely, my dear Zwingli, that you be open and share a few words with me so that I can understand your position clearly concerning what it is that we confess when we confess that Christ descended into hell. Today, there are not a few learned who invent wonderful tales to stir up readers and in the meantime goad one another in their desire for a prize [for their inventiveness].
>
> Goodbye.
>
> Yours, Heinrich Bullinger.
>
> 8 November 1528.[2]

No reply from Zwingli has been preserved, unfortunately. Interestingly, though, in his *In D. Petri apostoli epistolam utranque, Heinrychi Bullingeri commentarius* of 1534 Bullinger goes into extensive exposition of the issue on pages 123 ff.[3] This suggests that sometime between 1528 and 1534, Bullinger came to some interesting conclusions either with the aid of Zwingli in a now lost letter or by his own intellectual acumen.

Letter Two – Bullinger to Zwingli:

> Grace and peace from the Lord.
>
> It has warmed up here and I [write] you [to inform you] that the son of the elder John Ging is worthy of [your] pity.[4] The plague had been overthrown, and even while it raged the necessities of performing the duties of the teaching office pressed in. Furthermore, since you are not aware of the great esteem in which you are held here: no one here believes anyone to be more trustworthy among us to carry out this difficult task more than you, Zwingli, learned sir.
>
> I was awoken [to his need] because he is a concern of yours and of the Church, and [pray] you are able and wish to administer [the aid requested]. Many of the things [related to his situation] are already well known to you.
>
> We beseech you, therefore, that you would give us, in the first place, the expenses in this matter of Christ's sheep, and finally in large part, [overlook] the rashness of our petition

---

2 Autograph: Zürich StA, E II 349, 275 1/2 S. 8°: S VIII 235; Z IX 597.

3 http://www.e-rara.ch/zuz/content/titleinfo/936667 (Accessed 8 August, 2016).

4 This letter seems to be a plea for some sort of financial aid for a person otherwise unknown. Bullinger argues that though he wishes not to disrupt Zwingli's studies, he is, in the opinion of all, the best person to approach with such a concern both because of his connection with the family and because of his well-known charitable spirit. This is a perfect example of how much we would benefit from a response by Zwingli to Bullinger's plea.

by which we dare not inhibit or interfere with your ability to study. The Lord Jesus preserve you to us for a long time.

24. November 1529.[5]

Yours H. Bullinger

Letter Three – Zwingli to Bullinger:

Grace and peace from the Lord, dearly beloved Heinrich.

This man, whom you see, Carlstadt, is a person who is as human as Luther is divine.[6] Carlstadt will preach when no one else will do it and he will say what no one else will say. This is what leads him to you by way of Basel. He is brave and because of it he is poor so do what you can and strive to relieve and rejuvenate him, not in order to have a claim on him, but that he may be [treated as one] of our own and eat with us.

Farewell in the name of the guarantor of our salvation and sanctification.

Zurich, 22. On the morning of June 1530.[7]

Yours, Huldrych Zwingli.

What these three letters demonstrate, I think quite clearly, is that the Reformers were interested in mutual aid and encouragement, along with theological cohesion. Bullinger's letter to Zwingli seeks theological guidance and that's the very sort of thing we would expect of mutually respectful theologians. But Bullinger's second letter to Zwingli and Zwingli's letter to Bullinger both show more earthy concerns: financial aid and charitable welcome.

In terms of Bullinger's wider correspondence and Zwingli's too there are numerous of examples of theological insight. But there are even more little windows opened to modern readers on the minds, dispositions, likes, dislikes, frustrations, triumphs and defeats of these great 16th century thinkers. Here in their correspondence we see the human side of these men. We have here, then, a solid point of contact with these men who lived 500 years ago. In a very real sense, we have the opportunity, as we read their letters of being 'a fly on the wall' in their study.

---

5 Autograph: Zürich StA, E II 339, 210 1/2 S. 4°, sehr gut erhalten, mit Siegelabdruck Gedruckt: S VIII 375 f; Z X 339.

6 Zwingli appears to mean that Carlstadt is the opposite of Luther and for that reason alone should be well received by them. Carlstadt was as despised by Luther as Zwingli was. It was, then, natural that Zwingli would see in Carlstadt something of an ally along the lines of 'the enemy of my enemy is my friend'.

7 Autograph: Zürich StA, E I 3. 1, Nr. 63 1 S. 4°, sehr gut erhalten, mit Siegelabdruck Gedruckt: S VIII 470; Z X 640f.

One stellar example of this is a letter written, but never sent, by Zwingli to Johannes Eck. In it he writes, in part:

> Look out, you impudent chap, now you will experience an examination which can't be borne by you, but only by a Hercules. You actually deserve it, that one would hurl against you everything that gives insult, derision, and offense... Is it not almost insane that you think so much of yourself, that you write against me to the Confederation in such a shameless, rude and disgusting manner? Were you born to cause only confusion everywhere? You lacked the strength to act, after you exposed your stupidity in the presence of all, and you also still need to abandon your wickedness, so that the world has not only Eck's foolishness, but also his meanness for a very long time as a deterring example before its eyes. They were silent once about evildoers such as Herostratus, Plemminius, Antonius and Catilina, but one day they will also speak about Eck, the embodiment of all scandal. Even from childhood your life was piggish, your tongue impudent, your mouth evil, your voice impure, your eyes ruttish, your forehead shameless. Your heart burned in such a manner from the craze for greed and fame, that you, as the prophet says, simply could not bear rest and peace. Therefore you went to Rome and, because you did not become a Bishop there, you returned again to Germany, in order to mix up everything. Can one among all mortals show another who has lived a life like your infamous life (scelestam)? Your belly is so devoted to voracity and lasciviousness that... you would have been a better raptor or ass than a human being. Everything manifests externally what it is internally; whether you look like a human or like an ape on the outside. You are indeed in action nothing other than a cow. You still need, as it appears to me, and everyone else, to be broken like a mule or a donkey. I could never find a man more miserable than you, even if I scanned the whole of Germany... Since one cannot bend you into shape with either mildness nor sharpness, nothing else can be done but to treat you like a runaway slave or a miller's ass which needs to be flogged with a club. Or is one to send you into the mad house? Oh, there is no mad house good enough to bring so wicked a man back to order. Even if one made every effort to restore him again, he will always be completely insane and raving; nothing different than a completely mad and common chap. You have always naturally been like that...[8]

The fire in Zwingli's soul at the mistreatment he received from Eck is on full display here but Zwingli's refusal to send the letter demonstrates, (presumably), the power of his faith to restrain his pen.

The correspondence of the Reformers also enables us to get a look into the most personal aspects of their lives. So, for instance, when Zwingli was under consideration for the Pastorate at the Great Minster in Zurich, word began to spread that he had engaged in illicit sexual activities with the daughter of the town barber. In response to the rumors, Zwingli wrote to Heinrich Uttinger the following missive:

> One of the most learned and amiable of our friends [Oswald Myconius] has written to me that a rumor has been spread in Zurich about me, alleging that I have seduced the

---

8 The translation is that of S.M. Jackson in his 'Huldrych Zwingli', Z VIII, 216–218.

daughter of a high official, and that this has given offense to a number of my friends. I must answer this calumny so that you, dear friend, and others, can clear my life from these false rumors … First, you know that three years ago I made a firm resolution not to interfere with any female: St. Paul said it was good not to touch a woman. That did not turn out very well. … As to the charge of seduction I needn't take long in dealing with that. They make it out to concern the daughter of an important citizen. I don't deny that she is the daughter of an important person: anyone who could touch the emperor's beard is important — barber forsooth! No one doubts that the lady concerned is the barber's daughter except possibly the barber himself who has often accused his wife, the girl's mother, a supposedly true and faithful wife, of adultery, blatant but not true. At any rate he has turned the girl, about whom all this fuss is being made, out from his house and for two years has given her neither board nor lodging. So what is the daughter of such a man to me? … With intense zeal day and night even at the cost of harm to his body, [I] study the Greek and Latin philosophers and theologians, and this hard work takes the heat out of such sensual desires even if it does not entirely eliminate them. Further, feelings of shame have so far restrained me that when I was still in Glarus and let myself fall into temptation in this regard a little, I did so so quietly that even my friends hardly knew about it. And now we will come to the matter before us and I will cast off what they call the last anchor taking no account of public opinion which takes a poor view of open resort to loose women. In this instance it was a case of maiden by day, matron by night, and not so much of the maiden by day but everybody in Einsiedeln knew about her … no one in Einsiedeln thought I had corrupted a maiden. All the girl's relations knew that she had been caught long before I came to Einsiedeln, so that I was not in any way concerned. … To close: I have written a good deal of facetious chatter, but these people don't understand anything else. You can say whatever you think suitable to anyone who is concerned.[9]

It is precisely this kind of insight into Zwingli and Bullinger (and Calvin and Luther and Oecolampadius and Bucer and all the rest) that a study of their correspondence allows us. The correspondence of Zwingli and Bullinger deserve wider attention if only because it introduces us to aspects of their lives we would otherwise never enjoy. Translators are encouraged in the strongest possible terms to turn their attention to the correspondence of the Reformers and provide the wider public the insights which till now have been too restricted to specialists alone.

---

9 G.R. Potter's translation and selection of the letter to Utinger, Z VII, 110f.

For Further Reading:

There is an absolute dearth of materials in English about Zwingli and Bullinger and an even bigger lacuna in texts by Zwingli and Bullinger. Most of the materials in English, in fact, stem from the 19th and 20th centuries. Only the present author's volume on Zwingli is more recent than 2004.

GORDON, BRUCE and EMIDIO CAMPI. (2004), Architect of Reformation: An Introduction to Heinrich Bullinger, 1504–1575. Grand Rapids: Baker Academic.

JACKSON, SAMUEL MACAULEY. (1901), Huldreich Zwingli: The Reformer of German Switzerland (1484–1531). Heroes of the Reformation. New York; London: G. P. Putnam's Sons; Knickerbocker Press.

SIMPSON, SAMUEL. (1902), Life of Ulrich Zwingli: The Swiss Patriot and Reformer. New York: Baker & Taylor Co.

WEST, JIM. (2011), "Christ Our Captain": An Introduction to Huldrych Zwingli. Quartz Hill, CA: Quartz Hill Publishing House.

ZWINGLI, HULDREICH. (1912), The Latin Works and The Correspondence of Huldreich Zwingli: Together with Selections from His German Works. Edited by Samuel Macauley Jackson. Translated by Henry Preble, Walter Lichtenstein, and Lawrence A. McLouth. Vol. 1. New York; London: G. P. Putnam's Sons; Knickerbocker Press.

— (1922), The Latin Works of Huldreich Zwingli. Edited by William John Hinke. Vol. 2. Philadelphia: Heidelberg Press.

— (1929), The Latin Works of Huldreich Zwingli. Edited by Clarence Nevin Heller. Vol. 3. Philadelphia: Heidelberg Press.

— (1899), The Christian Education of Youth. Translated by Alcide Reichenbach. Collegeville, PA: Thompson Brothers.

The material available in German is much more abundant. Chiefly readers are advised to purchase the following:

OPITZ, PETER. (2015), Ulrich Zwingli: Prophet, Ketzer, Pionier des Protestantismus. Zurich: Theologischer Verlag.

Finally, a very new very large volume covering the entire topic of the Reformation in Switzerland has been published by Brill and it is utterly indispensable:

BURNETT, AMY NELSON and EMIDIO CAMPI, eds. (2016), A Companion to the Swiss Reformation. Leiden: E.J. Brill.

Rebecca A. Giselbrecht

Cliché or Piety: Heinrich Bullinger and Women in Alsace

The website for forgotten books has digitalized the little book containing the biography of Anna Alexandria zu Rappoltstein (1504–1581).[1] Published in 1900 in *Frakturaschrift* (that is, German typeface), it is a little forty-eight-page pamphlet. The source material that Heinrich Rocholl, the biographer, quotes is mostly Reformation history written in the late nineteenth century.[2] The problem with many texts from his time is not merely their moral didactic intention but more so that this influences our ability to determine their historical veracity. For instance, Heinrich Rocholl is justified to claim,

> Such a moving life of an evangelical woman is embodied in the name of this Anna Alexandria! She is truly worthy to be named among the first to confess the true gospel from the time of the Reformation; she stands as a noble ruler, true mother, and strongly believing Protestant; the following shall serve to reclaim her forgotten image.[3]

However, his enthusiasm irritates our contemporary sober sense of historicity. To Rocholl's merit, many of the documents he cites are attributed to the archives in Colmar in Alsace where they are still extant. He also mentions a large volume of correspondence originally from Anna Alexandria zu Rappoltstein including her correspondence with Matthias Erb (1494–1571) and her exchanges with Heinrich

---

1 The book is available online at: www.forgottenbooks.com/books/Anna_Alexandria_Herr-in_zu_Rappolstein_1100042270. For complete book see footnote 2.
2 In 1900, Heinrich Rocholl was commissioned by the Verein für Reformationsgeschichte to write a booklet on Anna Alexandria herrin zu Rappoltstein. An exception to many early twentieth-century authors, he does cite some of his references. However, the booklet is not a summary of the extensive correspondence that Anna Alexandria maintained. The letter exchanges with Zurich are merely mentioned in his biography. See: Heinrich Rocholl, *Anna Alexandria Herrin zu Rappoltstein, eine evangelische Edelfrau aus der Reformation im Elsass* (Halle: Verein für Reformationsgeschichte, 1900). Anna Alexandria's correspondence with Zurich is research that Hans Ulrich Bächtold gathered for his essay in 2001; whereby, the current author enlarged on this to include other letters and z. Rappoltstein's own writings. See: Bächtold, "Frauen schreiben Bullinger," 143–160.
3 *Rocholl, Anna Alexandria Herrin zu Rappoltstein.*

Bullinger (1504–1575).[4] In addition, there are several letters from Rudolf
Gwalther (1519–1585) in the collection from the Zurich Reformers, as well as
others to family members and for business purposes. In the following, we will
focus on the correspondence and the functional role of piety in the correspondence.

Anna Alexandria remains a mostly unknown reformer. Hans Ulrich Baechtold, however, dedicated half of his essay about Bullinger's correspondence with
women to Bullinger's exchanges with Anna Alexandria zu Rappoltstein.[5] She is
mentioned in a few contemporary essays, but there is no general assessment of
her role in the Reformation in Rappoltstein to date. In his essay, Baechtold
summarizes Anna Alexandria in relation to Bullinger,

> With Anna Alexandria zu Rappoltstein, a strong personality appears in Bullinger's
> correspondence, a woman – pious and rigorous at the same time – who perseveres to
> achieve her goal. She follows church and political developments with interest and a
> sharp eye, and she addresses their problems.[6]

After such apt praise, Baechtold's conclusion, especially since he is writing about
women's letters, is rather unexpected.

> In this case, it is completely unclear to what extent one can speak of a "Women's letter
> exchange." Naturally, the content is heavily weighted in the area of counseling, and
> Anna Alexandria's strongly trained sense of family. Nevertheless, partnership as a
> company of common interest among the shapers and receivers of the Reformation is
> decisive for their partnership.[7]

A full-fledged biography of Anna Alexandria zu Rappoltstein and an edition of
her prayer book and confession of faith are currently being written by this author.
Indeed, only an examination of some of her correspondence with Bullinger and
Gwalther is possible here. Nevertheless, these will help establish Rappoltstein's
appropriation of and participated in the Zurich Reformation – her testimony and

---

4 Hans Ulrich Bächtold, "Frauen schreiben Bullinger: Bullinger schreibt Frauen. Heinrich
  Bullinger im Briefwechsel mit Frauen, insbesondere mit Anna Alexandria zu Rappoltstein, in
  Die Zürcher Reformation: Ausstrahlungen und Rückwirkungen, ed. Alfred Schindler and Hans
  Stickelberger, Zurich: TVZ, 2001, 143–160, 148, nt. 24, Colmarer Bezirksarchiv E 578.
5 Bächtold, "Frauen schreiben Bullinger," esp., 147–55.
6 Bächtold, "Frauen schreiben Bullinger," 154: "Mit Anna Alexandria zu Rappoltstein tritt im
  Bullinger-Briefwechsel eine starke Persönlichkeit in Erscheinung, eine Frau, die – fromm und
  energisch zugleich – ihre Ziele mit Ausdauer anstrebt. Sie verfolgt mit Interesse und wachem
  Blick die kirchlichen wie auch politischen Entwicklungen, und sie hinterfragt die Probleme."
7 Bächtold, "Frauen schreiben Bullinger," 155: "Wie weit man in diesem Fall von "Frauen-
  briefwechsel" sprechen muß, ist gänzlich unklar. Natürlich fällt der inhaltlich gewichtige
  Anteil an Seelsorgerlichem oder Anna Alexandrias stark ausgebildeter Familiensinn ins Ge-
  wicht. – Entscheidend jedoch in dieser Briefbeziehung ist die Partnerschaft als Interessen-
  verband unter Gestaltern und Erhaltern der Reformation."

religious piety are of interest. Particularly, what secular scholars tend to categorize as religious clichés will be assessed.

Bloodlines

Anna Alexandria was of royal blood and belonged to the *Grafengeschlecht von Fürstenberg*. She was born on 5 November 1503 to Wolfgang, Graf of Fürstenberg, and highest Roman in Alsace. Anna Alexandria's mother was the *Gräfin* of Solms – a pious Catholic woman – who venerated Saint Anna. Anna Alexandria zu Fürstenberg married Ulrich von Rappoltstein on 10 August 1522. Although her work as a reformer is yet to be argued, Rappoltstein is highly praised for her virtues in all of the chronicles.[8] In the French history, *Entre la Gloire et la Vertu: Les Sires de Ribeaupierre: 1451–1585*, however, her life takes up two paragraphs with the sub-title "Die alte Frau von Rappoltstein" – the old woman from Rappoltstein.[9] The historical work does not discuss her piety.

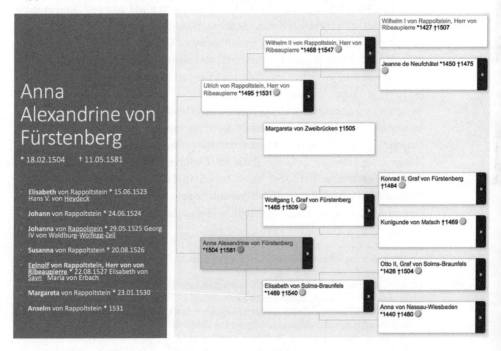

Anna
Alexandrine von
Fürstenberg

* 18.02.1504   † 11.05.1581

Elisabeth von Rappoltstein * 15.06.1523
Hans V. von Heydeck

Johann von Rappoltstein * 24.06.1524

Johanna von Rappoltstein * 29.05.1525 Georg
IV von Waldburg-Wolfegg-Zeil

Susanna von Rappoltstein * 20.08.1526

Eginolf von Rappoltstein, Herr von von
Ribeaupierre * 22.08.1527 Elisabeth von
Savn Maria von Erbach

Margareta von Rappoltstein * 23.01.1530

Anselm von Rappoltstein * 1531

Wilhelm I von Rappoltstein, Herr von
Ribeaupierre *1427 †1507

Wilhelm II von Rappoltstein, Herr von
Ribeaupierre *1468 †1547

Jeanne de Neufchâtel *1450 †1475

Ulrich von Rappoltstein, Herr von
Ribeaupierre *1495 †1531

Margareta von Zweibrücken †1505

Konrad II, Graf von Fürstenberg
†1484

Wolfgang I, Graf von Fürstenberg
*1465 †1509

Kunigunde von Matsch †1469

Anna Alexandrine von Fürstenberg
*1504 †1581

Otto II, Graf von Solms-Braunfels
*1426 †1504

Elisabeth von Solms-Braunfels
*1469 †1540

Anna von Nassau-Wiesbaden
*1440 †1480

8 Rocholl, *Anna Alexandria Herrin zu Rappoltstein*, 13.
9 Jordan, Benôit, La noblesse d'Alsace entre la gloire et la vertu: Les Sires de Ribeaupierre, 1451–
   1585 (Strasbourg: Editions Société Savante d'Alsace, 1991), 33.

Anna Alexandria zu Rappoltstein secretly read the Bible and Luther's publications, and she came to know that her husband was doing the same thing.[10] Much like Renée de France, Justina von Lupfen, and any number of people during the early years of the Reformation, Ulrich v. and Anna z. Rappoltstein were forced to hide their true Reformed convictions for political reasons. Anna z. Rappoltstein's husband Ulrich died in 1531 when their son Egenolf, who was born on 22 August 1527, was four years old. Ulrich von Rappoltstein's father Wilhelm II ruled until Egenolf was able to. Egenolf von Rappoltstein initially was trained silently in the Lutheran ways, and then the Zurich reformer's theological positions. After Wilhelm II passed away on 7 October 1547, Egenolf reigned. Anna z. Rappoltstein was educated, and intellectual; she also wrote prayers. Some of her prayers survived and now shape a little bundle in the archives of Colmar, but there is also a bound book[11] as well as her personal confession of faith.[12] The prayer book she wrote for her son Egenolf's wedding is titled, *A Book of New and Beautiful Prayers with Many Psalms to Use and Ask for God's Grace and Help in Everything.*[13] The volume is 167 pages handwritten in early New High German.

Hans Ulrich Baechtold suggests that Anna Alexandria zu Rappoltstein came into contact with Heinrich Bullinger through Matthias Erb, who served in Alsace as a pastor and superintendent by authority of Georg, Graf von Württemberg, from 1539 in Reichenweier (Riquewihr), and also for Rappoltsweiler/Ribeauvillé until he was sent away in 1561. Erb lived the rest of his life until he passed away in 1571 in Rappoltsweiler/Ribeauvillé.[14] Anna Alexandria zu Rappoltstein's daughters made contact with Bullinger when Heinrich and Anna Bullinger as well as Rudolf Gwalther with his family were on vacation at the spa in Baden by Zurich.[15] In any case, the letters from Rappoltstein's daughter Elisabeth von Heideck to Bullinger precede those of Rappoltstein. Elisabeth von Heideck, Rappoltstein's daughter, sent three letters to Bullinger; Anna Alexandria zu Rappoltstein sent Bullinger 15 letters, and he sent her 10.[16] Elisabeth's letters will be examined first for traces of religious language.

---

10 Rocholl, *Anna Alexandria Herrin zu Rappoltstein*, 13.

11 Bezirksarchiv zu Colmar E 648.

12 Rocholl, *Anna Alexandria Herrin zu Rappoltstein*, 19.

13 Rocholl, *Anna Alexandria Herrin zu Rappoltstein*, 17: "Ein Bettbüchlein neuer schöner Gebete mit etlichen Psalmen für allerlei Anliegen bei Gott um Gnade und Hilfe anzusuchen und zu bitten." R. Giselbrecht is currently editing the book.

14 Bächtold, "Frauen schreiben Bullinger," 148, nt. 24.

15 Bächtold, "Frauen schreiben Bullinger," 149, nt. 25: "Elisabeth, Witwe von Johannes, Herrn von Heideck (d. 1554), und ihre jüngere Schwester Johanna, verheiratet mit Georg, Truchseß und Feihherr von Waldburg, vgl. Kindler von Knobloch, Geschlechterbuch (Anm. 22), 336, hatten während eines mehrwöchigen Badeaufenthaltes im aargauischen Baden im September 1560 Bullinger besucht."

16 See Appendix for complete list of letters.

Elisabeth von Heideck

Before Bullinger's correspondence with Anna Alexandria zu Rappoltstein is introduced, it is worthwhile to analyze what can be gleaned from her daughter
Elisabeth von Heideck's exchanges with Bullinger and to establish Elisabeth's
self-identity as well as can be done with three letters and some background
information. The reformed network developed internationally through personal
relationships because Rappoltstein's daughter's visited the spa in Baden outside
of Zurich. Elisabeth's exchanges with Bullinger are typical, in that one of the main
features of practically every letter from Bullinger to and from women is the
exchange of books. Plainly, Bullinger influenced and taught men and women by
guiding their reading programs, as seen in his exchange with Lady Jane Grey, with
Justina von Lupfen, among other women; the Rappoltsteiners were no exception.
Elisabeth was part of the Protestant movement; nevertheless, her mother was
always concerned that she remain true to the cause.[17] The religious language is
ever present in all of their extant exchanges, but what we want to know is whether
their language is a cliché or truthful expression of their religious intentions and
concerns.

Elisabeth von Heideck wrote to Bullinger on 29 September 1560 and began her
letter with the same greeting that she used for most of her letters, "Grace and
peace from God through Jesus Christ, our Lord, and everything honorable, loving
and good that I have be yours forever."[18] Most of v. Heideck's letters bear the
same post-script; but does this mean that it was a cliché or does it express her
religious convictions? She thanks Bullinger also in the name of her sister for
Johan Wolff's book that Bullinger sent them. She promises, "So God will, I shall
read it earnestly and diligently in the hope that God, the Father of all grace, will,
through his Holy Spirit share his grace with me, that thereby my effort [to read the
book] will not be fruitless."[19] She wants to pay Bullinger for the book and sends
greetings to Bullinger's wife and children.[20] Finally, the letter full of references to
God, ends with von Heideck's blessing for Bullinger and his wife, and entire
household.[21]

---

17 Elisabeth zu Heideck to Heinrich Bullinger, 3 February 1564.
18 Elisabeth zu Heideck to Heinrich Bullinger, 29 September 1560, Zürich ZB, Ms. 80, 643r.-v:
"Gnod und frid von got, dem vatter, durch *Jessum Christum* und was ich alles liebs und gutz
vermag sey eich zuvor, erenthaffter(a), lieber her Heinrich Bullinger."
19 Elisabeth zu Heideck to Heinrich Bullinger, 29 September 1560: "Ich will es auch, ob got will,
mit fleiß und ernst(g) leßen, bin auch der hoffnung, got, der vatter aller gnode[n](h) wird
durch seinen heiligen geist sein gnod mittheillen, das es bey mir nicht on fruchten wete(i)
abgon."
20 Elisabeth zu Heideck to Heinrich Bullinger, 29 September 1560.
21 Elisabeth zu Heideck to Heinrich Bullinger, 29 September 1560.

Once again Elisabeth thanks Bullinger for sending books in her letter from 5 October 1560.[22] Her religious salutation remains consistent with her other letters. She has been thinking about Bullinger's beloved housewife and sends her a piece of something wooden – the noun is illegible. In addition, she assures Bullinger that he and his wife are in her prayers because, "True as can be, these times are very difficult, as you know better than I am able to write to you."[23] Her apologies that she and her sister were returning home without stopping by for a visit in Zurich as they had planned complete the body of her letter. Again she blesses the family.

The next letter Elisabeth wrote to Bullinger is dated 3 February 1564, three years after her mother Anna Alexandria zu Rappoltstein began corresponding with Bullinger.[24] In her letter, Elisabeth wishes Bullinger, his wife, and his family a blessed New Year. She writes that she was happy to receive a letter from her mother reporting that Bullinger's health had improved, "God and Christ alone can comfort us, according to Scripture."[25] Then she writes Mt. 11:28–30 as comfort to Bullinger, "Come to Me, all who are weary and heavy-laden, and I will give you rest. Take my yoke upon you and learn from Me, for I am gentle and humble in heart, and you will find rest for your souls. For My yoke is easy and My burden is light." The young Elisabeth sending the great Bible scholar biblical comfort is endearing; it is also a mark of her self-conscious profession of faith and application of her knowledge of scripture in the correspondence — it is her testimony and no cliché. Near the end of the letter, she begins to complain about the situation at her church; true to the Reformed perspective, Elisabeth does not agree that anyone should have to make a confession to a clergyman before being allowed to receive the Eucharist.[26] Her worries connect well to reflect her mother's worries about *her little church*.

Anna Alexandria zu Rappoltstein and Heinrich Bullinger

Bullinger's letter to Anna Alexandria zu Rappoltstein from 20 March 1563 is in reply to her concern regarding her daughter, who had moved to Behmer Wald where the church was not reformed. Bullinger replied with an entire page of comforting words for Anna Alexandria zu Rappoltstein. He goes into great detail appealing to Old Testament figures — Abraham, Jacob, Isaac and Rebecca, Jo-

---

22 Elisabeth zu Heideck to Heinrich Bullinger, 5 October 1560, Zürich ZB, Ms. F 80, 645r.-v.
23 Elisabeth zu Heideck to Heinrich Bullinger, 5 October 1560: "Dan worlichen die leiff eitz dißer zeit gantz schwer sind, wie ir dan wol selb besser wist, dan ich eich zuschreiben kendt."
24 Elisabeth zu Heideck to Heinrich Bullinger, 3 February 1564, StA E II 361, 140.
25 Elisabeth zu Heideck to Heinrich Bullinger, 3 February 1564.
26 Elisabeth zu Heideck to Heinrich Bullinger, 3 February 1564.

seph — all of whom left their fathers and mothers for new lands, "but in the end, all of us will live together in joy."[27] Elisabeth v. Heideck was a member of the reformed camp going into a foreign land with the good news of the gospel. Bullinger's arguments supported by scripture are known to scholarship. However, the absoluteness of the faith that lies behind his work are all too often secondary to military, political, and power issues that interest our contemporaries; the pious spiritual reality of the Reformation is all too often second and categorized as clichés rather than central to the actual authorial intent.

The evidentiary value of exchange has not been explicitly discussed thus far; however, paying for books, owing something to someone else for their kindness or material gifts – wanting to send gifts of thanksgiving – is also present in most reformed women's letters. More so, however, the religious content, spiritual counseling, and religious direction of every letter is the glue that holds the Reformed correspondence together. Elisabeth von Heideck is no exception with her concern for scripture, desire to understand theology better, and her commitment to do so "God willing." Her concern for the church and its doctrine are also a hallmark of women's correspondence with the Zurich reformers. However, the prevalence of prayers and blessings for others and the need to ask others to pray is perhaps the most common factor in v. Heideck's letters and is representative of what the other women in *the reformed circle* were writing. There is every reason to believe that Elisabeth's self-understanding was fundamentally comprised by her female religious identity as a witness to her belief.

An impressive network of reformers grew from Elisabeth and her sister's meeting with the Bullingers. As already mentioned, Rappoltstein and Bullinger exchanged letters for more than ten years, and I am editing these as well as her other writings. In this sense, Rappoltstein's exchanges represent evidence that women appropriated and participated in the Zurich Reformation, even as reformers – women's testimonies, faith language, and opinions are available and can be interpreted. The following will examine some of the letters that typify the exchanges between Rappoltstein with Rudolf Gwalther and Heinrich Bullinger. All of the exchanges between Zurich with Rappoltstein take more or less the same shape. The letters usually begin with "Grace and peace from God the Father through *Jesus Christ* our redeemer. Amen. Along with my friendly greetings in the Lord *Christ.*"[28] Notice that her salutation differs from her daughter's and my

---

27 Heinrich Bullinger to Anna Alexandria zu Rappoltstein, 20 March 1563, ADép E 726, 13, 1–3, "Und ob iren gnaden ettwas menschlichs ztfiele das sy kranck wurde in unfaal kåme (darvor sy gott trüwlich behrte) oder far sturbe oder das u[wer] g[naden] sturbe sy in disem ib nitt me ansshe so ist es doch one allen zwyfel das wir dvrt ewig(c) in frvuden by einander whonen werdent."

28 Anna Alexandria zu Rappoltstein to Rudolf Gwalther, 22 January 1561, StA, E II 338, 1596r.-v.:

research shows that her preface and salutation also differ from those of other women in her circle. The first extant letter she sent to Zurich was, not to Bullinger, but rather to Rudolf Gwalther. Rappoltstein's letter from 22 January 1561 begins,

> I cannot, not write to you, since I desire to know how you and the people you love are doing. The lovely book that you sent to me reminds me of you. It is in my living room and continuously reminds me of you. I pray to the Lord of hosts that you have a long life so that you can write more of these books in the spirit of God, for the poor, those in need of comfort, for the comfort of the grieving, and for their well being.[29]

All of her letters include a section on books that need to be sent or the reception of other books. Anna Alexandria zu Rappoltstein's main points of discussion, however, are usually her questions pertaining to correct doctrine, church rules, and church leadership. In her 22 January 1561 letter, she laments the situation in "her little church" to Gwalther,

> This Christmas a lot happened to change the Lord's Supper. The preacher gave only five people the Eucharist. Many people went forward to receive the Eucharist but the pastor pushed them back and said, "I'm not giving it to you, because you did not come before; you did not purify yourself. In other words, you want to give others the impression that you are following the rules, and that is why I won't give it to you." These members left the church with tears in their eyes. We are all upset. I listened to four of the preacher's sermons, and they made me cry because they brought up things that were already put aside by the grace of God. The Lord of all things does not want us to turn from him. The dear old preachers are in great danger and are being persecuted, hunted. May the dear Lord have mercy on them and us.[30]

"Gnad und fryd von gott, dem vatter, durch *Jesum Christum*, unssern erlösser. Amen. Sampt minen fruntlichen gruß in heren *Christo*, ersamer und wolgelertter herr *Rudolff Walter*."

29 Anna Alexandria zu Rappoltstein to Rudolf Gwalther, 22 January 1561: "Ich kann nicht underlassen, euch zu schrieben, diewill ich so gewiss bottschafft zu euch hab, damit ich erfaren mege, wie ir sampt den euwern geliebten leben, dan ich nit in dem zit mines lebens euwer nymer vergessen will noch kann, dan die schonen büchlin, so ir mir zugeschieckt haben, synd f – mir ser lieb, und bit den hern aller herscharen, daz ir lang lebt, damit ir disser gotselligen(a) bucher noch vil schrieben megen, den armen, trostlossen, betrubten gewissen zu trost und heil."

30 Anna Alexandria zu Rappoltstein to Rudolf Gwalther, 22 January 1561: "Ich kann auch nit underlassen, euch zu klagen, wiewol ich weis, ir sy vorhyn bericht syt, wie es in unserr kyrchen also ubel stat, daz es gott ym hymel geklagt sye, mir habens leider wol verdient, daz daz klar, leutter wortt uns genomen ist, und ist unsser kirch ser zertrentt, es ist jetz in dissen win-nachten vil enderung beschehen mit dez heren nachtmall. Daz hat man dennoch niemand geben wellen, dan denen, die sich am aben dem bredigcanten erzeigt haben, daz synd 5 perschonen gewesen. Es synd etliche alte perschonen hinzugangen, hat der bredygcant mit der hand hindersich gestossen und gesagt: 'Ich gyb dirs nit, dan du bist nechten nit komen, daz du dich gereinigt hast und bist auch ungehorsam erschinen, darum gyb ich dirs nit.' Synd die und andere mit weinenden augen zu der kyrchen hinaußgegangen, daz nieman von der gemein blyben ist dan 5 perschonen, denen er daz nachtmall geben hat. Dezhalben wir in grosser bekumerniß synd. Ich hab bischer nit wellen by iren bredigen syn. Ich hab mir 4 bredigen gehärtt, die haben mir die augen ubergetryben, dan ich wol gehört, daz vil wider

Anna Alexandria zu Rappoltstein ends her letter with a promise to pray for Gwalther and commits him and his entire family under God's *wing*. She sends him a hat and two pieces of cloth, which were to be of practical service to him.[31] The piety and biblical ideas appear to belong to her uniquely, likely a product of her scriptural studies and interpretations.

Anna Alexandria zu Rappoltstein addresses the Lord's Supper controversy in her letter to Gwalther and continues to do so later with Bullinger. Moreover, she also discussed her doctrine of the Eucharist in her *Confession of Faith*.[32] Rappoltstein wrote her confession in a little pamphlet titled confession, which she may well have written together with her husband before he passed away.[33] A portion of the text of her confession that discusses the Eucharist is worth evaluating in terms of Rappoltstein's self-identity as a reformer, her theological dedication, and prowess. The section again, merely represents the larger handwritten manuscript.

> I confess that the Lord's Supper is the other sign of God's covenant/testimony to the Church of Christ; that Christ is in his church with his majesty, power, and grace. And that eternal life cannot be attained by any other fare except for his body and blood, which he sacrificed for us on the cross, that it is not necessary that his life blood is visible and invisible, physical and fleshly. It is important that it was raised to heaven and eaten with the mouth on this earth, that is, spiritually eaten. Thus, through the Holy Spirit our existing faith is strengthened in our hearts, which include all gifts, earnings, favor, community, and goodness in his broken body and in his spent blood. All Scriptures testify that Christ with his flesh and blood is spiritual food for our souls.[34]

---

herfurgebracht wirdt, daz einmal von den gnaden gottes hingelegt waz. Der herr aller deing welle uns nit von im abwichen lassen. Es sind auch die lyeben alten predicanten in grosser gefar, warden mit gedult alle stund, wan sy verjagt werden, dan sy vil angefochten werden. Da vil von zu schreiber wer, aber der feder nit(b) zt vertruwen. Der liebe gott welle sich irer und unser aller erbarmen."

31 Anna Alexandria zu Rappoltstein to Rudolf Gwalther, 22 January 1561: "Auch, liebe her, ich schicken euch ein schlecht hüblin sampt ein wenig fatzenletlin zu eim gruß mit bitt, von mir in gutten auffnemen, dan es nun ..., daz ir sehen, daz euwer nit vergys."

32 Bibliothèque de Colmar MS 230, 85.

33 Rocholl, Anna Alexandria Herrin zu Rappoltstein, 20.

34 Rocholl, *Anna Alexandria Herrin zu Rappoltstein*, 22: "Vom Nachtmahl bekenne ich, dass es das andere Bundeszeichen der Kirche Christi sei; dass Christus mit seiner Majestät, Gewalt und Gnade in seiner Kirche sie und die selbige mit keiner anderen Speise nebst Trank zn dem ewigen Leben erhalte, denn mit seinem Leib und Blut, das er am Kreuz für uns geopfert hat, dass nicht not ist, dass sein Leben und Blut, sichtbarlich und unsichtbarlich, leiblich und fleischlich, wissentlich, wie es zu Himmel gefahren, auf Erden mündlich gegessen werde, sondern geistlicher Weise, so der beständige Glaube in unserm Herzen gestärkt durch den heiligen Geist, fassest alle Gaben, Verdienst, Gunst, Gemeinschaft, Guttat in seinem zerbrochenen Leib und in seinem vergossenen Blut. Es zeigen alle Schriften, dass Christus mit seinem Fleisch und Blut eine geistliche Speise unserer Seele sie." The text is located at the Bezirksarchiv zu Colmar E. 648.

The emphasis on spiritual eating leaves no doubt but that Rappoltstein had definitely appropriated the Zwinglian, Zurich understanding of the Lord's Supper. The political back-and-forth and struggle between the Lutheran, Zwinglian, Calvinist and Old Church are one reason for her confession, which underscores her position in the church as both a spiritual and organizational leader of its new direction.

Baechtold probed the exchanges between Rappoltstein and Bullinger within their historical context in terms of the overarching interconnectivity between the regions of Alsace and Zurich. In particular, he notes that Bullinger supported Rappoltstein in the midst of her feelings of isolation when the governing Habsburgers under Kaiser Ferdinand made Zwinglianism illegal. His argument is sensitive to the notion of her self-identity as the chosen protector of *her little church*. Not all of the letters can be presented here, but the following overview will excerpt the epistles content and their conversations as a foundation to support the idea that Rappoltstein's religious self-identity was the more central motivational impetus for her decisions than her political position – marks of her piety and no cliché.[35] That is to say, she assumed that spiritual welfare is a primary ideological good and necessity for being the protectorate of the people she assisted her son to rule. As the letters make clear, Rappoltstein wanted to see the entire region that her son presided over reformed. In order to achieve her goal, she protected young pastors, encouraged her son, built schools, and obtained stipends for two of the promising young men of her region to study theology in Zurich.[36]

The first letter in Bullinger's correspondence with Rappoltstein was sent on 23 March 1561.[37] Bullinger goes into great detail about the cure she sent him for his ailment. He writes about all of the medicines he has applied to no avail, but is more than happy to try hers. The problem was most likely his headaches or even migraines. As was his tradition with the men he corresponded with, Bullinger sent Rappoltstein two books on the church counsels, which he does not want any money for. He mentions that he cannot send his sermons on Jeremiah to her just yet because they are in Latin. Of course, this means that Rappoltstein did not have the complete set of language skills of her male companions, that is, she was not completely educated to the level of an intellectual man with Latin skills, which was not unusual for women in the Germanic provinces.

Bullinger's second letter to Rappoltstein on 26 May 1561 is to tell her that books are arriving for her and her daughters.[38] He goes into great detail con-

---

35 Bächtold, "Frauen schreiben Bullinger," 151.
36 Bächtold, "Frauen schreiben Bullinger," 151.
37 Heinrich Bullinger to Anna Alexandria zu Rappoltstein, 23 March 1561, ADép E 726, 13, 1–3.
38 Heinrich Bullinger to Anna Alexandria zu Rappoltstein, 26 May1561, ADép, E 578, 10, 1–3.

cerning Christ's bodily resurrection and Jesus being in heaven, arguing, in the next paragraph, against the Lutherans and the Augsburg Confession. Bullinger is sorry that the Lutheran versus Zwinglian conflict has not been resolved; nevertheless, he is pleased that Philip of Hessen and the *Pfaltzgraf* are on their side. Both of these points are central to his letter, which we must assume at least he felt interested Rappoltstein. He proceeds to provide what sounds a lot like missionary news: France is doing well; the gospel is thriving there; nothing yet about the Council of Trent; Italy is preparing for war; the Helvetians seem to be making progress. If she understood what Bullinger was saying, Anna Alexandria zu Rappoltstein appears to be deeply involved in spreading *right religion* and possessed the theological acumen to process the developments. Her replies support this observation and evidence a cognitive exchange with Bullinger on several levels, including the theological, which required her linguistic mastery of the Reformer's pious vernacular.

The level of intellectual intensity and interest in church growth does not decline in any way throughout the years that Rappoltstein and Bullinger corresponded. A summary of two letters from Rappolstein and one from Bullinger must suffice here to evaluate Rappoltstein's self-identity and the nature of, one might say, the apostolic nature of the religious testimony of a Reformed woman at least in what she wrote.

On 24 July 1561, she begins her letter with a prayer for Bullinger's longevity so that "many may be comforted and strengthened in their faith because the times are difficult and Satan is pressing in, over and over again. The Day of the Lord will be shortened because of the chosen; otherwise no one would be saved."[39] Then she asks Bullinger to find a publisher for Matthias Erb's book of comforting words in times of distress. Here we recognize the interest she has in promoting others and spreading the Reformation. Afterwards, Rappoltstein requests Bullinger purchase the book about the councils for her. Finally, there is news of progress and regression in the Reformation efforts and financial issues to negotiate in which Rappoltstein as usual looks for Bullinger's advantage.[40] There is no noticeable difference between how Rappoltstein and Bullinger correspond and that of Bullinger's other close men friends.

In her next letter to Bullinger on 10 August 1561, Rappoltstein is emotional and enraged about the pastors that are not getting along together in her little church.[41] The problem is in the town of Bergwerk, which lies basically on an adjacent hillside to her castle. She is beside herself; the preachers will not even speak to each other much less cooperate together for the cause. The letter in-

---

39 Anna Alexandria zu Rappoltstein to Heinrich Bullinger, 24 July 1561, StA, E II 361, 132.
40 Anna Alexandria zu Rappoltstein to Heinrich Bullinger, 24 July 1561.
41 Anna Alexandria zu Rappoltstein to Heinrich Bullinger, 10 August 1561, StA, E II 361, 134.

cludes her book requests and a discussion of the matter of transferring funds as usual.

Bullinger's reply on 15 August 1561 is most interesting.[42] He suggests that her son Egenolf III Landgraf von Rappoltstein (1527–1585) should seek help from the Palatinate. Addressing the problem among the pastors in the region ruled by the Rappoltsteins, Bullinger works out a complete plan of action and shares it with Rappoltstein. First, she should seek to unify the pastors together among themselves. But, "if they no longer build, but only destroy," she should send them to other places.[43] Then she and her son must seek others who can work together, and these should be men of peace who teach the gospel, not the Augsburg Confession; especially, not Augsburg Confession's arguments in regard to the Lord's Supper – adhering to the pope's teachings. She must be very careful that the government does not see this as a schism. But, first of all, seek unity. He ends by telling his friend Anna that she should encourage the youth and serve as their leader. Close to the end of his letter, Bullinger complains of a headache. Then, once again, the missionary news: the pope is in a bad mood, there is persecution in Calabria, Philip of Hessen is asking for help to hold back the Turks; Spain has introduced the inquisition.[44] The theological and religious finally mix to be a complete way of life that does not exclude politics, habitus, real life. The religious language is applying words for faith to engage concepts and the problems of a world –namely, applying the common Reformed theological content the two reformers shared.

Anna Alexandria zu Rappoltstein answered Bullinger on 5 October 1561, "Grace and joy from God, the Father, through Jesus Christ our redeemer, together with my friendly greetings, most scholarly, dear, Mr. Bullinger." The other letters (through 1571) also merit attention, but the exchange to this point will suffice for interpreting whether the religious language among the reformed men and women were simply cliché socially adapted vernacular adornments or actually the concrete substance of their reform project.

A provisional summation of Anne Alexandria's testimony emerges from what she wrote to Bullinger on 5 October 1561:[45]

> I cannot hold back from telling you how Satan is practicing great divisiveness between the Germans and the French practices in Bergwerk, so that our dear God mourns. May he pour out his godly peace. I thought that the whole thing had to do with the rules of church order, but I have come to understand that those on the German side cannot bear the French. The greed of most is responsible for this because they complain about them saying the Calvinists are richer than they themselves. To this I say, this is true because they are not wine drinkers, not lazy and acting against God, and because of the church

---

42 Heinrich Bullinger to Anna Alexandria zu Rappoltstein, 15 August 1561, ADép, E 726, 18.
43 Heinrich Bullinger to Anna Alexandria zu Rappoltstein, 15 August 1561.
44 Heinrich Bullinger to Anna Alexandria zu Rappoltstein, 15 August 1561.
45 Anna Alexandria zu Rappoltstein to Heinrich Bullinger, StA, E II 361, 135r.-v.

[wherein] they have more order, particularly in how they practice the Lord's Supper – may God hear this lamentation.[46]

Bullinger's reply was mentioned above in relation to his comforting explanation of Abraham and Sarah and how God sends his people out into the world for his own purposes. In this same letter, Bullinger praises the Heidelberg Catechism that he received from the Palatinate and suggests that Anna Alexandria and her son use the Catechism for their church and schools.[47]

The correspondence between Rappoltstein and Bullinger continued for another ten years. However, to interpret her testimony is already visible in the exchanges above – her usage of biblical language, pious expressions, and theological ideology were certainly not clichés, there was no reason for her to use them other than her convictions. Anna Alexandria zu Rappoltstein testified to her belief as the champion of her little church, guiding her husband and son as they governed. Rocholl says that she was a champion of the underdogs and "Pushed back with all of her power against the persecution and eviction of the Anabaptists, Calvinists, and other sects."[48] Egenolf did not implement the Heidelberg Catechism, which in the politics of Rappoltstein might have caused war. He allowed the Augsburg Confession Variata for the surrounding churches and had the preacher in his own little church teach from the Heidelberg Catechism until he died in 1585.[49]

---

46 Anna Alexandria zu Rappoltstein to Heinrich Bullinger, StA, E II 361, 135r.-v: "Ich kann nitt unerlassen, euch zu ber–tigen, wie der satan so mit grosser ungestumigkiet sich für und and in dem beckwerck sych ubet zwische der teuschen und der welschen sitten, daz es unsserm lieben gott geklagt sy. Der welle auch syn göttlichen fryden geben. Ich hab vermeint, es sy(a) der unfryden umb der kyrchen ordnung allenin zu thun, so verstehe ich wol, daz die auff der, teuschen sytten die welschen nit lyden wellen. Da ist der gytz der merntteheill daran shuldig, dan sy furen ein klag wider sy, sagen, die calvinischen dye werden richer dan sy. Da sag ich, das thutt, daz sy keine winseuffer syen, daz ir nit unnützlich und wider gott verthunt, da ist man in ser vind umm der kyrchen willen, haben sy auch besser ordnung dan auff der teuschen sytten, vorab in dez heren nachtmall, gott sy es geklagtt."
47 See: Albrecht Wolters, *Der Heidelberger Katechismus in seiner ursprünglichen Gestalt, nebst der Geschichte seines Textes im Jahre 1563* (Bonn: Adolph Marcus, 1864). It is essential to note that the authoritative publication, the third edition of the Heidelberg Catechism, included the church ordinances, and one of them was *Pfalzgrave Fridericks, churfürsten, aufgerichte christliche eheordnung* from 30 July 1563 – the ordinances of marriage.
48 Rocholl, *Anna Alexandria Herrin zu Rappoltstein*, 37: "Dagegen drang sie mit allem Eifer auf die Verfolgung und Verteibung der Wiedertäufer, Calvinisten und anderen Sekten."
49 Rocholl, *Anna Alexandria Herrin zu Rappoltstein*, 43–44: "Es wäre aber ein arger Missgriff gewesen, wenn die Rappoltsteiner Herrschaften dem Rate Bullingers gefolgt wären. Denn die Einfischeimer Regierung stand auf der Lauer, um Egenolf die Anklage zu stellen, dass er sein Augsburger Konfessions Verwandter sei, vielmehr Heimlich dem Zwinglianismus und Calvinismus anhange, um durch sein ganzes Reformationswerk brach zu lebte – er starb im Jahre 1585."

Until her own death in 1581, Rappoltstein testified to her beliefs to the extent that she should be referred to today as a reformer, missionary, and theologian. Her method always included seeking counsel from experts, and her determination to follow that counsel was consistent. One reason she may be forgotten in today's historiography is because Alsace is a mosaic of Roman Catholics and Lutherans, with but a small enclave of Reformed Churches. No doubt Anna Alexandria zu Rappoltstein was an original witness convicted and loyal to the Zwinglian Reformation and the Reformed Church once she was convinced of its *rightness*. Here, Hans Ulrich Baechtold deserves special mention for his assessment that women's letters almost always have a personal and practical note to them. Just so, Rappoltstein also counseled and showed earnest concern for Bullinger's physical and emotional welfare, his family, and his personal struggles.

Joe Mock

Bullinger and The Lord's Holy Supper

1.   Introduction

The thesis of this essay is that Bullinger was a major contributor and stimulus to Zwingli as he developed his understanding of the Eucharist and the covenant as the underlying theme of the biblical canon. Comparing Bullinger with the other reformers with respect to his understanding and practice of the Eucharist reveals that he resisted any compromise concerning the relevant biblical texts and the terminology used either for ecumenical or political expediency.

The events following the Marburg Colloquy of 1529 and the dynamics of the ongoing strained relationship between Wittenberg and Zurich meant that any attempt towards a pan-Protestant movement would not prove to be successful. That the relationship between Wittenberg and Zurich had deteriorated was reflected in Luther's ire expressed in his *Kurzes Bekenntnis vom heiligen Sakrament* (1544) and the feisty response of Bullinger on behalf of the ministers of Zurich in the *Wahrhaftes Bekenntnuss* (1545). In the wake of Marburg, Zurich's refusal to endorse either the *Confessio Augustana Invariata* (1530) or the *Confessio Augustana Variata* (1540)[1] or, for that matter, the *Wittenberg Confession* (1536) were major hurdles to closer ties between Wittenberg and Zurich during challenging times for the reformation in Europe. This was despite the sustained efforts of Bucer over many years (Thompson: 2005, 3–16; Burnett: 2011a, 68–69). In his letter to Bonifacius Amerbach dated 14 March 1545 Bullinger lamented that "He (i.e. Luther) has ranted and raved in public writings against the living and the dead to such an extent that we cannot conceal it. We respond, however, modestly, I imagine, for these very good men and especially for the church for which we are ministers, defending our integrity and that of others in a forthright manner."[2] That Bullinger wanted to clear the air, once and for all, between Wittenberg and

---

1 Calvin signed the *Variata*.
2 Cited in James D. Mohr (1972), Heinrich Bullinger's Opinions Concerning Martin Luther (MA-thesis), Kent State University Graduate School, 56.

Zurich with respect to the *Abendmahl* can be clearly seen in the fact that Bullinger appended Luther's *Kurzes Bekenntnis* to his *Wahrhaftes Bekenntnuss* in order to demonstrate and confirm that the Zurichers had read it carefully yet, at the same time, he begged Luther to carefully examine the measured reply of the Zurichers whom Luther claimed were "heretics." Since the basis of the *Wahrhaftes Bekenntnuss* was the faithful interpretation of Scripture the hope was that Luther would consider it carefully.What was so critical for the reformation with respect to the understanding, significance and practice of the Lord's Supper or Eucharist? W. Peter Stephens has suggested that the central issue at Marburg was not so much the Eucharist itself but the understanding of salvation (Stephens: 1991). Zwingli feared that an over-emphasis on the Eucharist as an instrument of grace could easily be interpreted in terms of the sacrament being regarded as an instrument of salvation which would then undermine the reformed understanding of justification and sanctification by faith alone. This appears to be reflected in Vermigli's analysis during the Oxford Disputation of 1549 where he stated: "In the first opinion, I cannot allow such a crass connection of the body of Christ with bread so that he is contained in it naturally, corporeally, and really... Moreover, such a presence is not necessary, and has no bearing on our salvation (Vermigli: 2000, 121)." McLelland, on the other hand, concluded that the dispute was essentially about Christology (McLelland: 1992, 180). This was reflected in the discussions about the "presence" of Christ in the Eucharist and, by extension, the role of ministers in the church.[3] On the one side, Zwingli and the Zurichers were accused of Nestorianism while, on the other side, Luther's rigid application of the *communicatio idiomatum* tended towards Eutychianism.

Since the issues surrounding the Eucharistic controversy were at the heart of reformed faith, it may appear somewhat curious that, apart from some smaller works that mention aspects of the Eucharist, Bullinger's first significant works on the Eucharist were produced as late as 1545, *viz.* the *Wahrhaftes Bekenntnuss* and the *Absoluta de Christi Domini et Catholicae Ecclesiae Sacramentis tractatio* (also known as *De Sacramentis*). This latter work was not originally intended to be published by Bullinger but was drafted as part of the discussions with Calvin that culminated in the *Consensus Tigurinus* of 1549. Significantly, this joint statement between Zurich and Geneva was produced in the shadow of the sessions of the Council of Trent that had deliberated on the sacraments. Bullinger's *Absoluta* was subsequently reflected in what he wrote about the Eucharist in *The Decades* (commenced in 1549), the *Catechismus pro Adultoribus* (1559) and *The Second Helvetic Confession* (written in 1562, revised in 1564 and published in 1566).

---

3 That the presence of Christ in the Eucharist and the role of ministers were hotly debated is reflected in Joel Van Amberg (2012), A Real Presence: Religious and Social Dynamics of the Eucharistic Conflicts in Early Modern Augsburg 1520–1530, Leiden: Brill.

Based on Bullinger's writings and the events underlying and surrounding them, this article concludes that, although there was much sharing and exchange of ideas with Zwingli, nonetheless, Bullinger essentially developed his understanding of the Eucharist independently. It was not the case that as Zwingli's *Nachfolger* Bullinger faithfully took over the baton and continued to teach Zwingli's view of the Eucharist which he eventually extended or extrapolated. Rather, in the years following the demise of Zwingli on the battlefield at Kappel-am-Albis in 1531, Bullinger did not write on the Eucharist. Indeed, at the first appropriate opportunity (1536), to the ire of Luther, Bullinger published Zwingli's *Christianae fidei brevis et clara expositio*. Written by Zwingli in the summer of 1531 this work expressed Zwingli's "positive" understanding of the Eucharist. In light of the claim that the death of Zwingli on the battlefield and the subsequent death of Oecolampadius were due to their teaching on the sacraments, Bullinger was keen to publish this work of Zwingli as soon as he adjudged the dust had settled. In point of fact, it was published soon after *The First Helvetic Confession*. When Bullinger himself began to write on the Eucharist he deliberately used the terminology and phrasing of Zwingli as much as possible. In this regard, Amy Burnett observed that Bullinger's "esteem and desire to uphold Zwingli's reputation made him sound more Zwinglian than he actually was." Burnett has rightly concluded that the major factor was Bullinger's "loyalty to Zwingli's reputation (if not precisely to his theology)" (Burnett 2007: 239). It was only well after Luther was no longer on the scene that Bullinger put into print his own understanding of the Eucharist. In tandem with Zwingli, Luther and Calvin, Bullinger sought to expose the errors of the teaching and practice of Rome concerning the Eucharist as well as to counter the views of the Anabaptists. But, for Bullinger, it was not so much a question of soteriology or Christology but that the church needed to hear afresh the intended purpose of the Eucharist from a biblical-historical, salvation-historical perspective from the canon of Scripture. More so than the other reformers, Bullinger underscored the covenant context of the sacraments. Moreover, Bullinger was insistent that care be taken in the terminology used so that, unambiguously, there was adherence to "the simplicity of the truth."

2.   Bullinger vis-à-vis Zwingli concerning the Eucharist

It is tacitly taken as a given by many that, as Zwingli's *Nachfolger*, Bullinger followed and subsequently developed Zwingli's understanding of the Eucharist and the theme of the covenant (Woolsey: 2012). For example, with respect to Bullinger's *Absoluta* (1545), Carrie Euler is of the view that "Bullinger took kernels of ideas from Zwingli's writings and expanded upon them in meticulous detail, offering classical, biblical, and patristic support for his arguments" (Euler: 2006, 185). Gottfried Locher coined the phrase "late Zwinglianism" to refer to the later phase of Zwingli's writings on the Eucharist (1530–1531) where he concluded there was noticeably more reference to the presence of Christ in the Eucharist as well as other aspects of the Eucharist which were followed and subsequently developed by Bullinger (Locher: 1979, 584–614; Sanders: 1992). However, the position advanced here is that it was actually Zwingli who gleaned much from Bullinger with respect to the Eucharist as well as the theme of the covenant. Bullinger's understanding of the Eucharist was intimately linked with his understanding of God's covenant which he viewed as foundational for God's plan of salvation from the Garden of Eden in Genesis 3 to the garden of Revelation 22. For Bullinger, the Eucharist is a covenant sign and seal of God's grace. Like Joachim Staedtke, the view advanced here is that Bullinger referred to the covenant *prior* to Zwingli (Staedtke: 1975, 227–228; Williams: 1975, 131). In an important entry in his *Diarium* dated 12 September 1524 Bullinger stated that "Zwingli disclosed his mind to me concerning what he understood about the sacrament of the body and blood of the Lord" in response to Bullinger's sharing "in good faith" of his own view of the Eucharist to Zwingli. Bullinger explained that his conclusions concerning the Eucharist from his own study of Scripture and his grasp of the theme of the covenant were reflected in the writings of both Augustine and of the Waldensians (Burnett 2011: 77–90, 103–104). Bullinger also noted in his *Diarium* that Zwingli "forbad me to explain this mystery to anyone" as he deemed it not the appropriate time to do so for Zwingli "desired to mention it himself at the proper time."[4]

Bullinger's discussion with Zwingli concerning the Eucharist took place after Zwingli's *Auslegen* (14 July 1523 – Article 18 refuted the Mass as a sacrifice of Christ)[5] and his *De canone missae libelli apologia* (9 October 1523)[6] and the letter of Cornelius Hoen concerning the Eucharist that had been brought to him in the summer of 1523 by Hinne Rode. This discussion also took place *prior* to Zwingli's letter to Matthew Alber at Reutlingen (16 November 1524) which was not published until March 1525, after Hoen's death in 1524. Zwingli employed this letter to Matthew Alber to underscore the differences between his understanding and practice of the Eucharist to that of Karlstadt's. Throughout 1524–1525 Karlstadt had distributed pamphlets which rather vehemently denied the bodily presence of Christ in the elements of the Eucharist (Linberg: 1979). Karlstadt's intemperate language forced Zwingli to write on the Eucharist in order to distance himself

---

4 Emil Egli (ed.), Heinrich Bullingers Diarium, Basel: Basler Buch und Antiquariatshandlung, 1904, 9, lines 14–18.
5 Z II, 118–157.
6 Z II, 620–625.

from Karlstadt and, in doing so, he took issue with the philological and syntactical approach used by Karlstadt for interpreting "this is" as referring to the body of Jesus and not the bread of the last Supper. In point of fact, many scholars draw the erroneous conclusion, in our opinion, that Zwingli came to understand from Hoen's letter that the *est* ('is') of the words of Christ in Matthew 26:26 should be taken, as a trope, to mean *significat* ('symbolizes'). This is based on their reading of Zwingli's letter to Bugenhagen (25 October 1525).[7] However, just citing a work does not necessarily indicate that Zwingli derived his ideas from it.[8] Zwingli made a point to cite Hoen's letter because he knew that both Bugenhagen and Luther had read it, for a group from the Low Countries led by Rode had shown Hoen's works and some of the works of Wessel Gansfort to Luther in 1521. Hoen's name was not cited when his letter was actually published. This has been traditionally explained in terms of protecting Hoen's name, even in death. The reference to the so-called letter from Hoen occurs after Zwingli had first urged Bugenhagen to read what Oecolampadius had written (*De genuina verborum domini, Hoc est corpus meum, iuxta vetissimos auctores expositione liber*, 1525) as well as Zwingli's *Subsidium sive coronis de eucharistia* (1525).[9] Furthermore, the reference to the letter occurs after Zwingli had stated, in summary, his main point and had illustrated it by commenting on Luke 8:11, Exod 12:11, Matt 11:14, Gal 4:24, John 15:1, John 6:55, Luke 12:50, John 4:32 and Luke 22:19. Zwingli was certainly not citing the letter as the basis for his understanding of the Eucharist.

Scott Gillies has correctly observed that Zwingli made "the covenantal discovery" in the summer of 1525 (Gillies: 2001). Prior to then, Zwingli had little emphasis in his works on the covenant as a biblical theme linking the Old and New Testaments. On 5 November 1525 Zwingli wrote his *Antwort über Balthasar Hubmaiers Taufbüchlein*[10] in response to Hubmaier's *On the Christian Baptism of Believers*. This has led many scholars to propose that Zwingli developed his thought on the covenant because of the growing influence of the Anabaptists (Lillback: 2001, 81, 82). But it might well have been the case that his interactions with Bullinger had already led him to grasp the significance of the biblical theme of the covenant, though he was yet to refer to it specifically in his works.[11] In *Reply to Hubmaier* Zwingli argued for the unity of the canon of Scripture with God's covenant of grace spanning the two ages of salvation history. On 27 May of 1525 Zwingli had written his *Von der Taufe, von der Widertaufe und von der*

---

7 *Responsio ad epistolam Ioannis Bugenhagii* – Z IV, 558–576.
8 Hoen's name is not actually mentioned by Zwingli but rather a reference to the letter of the "learned and pious Dutchman whose work was indeed published anonymously."
9 Z IV, 458–504.
10 *Antwort über Balthasar Hubmaiers Taufbüchlein*, Z IV, 585–647.
11 See in the present volume the essay by Pierrick Hildebrand on Zwingli's understanding of covenant.

Kindertaufe.[12] Bullinger was to remark later that the arguments Zwingli used in this work came from him (Simpson: 1902, 154).

Particular attention and consideration should be given to the letter from Leo Jud to Bullinger dated 1 December 1525 (Gäbler/Zsindeley: 1973, 81–82). In this letter, Jud thanked Bullinger for his letter to Zwingli in which Bullinger drew Zwingli's attention to quotes from both Lactantius and Tertullian supporting the covenant unity of Scripture which Zwingli had incorporated in his *Reply to Hubmaier.* Although this particular letter from Bullinger to Zwingli is no longer extant, it is clear, nonetheless, that the letter from Jud to Bullinger appeared to acknowledge Bullinger's input into Zwingli's growing and developing understanding of the theme of the covenant.

Jack Cottrell's oft-cited conclusion concerning the priority of Zwingli to Bullinger with respect to understanding the importance and significance of the covenant is based on a 1527 work of Bullinger in which he compared Zwingli's rediscovery of the biblical theme of the covenant at the time of the Reformation to Josiah rediscovering the Book of Deuteronomy (Cottrell: 1971, 338–339; 1975, 75–83). However, Cottrell has given insufficient weight to the dynamic that, prior to the war at Kappel-am-Albis in 1531, Bullinger was willing to be deliberately self-effacing in order to promote the positive contributions of Zwingli for the sake of the Zurich reformation. For Bullinger, to give credit whenever possible to Zwingli was viewed by him as a pivotal means of uniting the Zurich church in a critical period as the 'forest cantons' had formed an alliance loyal to Rome only a few years previously. Understanding this wider background while, at the same time, bearing in mind Bullinger's fondness for seeing models in Old Testament history for leadership in the reformation church, it is not surprising that Bullinger termed Zwingli a 'Josiah' type figure. Moreover, it is well documented that Zwingli was often referred to as a 'prophet.' Indeed, Bullinger's main work on the prophetic office was a posthumous defence of Zwingli's prophetic office (Timmerman: 2015, 83).

A consideration of the covenant with Adam in both Zwingli and Bullinger provides a window through which to gauge the mutual interaction between them (Mock: 2011). The first time that Zwingli appeared to have referred to the infralapsarian covenant with Adam was in his refutation of the Anabaptists, *In catabaptisarum strophas elenchus* (31 July 1527).[13] In this work, Zwingli referred to a covenant of grace with Adam expressed through the *protoevangelium* of Genesis 3:15.[14] In this connection, Stephens summarizes Zwingli's understanding of the link between the covenant and baptism as follows: "In *A Refutation* in 1527

---

12 Z IV, 206–337.
13 Z VI, 21–196.
14 Z I, 157.

he pointed out that the covenant was in fact with Adam in the first instance. There is only one covenant as there is only one God, and he is 'as much our God as he was Abraham's, and we are as much his people as was Israel'" (Stephens: 1992, 91) What Zwingli underscored is the continuity between Israel and the people of God post Christ.

Bullinger, for his part, first referred to the covenant with Adam in *Von dem Touff* (1525; Vom Berg/Schneider/Zsindeley: 1991, 71–85) and *Antwort an Burchard.*(1526; Vom Berg/Schneider/Zsindeley: 1991, 140–172). In the former work, addressed to Heinrich Simler, Bullinger pointed out that God "made a covenant, testament or will with the fathers, Adam, Enoch, Noah and especially clearly and explicitly with Abraham and his seed for eternity" (Vom Berg/ Schneider/Zsindeley: 1991, 72). Although it is true that Zwingli did refer to the covenant as early as his *Supplicatio ad Hugonem episcopum Constantiensem* (2 July 1522)[15] as well as in the Eighteenth Article of his *Auslegen* (14 July 1523), the terms for "covenant" used there are no real reference to the biblical theme of the covenant undergirding the overall message of the canon.

As noted above, many scholars argue for a "symbolic" period in Zwingli's understanding of the Eucharist followed by a "later" period (Sanders: 1992, 308–310). However, this is an over-simplification as the contexts of Zwingli's works need to be duly considered. Furthermore, against the view that Zwingli only considered the presence of Christ in the Eucharist in his later writings is the observation of Peter Stephens:

> Zwingli's view of the eucharist is presented more positively in his later writings in 1530 and 1531. This is in part because he states what he believes rather than what he does not believe and in part because he gives priority to the first rather than the second. There is no real change in substance in what he says, except perhaps the role given to the senses, but the writings are statements of faith rather than primarily attacks on his opponents (Stephens: 1986, 250).

The liturgy for the Eucharist (*Aktion oder Brauch des Nachtmahls*) first introduced by Zwingli on 13 April 1525 assumed Christ's presence.[16] Thus, against the oft cited criticism that the sacraments were "empty signs" for Zwingli, Peter Opitz cited Zwingli's declaration that "I believe that Christ is truly in the Supper, nay, I do not believe it is the Lord's Supper unless Christ is here."[17]

---

15 Z I, 220.

16 Z IV, 13–24. For an English translation see Jim West (2016), Huldrych Zwingli: The Implementation of the Lord's Supper, Atlanta: Pitts Theological Library.

17 Peter Opitz, "At the Table of the Lord: To Zwingli's View on the Lord's Supper" – paper delivered at the Sixteenth Century Society Conference at Montreal in 2010. The citation is from Zwingli's *Christianae fidei brevis et clara expositio ad regem Christianum*, Z VI/V, 90.

There was thus a measure of partnership between Bullinger and Zwingli in hammering out an understanding of the Eucharist with Bullinger taking a lot of the initiative. Zwingli invited Bullinger to attend the Marburg Colloquy but he had to decline because he had just got married and couldn't leave the responsibilities of his pastoral ministry at Bremgarten. Would history have turned out differently had Bullinger been present at Marburg? What is unmistakeable, as Jon Balserak has noted, is that both Zwingli and Bullinger acted as prophets in opposing the idolatry of the Mass (Balserak: 2014, 55–65). In sum, therefore, we would expect to see both continuity and development between Zwingli and Bullinger in the following aspects of the understanding of the Eucharist and its practice: 1. the definition of a sacrament, 2. the relationship between the sign of the sacrament (*signum*) and the spiritual reality thereby signified (*res signata*), 3. the relationship between the sacrament and grace, 4. the relationship between the sacrament and the faith of the believer, 5. the role of the Holy Spirit in the sacrament, 6. the presence of Christ in the Eucharist, 7. the sacraments as badges of Christian profession, 8. union with Christ/incorporation with Christ, 9. fellowship with God.

3. Bullinger and the Eucharist

The First Helvetic Confession (1536), of which Bucer and Bullinger were included among the authors, revealed considerable continuity with Zwingli's thought and was characterized by its positive tone. Prior to this, in 1534 the Zurich ministers had sent Bucer the *Zurich Confession* indicating that Zurich would not go beyond what was outlined in it. The *Zurich Confession* stated that "The true body of Christ ... is truly present, given, and distributed to believers."[18] In Bullinger's commentary on 1 Corinthians (1537) he not only referred at length to Zwingli and Oecolampadius and spoke of the bread as a *signum* and *figura* and of the body of Christ but also echoed Zwingli's concept of *fidei contemplatio* (Baschera: 376). The same ideas featured in Bullinger's *De scripturae sanctae authoritate* (1538), his *De origine erroris in negocio eucharistiae ac missae* (1539) and in his commentary on Matthew (1542). It is not surprising, therefore, that when Bullinger wrote about the sacraments and the Eucharist in *The Decades* he mentioned Zwingli (whom he referred to as 'the faithful minister of Christ') multiple times and included several quotes from his works.

---

18 Endre Zsindeley/Matthias Senn/Jakob Kurt/Hans Ulrich (ed. 1989), Band 4: Briefe des Jahres 1534, Zürich: TVZ, 422.

3.1 Bullinger primarily regarded the sacraments as covenant signs, testimonies and seals given by God to bind and cement his relationship with the elect and remind them of his covenant faithfulness and to challenge them to keep covenant faithfulness. This was reflected, for example, in the frequent use of the words for "covenant" in *The Decades* in the sermons on the sacraments and on the Eucharist.[19] In his commentary on 1 Corinthians he referred to the Eucharist as a "sign of the eternal covenant" (Baschera: 383). His discussion of the Eucharist in his commentary on Matthew emphasized the covenant. Commencing with early works such as *De sacrificio missae* (1524; Vom Berg/Schneider/Zsindeley: 1991, 40) and *De institutione eucharistiae* (1525; Vom Berg/Schneider/Zsindeley: 1991, 90), Bullinger highlighted the link between the Eucharist and God's eternal covenant. In discussing the Eucharist he linked it to the eternal covenant that commenced with Adam in which God accommodated himself to mankind. For Bullinger, the celebration of the sacraments were opportunities for both re-membering what God had done in Christ, what is yet to be fulfilled in Christ at the *eschaton*,[20] but also an opportunity for covenant renewal. He pointed out that the word in the sacraments is "a remembrance and a renewing of the benefits and promises of God" (*Decades:* 890).[21] More so than the other reformers he often referred to the covenant when he discussed the sacraments, especially the Eu-charist. Repeatedly he referred to the parallel between baptism and circumcision and between the Eucharist and Passover. They have the same "substance" while "in signs they are diverse, but in the thing signified equal" (*Decades:* 923). He explained that "the Lord himself by the institution of his sacraments has bound himself unto us, and we again by the partaking of them do bind ourselves to him and to all the saints" (*Decades:* 882). In particular, Bullinger referred to the Eucharist as the *testamentum* of God and of our Lord (*Decades*, 996)[22] where Christ is the testator while all the faithful that belong to Christ are appointed as the heirs and are "partakers and heirs of all of God's goodness" (*Decades:* 934). He also referred to the Eucharist as a *synaxis* to underscore covenant communion with God and fellow believers (*Decades:* 944). Just as his exposition of Genesis 17 in *De testamento* warned against despising and not taking circumcision seriously

---

19 In sermons V.6, V.7 and V.9 the following words are used: *foedus* (30x), *testamentum* (20x), *pactum* (3x), *pactio* (3x), *conventio* (1x), *transactio* (1x), *confoederatus* (1x).

20 Cf. Bullinger's understanding of history and the importance of the book of Revelation.

21 Peter Opitz (2008), Heinrich Bullinger Werke Theologische Schriften Band 3 Sermonum Decades Quinque de Postissimus Christianae Religonis Capitibus (1552), Zürich: TVZ, 1015. Translations of *The Decades* are those of the author.

22 *Vide* Opitz (2004: 454,455).

in the old covenant, so in *The Decades* Bullinger warned about the right attitude of receiving and appropriating baptism and the Eucharist in the new covenant.[23]

3.2 Following Augustine, Bullinger explained that the sacraments "consist of two parts, the sign and the thing signified" (*Decades:* 904). Bullinger further pointed out that the Swiss use the term *wortzeichen* to indicate the intimate link between the word of God and the signs he gives the elect. Thus *The Second Helvetic Confession* referred to the sacraments as "added to the word", i. e. they supplement the word. Article 2 of the *Consensus Tigurinus* explained that sacraments are "supplements to the gospel." They are "visible words." They are signs of God's grace. Furthermore, "the word of God makes them sacraments." Although distinct, because they are "coupled" together or "united by a mystical signification" then "the name of the one is given to the other" (*Decades:* 910). In other words, because the signs and the thing signified are sacramentally joined together so signs take the name of the thing signified.[24] Bullinger also countered charges of "empty" and "bare" signs by declaring that "they who are partakers of the sacraments do not receive nothing" (*Decades:* 933). The sacraments are not superfluous (*Decades:* 953).

3.3 For Bullinger, the sacraments are signs and seals of God's grace. But, as he underscored in the title of sermon V.7 of *The Decades*, "they do not, in themselves, give grace neither is grace included in them" (*Decades*, 918). This was made abundantly clear in Article 17 of the *Consensus Tigurinus*. He also pointed out that Augustine had been misinterpreted as teaching that the sacraments give grace. As has been well documented, Bullinger was averse to referring to the sacraments as *instrumenta* ('instruments') of grace as well as the use of the verb *exhibere*. In the *Consensus Tigurinus* he preferred the terms *organa* ('implements') and *adminincula* ('aids') with the understanding that Christ (not the minister) employs them and makes them effective while only God (not the sacrament) is the subject of the verb *exhibere*.

3.4 For Bullinger, faith in the heart of the believer was paramount in the context of partaking of the Eucharist. In *De testamento* and *The Old Faith* Bullinger had repeatedly highlighted the notion of true Israel within Israel. He reiterated that the Israelites wrongly viewed circumcision and the Passover as works to be done rather than regarding them as God's covenant signs and seals through which they receive God's blessings through faith. Thus, he taught that in the Eucharist only

---

23 There is a section in sermon V.7 of the *Decades* that warns against an attitude of indifference to the sacraments – *Decades*, 954.
24 *The Second Helvetic Confession*, chapter XIX.

those with true faith benefited from partaking of the sacrament. This was diametrically opposed to the *ex opere operato* understanding of the Mass. Christ's presence in the Eucharist is only apprehended through faith. Bullinger agreed with Calvin that through the sacraments "God exercises his people, first to build up and encourage their faith ..." (*Decades:* 879). He cited Augustine in this regard: "Moreover, faith in Christ and his sacraments is to believe in him who justifies the ungodly, to believe in the Mediator, without whose intervention we are not reconciled to God" (*Decades:* 951).

3.5 Like Zwingli, Bullinger highlighted the role of the Holy Spirit in the Eucharist. For example, in *The Second Helvetic Confession* he referred to God's action in the sacraments in terms of the manner in which he "strengthens and increases our faith through the working of God's Spirit in our hearts." It is Christ who "pours himself into us not in fact by signs lacking life, but by his Spirit and makes us sharers in all his good things" (*Decades:* 1026). Moreover, Christ's presence through the Spirit would be more profitable to the church than his bodily presence" (*Decades:* 1026). Articles 3, 6, 8, 12, 15, 16 and 23 of the *Consensus Tigurinus* underscored the primacy of the Holy Spirit in the Eucharist. Although the sacraments may be termed "seals", properly speaking the Holy Spirit alone is the seal of God's covenant through whom he acts in the celebration of the Eucharist. In the Eucharist the soul of the believer is nourished through the power of the Holy Spirit.

3.6 Regarding the vexed issue of the presence of Christ in the Eucharist, the wise words of Amy Burnett with respect to avoiding the use of the English phrase "real presence" ought to be noted (Burnett: 2011b, 9). The hand of Bullinger was clearly to be seen in Article 21 of the *Consensus Tigurinus* which stated that the "notion of any kind of local presence ought especially to be set aside... Christ, so far as he is man, is to be sought nowhere other than in heaven."[25] In the same vein as Zwingli, Bullinger took exception to the concept of the ubiquity of Christ's body and this is reflected in his sermons on the Last Judgment (Gordon: 2002, 35). In *The Decades* Bullinger pointed out that he is not against the notion of Christ's presence in the Eucharist but, rather, opposed to any notion of Christ's *bodily* presence. Writing about both baptism and the Eucharist he stated that Christ "is not present bodily, essentially or really" (*Decades:* 891). What he affirmed was the "spiritual, divine and quickening presence of Christ" in the Eucharist (*Decades:* 1026). In the Eucharist Christ is absent corporeally but present spiritually with the result that "we do not have the Supper without

---

25 English translations of the *Consensus Tigurinus* are taken from Campi /Reich: 2009, 258–267.

Christ."[26] Furthermore, he rejected any charge of Nestorianism. In an apparent reference to Calvin who reiterated that God does not deceive but gives what he promises, Bullinger pointed out that God does indeed give us the flesh of his Son to eat. That is to say, his body sacrificed on the cross once for all is "received spiritually, not bodily" for it "is eaten spiritually by faith, not with the corporeal mouth" (*Decades:* 1032). Thus, Bullinger differentiated between bodily eating, spiritual eating and sacramental eating. Bullinger's understanding of John 6, Matthew 18:20 and Matthew 28:20 undergirded how he viewed the Eucharist:

> Therefore as we are not without or void of Christ before the Eucharist, but we are vivified by him as his members or partners, so that in the very act of or celebration of the Supper the promise is renewed to us as we renew and continue our communion in Christ spiritually by the body and blood of Christ in which we stand, truly participating through faith in his life and all his gifts (*Decades,* 1015).

In addition to texts such as Matthew 18:20, Matthew 28:20 and John 14–16, like Zwingli, Bullinger placed particular importance on the discourse in John 6 concerning feeding on Christ by believing on him, on Christ's presence generally and for Christ's presence in the Eucharist. Unlike other confessions where scripture references are proof texts or footnotes, Bullinger cited John 6: 35, 56, 57, 63 in the actual text of *The Second Helvetic Confession.*

3.7 In a similar manner to Zwingli, Bullinger also emphasized the sacraments as marks and badges of a Christian's profession. Not only did he cite Zwingli (*Christianae fidei expositio*) with respect to *sacramentum* meaning an oath (*Pflichtzeichen*) but he also explained that the sacraments separate believers from non-believers as they point to unity in the body of the one true God (*Decades:* 949). Article 7 of the *Consensus Tigurinus* stated that the sacraments are "marks and tokens of Christian profession." *Contra* Luther, Bullinger declared that neither the ungodly (*impii*) nor the unworthy (*indigni*) receive the substance of the Eucharist. He further out pointed that in coming to the Eucharist the believer is to consider soberly whether he or she "is in the number of those who have been delivered by Christ and saved."[27] In other words, the Eucharist is both a badge of Christian confession and a sign of the elect of God.

3.8 A window into how Bullinger understood union with Christ can be opened from the vantage point of the *Consensus Tigurinus.* Significantly, Article 5 is concerned with "How Christ communicates himself to us" and states "For he does not pour forth his life into us unless he is our head." Article 6 states "The

---

26 *The Second Helvetic Confession,* chapter XXI.
27 *The Second Helvetic Confession,* chapter XXI.

communion we have with the Son of God is spiritual union when, by his Spirit dwelling in us, he makes all believers capable of the good things which reside in him." Article 9 points out, concerning believers, that "as long as they have been made partakersof Christ, continue and renew that fellowship." Article 10 states that "faith makes us partakers of Christ." Article 14 states that it is "Christ alone who makes us partakers of himself in the Supper." Article 19 states "Thus in the Supper Christ communicates himself to us, even though he had previously imparted himself to us, and dwells perpetually in us."

3.9 Peter Opitz's comprehensive monograph on *The Decades* identifies fellowship with God as the underlying theme of the whole work. He concludes that, for Bullinger the Eucharist signifies becoming one body in fellowship with God (Opitz: 2004, 453–455). The key to a restored fellowship with God after the Fall is union with or incorporation into Christ who became man for the salvation of the world. Just as Bullinger linked baptism with the *circumcisio Christi* or the circumcision done "without hands" by Christ through the Holy Spirit on the heart of the believer so he viewed the blessings of the Eucharist as the "true letters and the tablets" (*verum literae et tabulae*) which are not only declared through the words of institution but are also written on the heart of the believer through the Holy Spirit. For Bullinger, the Eucharist symbolizes incorporation into Christ and the receiving of the *omnia Christi bona* and, thereby, a restored relationship with God.

## 4.	Bullinger vis-a-vis Luther concerning the Eucharist

As attested in his *Diarium* entry (*Diarium*: 6), Luther's *De Captivitate Babylonica Ecclesiae Praeludium* (1520) made a profound impact on the young Bullinger. Not only did Bullinger discover in this seminal work a trenchant criticism of the sacerdotalism of the medieval sacramental system but also an understanding of salvation by faith alone and Scripture as the sole rule of authority for the church. In this connection, Garcia Archilla has argued that: "The parallels between Luther's *Babylonian Captivity* and Bullinger's *The Old Faith* are so striking as to leave little doubt as to who is really the founder of covenant theology" (Garcia Archilla: 1992, 11, n6). While it is true that Luther used the word *testamentum* in tandem with *promissio* to refer to the Eucharist there is a profound difference in Bullinger's use of the terminology for "covenant." For example, as McGrath has suggested, the early Luther employed the tenets of nominalist *pactum* theology in formulating his doctrine of justification. In this regard, Luther asserted:

Even grace and faith, through which we are justified today, would not justify us of themselves (*ex seipsis*), without God's covenant. It is precisely for this reason, that we are saved: God has made a testament (*testamentum*) and covenant (*pactum*) with us, so that whoever believes and is baptized shall be saved. In this covenant God is truthful and faithful and is bound by what he has promised (McGrath: 1985, 88, 89).[28]

As well as Luther, Bullinger also emphasized the *protoevangelium* of Genesis 3:15 and used *testamentum* to translate both *berith* and *diathēkē*. But his source was both Irenaeus and Augustine. Although Luther did on one occasion juxtapose the terms *pactum*, *foedus* and *testamentum* he did not view the terms *foedus* and *testamentum* as interchangeable. Bullinger, on the other hand, viewed these terms as interchangeable. In his exposition on the covenant (*De testamento seu foedere Dei unico et aeterno*, 1534) Bullinger revealed his preference for the term *foedus*, his relatively frequent use of the word *testamentum* and the deliberately sparing use of *pactum* in order to minimize any reading of nominalist *pactum* theology into his works (Mock: 2013, 28–31).

Bullinger continued to display deference to Luther as a person even though there were differences theologically. In his discussion of the Eucharist, Bullinger did not refer to Luther by name but as an "adversary" (*Decades*, 1021). But he rather pointedly referred to the Lutheran view in terms of "crying out and repeatedly crying out, 'This is my body,' 'This is my blood;' 'This is,' 'This is,' 'This is,' 'This is,' 'Is,' 'Is,' 'Is' while we repeat, 'The word was made flesh,' 'was made,' 'was made'" (*Decades*, 1017).

5.   Bullinger vis-à-vis Calvin concerning the Eucharist

In the wake of his *Antidotes* (1547) against the decrees of Trent on the Mass, Calvin was eager to forge an agreement with Zurich on the Eucharist despite Bullinger's apparent lack of urgency to do so (Campi/Reich: 2009; Campi: 2014: 83–121). Indeed, over several decades, Calvin was willing to be flexible and malleable with respect to his teaching on the Eucharist because of his fervour for evangelical union (Holder: 2016). Bullinger baulked at using the word *instrumentum* and replaced it with *organum*. He also insisted that only God could be the subject of the verb *exhibere*. Peter Stephens observed of the *Consensus Tigurinus* that not only is Christ the focus of the opening articles but that "It could be described as a Calvinian view expressed within the constraints imposed by Bullinger's theology or Bullinger's view stretched to embrace Calvin" (Stephens 2006: 67). However, that Calvin's motive was primarily ecumenical and political is evident from Calvin's subsequent works in response to the fierce

---

28 W.A. 3:.289.1–5.

charges of "Zwinglianism" from Joachim Westphal and Tilemann Heshusius. These latter works of Calvin display significant divergence from the *Consensus Tigurinus.*

Calvin repeatedly stated that God does not "deceive" so that the sacraments actually "provide" and "pass on" (*apporter et communiquer*) what they signify. Hence Gerrish termed Calvin's understanding of the Eucharist as "instrumental symbolism." For Calvin, through the Holy Spirit, the believer ascends to heaven in the Eucharist to feed on Christ's body (Zachman: 2016, 67). That is why he emphasized the *epiclesis* and the *sursum corda.* Moreover, Calvin's commentary on 1 Corinthians and his sermons on 2 Timothy 2:8–10 and Titus 1:7–9 demonstrate unequivocally that Calvin believed in "really" and "truly" feeding on the substance of Christ's body. He admitted that he couldn't understand how but just stated that he "experienced" it (*Institutes* IV.17.32). Hence Thomas Davis correctly observes of Calvin:

> That is why Calvin insisted on substantial partaking of the body of Christ in the Eucharist, for it is the human body of Christ that is the accommodated instrument of God's salvation. It is the thing by which righteousness comes to believers (Davis: 2008, 87).[29]

Calvin saw an intimate link between the Eucharist and union with Christ. He viewed the Eucharist as a meal that believers feed on as they grow in union with Christ. This was one reason he wanted the Eucharist to be celebrated weekly. As many scholars have noticed, from beginning to end, union with Christ was given priority in Calvin's thought. His very first theological work, *Psychopannychia*, illustrates (*contra* the Anabaptists) that he could not conceive in any way of life separated from union with Christ. For Calvin, union with Christ must be continuous with Christ in the life to come. The Eucharist, for Calvin, was an important means of growing in union with Christ by feeding on him bodily.

> Despite some theological differences with him, nonetheless, Bullinger displayed his admiration for Calvin by ending his sermon on the Eucharist with a lengthy quotation from Calvin (*Decades:* 1041).

---

29 Cf. the helpful overview in Anthony N.S. Lane (2007), Was Calvin a Crypto-Zwinglian?, in: Mack, C. Holt (ed,), Adaptations of Calvinism in Reformation Europe: Essays in Honour of Brian G. Armstrong, Aldershot: Ashgate, 21–41.

6.   Bullinger vis-à-vis Bucer concerning the Eucharist

Martin Bucer's almost tireless efforts at Eucharistic concord have been surveyed
in detail (Eells: 1931). In his zeal for such concord, for example, to Bugenhagen's
ire, he modified Bugenhagen's views when he translated Bugenhagen's work on
the Eucharist. His interaction with Bullinger concerning the Eucharist has also
been scrutinized (Burnett: 2007). Furthermore, Bullinger's impatience, irritation
and suspicions of Bucer's motives have been well documented. Bucer also attempted collaboration with Catholic theologians in order to formulate common
statements on aspects of the Eucharist. In this regard there seems to be a definite
change in his understanding of the Eucharist beginning with his *Psalms Commentary* (1529), his *Defensio adversus Axioma catholicum* (1534) and his *Romans
Commentary* (1536). His effort at the Colloquy at Regensburg (1541) even led the
papal nuncio to remark that Bucer had professed of himself: "I, for my part,
would admit the (Roman) Canon!" (Thompson: 2005: 181).

Bucer emphasized the *unio sacramentis* (sacramental union) and that ministry of the Word and sacrament were foundational for the believer to grow in
communion with Christ. He explained the sacramental union in terms of *unio
pacti exhibiti* whereby the body of Christ is given as food for the believer. Ian
Hazlett coined the phrase "analytical mystical realism" to describe Bucer's understanding of eucharistic communion which Bucer referred to as "the food of
the new internal man, the food of eternal life, the strengthening of faith by which
the just man lives, the increase of new life, the life of God in us" (Hazlett: 1994,
74,75).

The differences between Bucer and Bullinger are rather striking and are well
illustrated by their respective commentaries on Romans. Bucer tended to be
verbose and flexible in his use of language whereas Bullinger focused on the
scopus of each section of the epistle. Bucer's flexibility with language can be seen
in the *Tetrapolitan Confession* (1530) which was not endorsed by Zurich. On the
other hand, Bullinger's doggedness for clarity of the terms used was reflected in
his aversion to colloquies (unlike Bucer) claiming that matters can be hammered
out via correspondence with a view to "simplicity of the truth." In the *Zurich
Confession* (1534) Bullinger and the other Zurich ministers impressed upon
Bucer the importance of writing clearly and without obscurity and ambiguity.[30]
In particular, Bullinger objected to Bucer's fondness for the terms *exhibere* and
substantia. Bucer was to interpret these terms as understanding the *First Helvetic
Confession* to be compatible with the *Wittenberg Concord* (Burnett: 2005). His *De*

---

30 Letters from the Zurich ministers to Bucer 15 December 1534 – Endre Zsindeley,/Matthias
    Seen/Jakob Kurt/Hans Ulrich (ed. 1989), Heinrich Bullinger Werke Band 4: Briefe des Jahres
    1534, Zürich: TVZ, 422.

vera et falsa caenae dominicae administratione (1546) discussed the Eucharist in terms of sacrifice (Thompson: 2005, 225–277).

7.   Bullinger vis-à-vis Oecolampadius concerning the Eucharist

Oecolampadius met Zwingli in late November 1524, which was *after* Zwingli's meeting with Bullinger referred to above, when they discussed the Eucharist. In the following year he wrote his *De genuina verborum Domini: Hoc est corpus meum, iuxta vetustissimos auctores, expositione liber.* In this treatise the body of Christ that was on view was not the ascended body of Christ but his body on the cross. For Oecolampadius the bread and the wine symbolize the body and blood of Christ who is present spiritually and whose body is eaten by faith. Following Tertullian, Oecolampadius interpreted *hoc est corpus meum* to mean "this is a symbol of my body" (i. e. *hoc est figura corporis mei*) rather than "this symbolizes my body" (i. e. *hoc significat corpus meum*) as Zwingli and Bullinger did. Like Zwingli, he believed that the natural body of Christ is in heaven (Piotrowski: 2012, 136). Oecolampadius retained the notion of sacrifice in the Eucharist seeing it as self-sacrifice of the believer to the Lamb of God who was sacrificed once and for all. Despite his careful attention to the church fathers (Northway: 2008), Bishop John Fisher of Rochester wrote the tome *De veritate corporis et sanguinis Christi in eucharistia* (1526) taking Oecolampadius to task for the way he handled the fathers. Oecolampadius was present at Marburg and Luther labelled him "Icarus" who had been led astray by "Daedalus" (Zwingli) because of the denial of the bodily presence of Christ in the Eucharist. His relationship with Melanchthon illustrates how he was viewed by the Wittenbergers (Fisher: 2015).

Oecolampadius' writings relevant to the Eucharist were clearly read by Calvin as indicated in his works against Joachim Westphal's *Farrago* (1552) and *Recta Fides de Coena Domini* (1553; Burnett: 2016). It is clear that Bullinger was aware of Oecolampadius' works. For example, Oecolampadius' commentary on Jeremiah was cited in Bullinger's *De testamento* (1534) while Bullinger wrote in the preface to the republication of Oecolampadius' commentaries on the prophets (Fisher: 2016, 68). However, it is not clear to what extent Bullinger consulted Oecolampadius' works that relate to the Eucharist. Nonetheless, it is evident that a significant difference between Oecolampadius and Bullinger was Oecolampadius' emphasis on excommunication for church discipline which appears to have been taken up by Calvin.

8.   Bullinger vis-à-vis Vermigli concerning the Eucharist

Perhaps Vermigli's most important work on the Eucharist was his *Defence of the Ancient and Apostolic Doctrine Concerning the Most Holy Sacrament of the Eucharist* (1559) which was directed against Bishop Stephen Gardiner. Since both he and Calvin were students of Bucer it is not surprising that there was considerable overlap in their respective views on the Eucharist (McLelland: 1957, 278–281). This is ably illustrated by the following quote:

> The point of the eucharist is for the believer to become a partaker more and more of the body and blood of Christ … and also for the attributes of Christ to become more and more part of the believer (Zuidema: 155).

Vermigli, who was present at the Colloquy of Poissy (1561), regarded the sacraments as visible words through which God, through accommodation to human frailty, communicated to his people. He insisted that the sacrament must be "intelligible" to the worshipper and employed Augustine's distinction between *usus* and *fructio*. He was fond of citing Theodoret to fathom the Christological aspects of the Eucharist. Like Bullinger, Vermigli emphasized the covenant in his understanding of the Eucharist and saw the equivalence of *testamentum* with *foedus* though his understanding of the link between the covenant and the sacraments was markedly different from that of Bullinger as Lillback has pointed out: "In Martyr's exposition, it is as if the sacrament has a covenant rather than the covenant having a sacrament (Lillback: 2004, 83). Peter Opitz describes Vermigli's grasp of communion with Christ in the Eucharist as a "bipolar" process. That is, the word of God and the institution of the Eucharist on one side with movement from the human side via *contemplatio fidei*. But this is with the understanding that it is the Holy Spirit that creates such faith in the heart of the believer (Opitz: 2009, 396,397). Vermigli acknowledged his debt to Bullinger whom he first met in 1543 and to whom he wrote (concerning the Oxford Disputation [1549]): "you have for so many years both taught and maintained that doctrine which I there undertook to defend" (McLelland 1957: 277). On hearing Vermigli give a lecture on 1 Corinthians 11 on 2 March 1949 one of Vermigli's students wrote the following to Bullinger:

> Martyr has openly declared to us all on this very day on which I write this letter, what was his opinion upon this subject and he seemed to all of us not to depart even a nail's breadth from that entertained by yourself. Nay, more, he has defended that most worthy man, Zwingli, by the testimony of your opinion, and taken part with him against his adversaries (Opitz: 2009, 397).

9. Conclusion

Bullinger's time at Kappel-am-Albis was a period of intense activity which set the die for his future works. The many works produced while he was *Antistes* at Zurich reveal no major development or change from this "purple patch" of his where he had worked out the broad outlines of biblical theology that would undergird his subsequent works. He was a major contributor to Zwingli's developing understanding of the covenant as the major theme of the canon and its connection to the sacraments, especially the Eucharist. For him, the Eucharist was primarily a covenant sign and seal of God's grace and the gift of salvation in Christ along with the *omnia bona* that the elect enjoy through union with Christ. As Bullinger always emphasized the *praxis pietatis* he viewed the Eucharist first of all as a visible word from God to the believer giving assurance of God's grace – given in Christ, continually given in Christ in the present through the Holy Spirit and to be consummated at the *eschaton*.[31]

Secondarily, he regarded the Eucharist as a word or pledge from the believer to God assuring him of covenant faithfulness and of binding the believer to God. In terms of the words of Matthew 17:5 on the front page of all of his works, the believer would declare that he or she would listen to and obey Jesus (*ipsum audite*). Furthermore, the Eucharist was to be celebrated together with fellow believers with the elect gathering together mirroring the pattern that all males under the old covenant were required to gather before Yahweh in Jerusalem at the three annual pilgrimage feasts. This may underlie the pattern in Zurich of celebrating the Eucharist three times a year.[32] In the Zurich liturgy there was neither an *epiclesis* nor *sursum corda*, but Psalm 113, the first of the *Hallel* psalms was recited to indicate the connection with the Passover. Significantly as well, the church in Zurich did not practise excommunication as did the church in Geneva. For, as he expounded in his *Tractatus de excommunicatione* (1568), Bullinger emphasized that the Eucharist, like the Passover in the Old Testament, was an opportunity for the elect to gather together to give thanks to God for the gracious gift of the forgiveness of sins (Baker: 1975).

First and foremost, Bullinger based his understanding and practice of the Eucharist on the clear interpretation of Scripture. His aversion to colloquies or joint confessions was due to the fact that consensus meant being flexible with biblical interpretation. That is why he did not see eye to eye with the tireless efforts of Bucer for Eucharistic unity and why he was highly annoyed at Beza and Farel for drafting the Göppingen Eucharistic Confession (1557). In *The Decades* he referred to the Eucharist as the "Lord's Holy Supper." His desire was that the

---

31 There was a definite note of the assurance of salvation because of the grace of God.
32 *De Ritibus et Institutis Ecclesiae Tigurinae Ludovici Lavateri Opusculum*, (Zurich, 1702), 59.

Eucharist be understood and practised through the words of Jesus recorded by the Gospel writers and explicated by Paul in the context of the salvation-historical message of the Bible as a whole.

Bibliography

BAKER, J. WAYNE (1975), In Defense of Magisterial Discipline: Bullinger's "Tractatus de Excommunicatione," in: Ulrich Gäbler/Erland Herkenrath (ed.), Heinrich Bullinger 1504–1575 Gesammelte Aufsätze zum 400. Todestag Erster Band, Zürich, TVZ, 141–159.

BALSERAK, JON (2014), John Calvin as Sixteenth-Century Prophet, Oxford: OUP, 55–65.

BASCHERA, LUCA (2012), Heinrich Bullinger Werke Theologische Schriften, Band 6: Kommentare zu den neutestamentlichen Briefen Röm-1Kor-2Kor, Zürich: TVZ.

BURNETT, AMY NELSON (2005), The Myth of the Swiss Lutherans: Martin Bucer and the Eucharistic Controversy in Bern, Zwingliana 32, 49–51.

— (2007), Heinrich Bullinger and the Problem of Eucharistic Concord, in: Emidio Campi and Peter Opitz (ed.), Heinrich Bullinger: Life, thought, Influence, Zürich: TVZ, 233–250.

— (2011a), Basel, Beza and the Development of Calvinist Orthodoxy in the Swiss Confederation, in: Irene Dingel/Herman Selderhuis (ed.), Calvin und Calvinismus: Europäische Perspektiven, Göttingen: V&R.

— (2011b), Karlstadt and the Origins of the Eucharistic Controversy: A Study in the Circulation of Ideas, Oxford: OUP.

— (2016), Exegesis and Eucharist: Unexplored Connections between Calvin and Oecolampadius, in: Herman J. Selderhuis/Arnold Huijgen (ed.), Calvinus Pastor Ecclesiae. Papers of the Eleventh International Congress on Calvin Research, Göttingen: V&R, 248–262.

CAMPI, EMIDIO/REICH, RUEDI (ed., 2009), Consensus Tigurinus: Heinrich Bullinger und Johannes Calvin über das Abendmahl, Zürich: TVZ.

CAMPI, EMIDIO (2014), Shifting Patterns of Reformed Tradition, Göttingen: V&R.

COTTRELL, JACK WARREN (1971), Covenant and Baptism in the Theology of Huldreich Zwingli (PhD-thesis), Princeton, 338, 339.

— (1975), Is Bullinger the Source for Zwingli's Doctrine of the Covenant?, in: Ulrich Gäbler/Erland Herkenrath (ed.), Heinrich Bullinger 1504–1575 Gesammelte Aufsätze zum 400. Todestag Erster Band, Zürich: TVZ, 75–83.

DAVIS, THOMAS J. (2008), This is My Body: The Presence of Christ in Reformation Thought, Grand Rapids: Baker,

EELLS, HASTINGS (1931), Martin Bucer, New Haven: YUP.

EULER, CARRIE (2006), Couriers of the Gospel: England and Zurich, 1531–1558, Zürich: TVZ.

FISHER, JEFF (2015), The Breakdown of a Reformation Friendship: John Oecolampadius and Philip Melanchthon, Westminster Theological Journal 77, 265–291.

— (2016), A Christoscopic Reading of Scripture: Johannes Oecolampadius on Hebrews, Göttingen: V&R.

GÄBLER, ULRICH/ZSINDELEY, ENDRE (ed. 1973), Heinrich Bullinger Briefwechsel Band 1, Zürich: TVZ.

GARCIA ARCHILLA, AURELIO A. (1992), The Theology of History and Apologetic Historiography in Heinrich Bullinger: Truth in History, San Francisco: Mellen Research University Press.

GILLIES, SCOTT A. (2001), Origin of the Reformed Covenant 1524-7, Scottish Journal of Theology 54, 21-50.

GORDON, BRUCE (2002), "Welcher nit gloubt der ist schon verdampt": Heinrich Bullinger and the Spirituality of the Last Judgment, Zwingliana 29, 29-53.

HAZLETT, IAN (1994), Eucharist Communion: Impulses and Directions in Martin Bucer's Thought, in: D.F. Wright (ed.), Martin Bucer's Reforming Church and Community, Cambridge: CUP.

HOLDER, R. WARD (2016), The Pain of Agreement: Calvin and the *Consensus Tigurinus*, Reformation and Renaissance Review 18, 85-94.

LILLBACK, PETER (2001), The Binding of God: Calvin's Role in the Development of Covenant Theology, Grand Rapids: Baker, 81, 82.

— (2004), The Early Reformed Covenant Paradigm: Vermigli in the Context of Bullinger, Luther and Calvin, in: Frank A. James III (ed.), Peter Martyr Vermigli and the European Reformations: Semper Reformanda, Leiden: Brill, 70-96.

LINBERG, CARTER (1979), Karlstadt's Dialogue on the Lord's Supper, Menonnite Quarterly Review 53, 35-77.

LOCHER, GOTTFRIED W. (1979), Die Zwinglische Reformation im Rahmen der europäischen Kirchengeschichte, Göttingen: V&R.

McGRATH, ALISTER (1985), Luther's Theology of the Cross, Oxford: Blackwell.

McLELLAND, J.C. (1957), The Visible Words of God: An Exposition of the Sacramental Theology of Peter Martyr Vermigli, A.D. 1500-1562, Edinburgh: Oliver and Boyd.

McLELLAND, J.C. (1992), Meta-Zwingli or Anti-Zwingli? Bullinger and Calvin, in: Eucharistic Concord in: Richard C. Gamble (ed.), Articles on Calvin and Calvinism vol. 13, New York: Garland Publishing, 179-195.

MOCK, JOE (2011), Bullinger and the Covenant with Adam, Reformed Theological Review 70, 185-205.

— (2013), Biblical and Theological Themes in Heinrich Bullinger's »De Testamento« (1534), Zwingliana, 40, 1-35.

NORTHWAY, ERIC W. (2008), The Reception of the Fathers & Eucharistic Theology in Johannes Oecolampadius (1482-1531) with Special Reference to the *Adversus Haereses* of Irenaeus of Lyon (PhD-thesis), Durham University.

OPITZ, PETER (2004), Heinrich Bullinger als Theologe: Eine Studie zu den «Dekaden», Zürich: TVZ.

— (2009), Search for the Main Roots of Vermigli's Eucharistic Theology in Torrance Kirby/ Emidio Campi/Frank A. James III (ed.), A Companion to Peter Martyr Vermigli, 387- 400.

PIOTROWSKI, NICHOLAS (2012), Johannes Oecolampadius: Christology and the Supper, Mid-America Journal of Theology 23, 131-137.

SANDERS, PAUL (1992), Heinrich Bullinger et le «zwinglianisme tardif» aux lendemains du «Consensus Tigurinus», Zwingliana, 19, 307-323.

SIMPSON, SAMUEL (1902), Life of Zwingli, the Swiss Patriot and Reformer, New York: Baker and Taylor, 154.

STAEDTKE, JOACHIM (1975), Die Theologie des jungen Bullinger, Zürich: Zwingli Verlag, 227–228.

STEPHENS, W. PETER (1986), The Theology of Huldrych Zwingli, Oxford: Clarendon, 250.

— (1991), The Soteriological Motive in the Eucharistic Controversy, in: Willem van't Spijker (ed.), Calvin: Erbe und Auftrag: Festschrift für Wilhelm Neuser zu seinem 65. Geburtstag, Kampen: Kok, 203–213.

— (1992), Zwingli: An Introduction to His Thought, Oxford: OUP, 91.

— (2006), The Sacraments in the Confessions of 1536, 1549, and 1566 – Bullinger's Understadning in the Light of Zwingli's, Zwingliana 32, 51–76.

THOMPSON, NICHOLAS (2005), Eucharistic Sacrifice and Patristic Tradition in the Theology of Martin Bucer, Leiden: Brill.

TIMMERMAN, DANIËL (2015), Heinrich Bullinger on Prophecy and the Prophetic Office (1523–1538), Göttingen: V&R, 83.

VERMIGLI, PETER MARTYR (2000), The Oxford Treatise and Disputation: On the Eucharist 1549, Kirksville, Missouri: Truman State University Press.

VOM BERG, HANS-GEORG/SCHNEIDER, BERNHARD/ZSINDELEY, ENDRE (ed. 1991), Heinrich Bullinger Werke Band 2: Unveröffentlichte Werke aus der Kappeler Zeit, Zürich: TVZ.

WILLIAMS, GEORGE H. (1975), The Radical Reformation, Philadelphia: Westminster.

WOOLSEY, ANDREW A. (2012), Unity and Continuity in Covenantal Thought: A Study in the Reformed Tradition to the Westminster Assembly, Grand Rapids: Reformation Heritage, 228–230.

ZACHMAN, RANDALL C. (2016), Did the Zurich Consensus create the possibility of future dialogue with Wittenberg?, Reformation and Renaissance Review 18, 59–71.

ZUIDEMA, JASON (2015), Peter Martyr Vermigli (1459–1562) and the Outward Instruments of Divine Grace, Göttingen, V&R.

Hywel Clifford

The 'Ancient Jewish Church': the anti-Unitarian exegetical polemics of Peter Allix

1. Introduction

Who was the first century Jew, Jesus of Nazareth? Have Christians understood the person they call 'the Son of God' and 'the Christ' accurately and appropriately? Or, to put the same questions into a singular and sharper focus: does the ancient Christian belief in the Trinity, and a divine Messiah, represent a false departure from the Jewish origins of Christianity, or were those beliefs a natural outflow from those origins? This is the fundamental question that Peter (Pierre) Allix (1641–1717) treated in his book *The judgement of the ancient Jewish church against the Unitarians in the controversy upon the holy Trinity and divinity of our Blessed Saviour* (1699). In some respects, *Ancient Jewish Church* (AJC) replays early Christian doctrinal controversies. But its distinctiveness is to be found in Allix's defence of Trinitarianism against Unitarians in late seventeenth century England, informed by his background and scholarly capacities. Allix was a Huguenot refugee well versed in Jewish literature, ancient and medieval, evidence whose deployment in the doctrinal disputes of the 1690s had become contested. The purpose of this brief study is to outline, analyse, and evaluate how Allix used this evidence. Since Allix is not as well known nowadays as other early modern Protestant Hebraists (e.g. Isaac Casaubon, the Buxtorfs, Louis Cappel), some select biographical details will first of all help to place AJC in context.

2. Biography: select details

The life of Peter Allix falls fairly neatly into two parts: residence in France and in England.[1] Allix was born in 1641 in Alençon (Normandy). Educated at the universities of Saumur and Sedan (both Protestant academies for the training of

---

1 For a biographical summary, on which much of this opening section depends, see Larminie: 2004. The DNB entry by W. G. Blaikie published in the later nineteenth century (1885–1900)

Huguenot pastors, modelled on that in Geneva), Allix showed distinction in the study of Hebrew and Syriac. Allix became pastor to the Reformed congregation at Grande-Quevilly, Rouen, and, due to his reputation for learning and preaching, succeeded in 1670 the renowned Jean Daillé as pastor to the main Huguenot church at Charenton, near Paris. Having written effectively in defence of Protestantism by his mid-thirties, Allix continued to repel Catholic challenges, such as the attacks of Jacques-Bénigne Bossuet, bishop of Meaux (Seine-et-Marne). Allix welcomed and conversed with scholars from the Sorbonne, and with visitors from England and Scotland; and he corresponded with the Oxford orientalist Robert Huntingdon. Allix began to collaborate with his colleague Jean Claude over a new French translation of the Bible, but this failed due to disputes in the congregation at Charenton over the controversial soteriological ideas of Claude Pajon.[2] Allix was himself labelled a Socinian (i.e. a non-Trinitarian) for supporting fellow Pajonist Norman Charles le Cène. From April 1683 Allix was suspected of imminent conversion to Catholicism. But the rumours were not trustworthy: that year, Allix was the moderator of the last provincial French Protestant synod, held in Lisy (diocese of Meaux), before which he often preached.

The major turning point in his life, as for many French Protestants, was the Edict of Fontainbleau in 1685 (under Louis XIV), also known as the Revocation of the Edict of Nantes, which cancelled the edict of 1598 (under Henry IV) that had granted Huguenots the freedom and right to worship without state intervention and persecution. Many fled France, including Allix, his wife Margaret (Marguerite), and their three children. But the ground had been laid for Allix's arrival in England. In addition to the contacts mentioned above, he had already had correspondence with Archbishop William Sancroft and Bishop William Lloyd (St Asaph, Coventry and Litchfield, Worcester). Lloyd was a tolerationist (i.e. of Protestant non-conformists), as was Gilbert Burnet (later bishop of Salisbury) who invited Allix to study in England. Allix secretly sent his books to England, and, when faced with the revocation in October 1685, he finally left France for England. Allix settled in London where, as a high profile refugee, he developed his contacts within the Church of England; he was heard conversing fluently in Latin with Sancroft at Lambeth Palace. Allix was granted a royal patent to set up in Jewin Street, Aldersgate, a new French church for French Protestant refugees (St Martin Orgar) that conformed to the Church of England rite, with a (con-

---

uses at least half of its space to list Allix's publications. Larminie more usefully places Allix's works in the developing context of seventeenth century theological disputes. Dunan-Page: 2006, 57.

2 On the background to this, see Grootjes: 2013, 75–80; on Allix specifically, see 77 n99, and 93 n49.

troversially, for some) re-ordained Allix as rector, assisted by four other ministers as curates.[3]

For Allix's support of William and Mary, following the Glorious Revolution of
1689, Allix was appointed treasurer of Salisbury Cathedral in 1690, at Bishop
Burnet's recommendation; and he was admitted as a residentiary canon there in
1695. But Allix probably spent most of the 1690s in London, where he had become
a well-known preacher.[4] Allix maintained his scholarly contacts: he corresponded with Huntingdon (now at Trinity College, Dublin) and the Oxford
Coptic specialist Thomas Edward; as well as with many others (e. g. John Locke).
In 1690, Allix was awarded a Doctor of Divinity degree from Emmanuel College,
Cambridge, incorporated at Oxford in 1692. Allix wrote many theological works,
although they received mixed responses in an era of fierce ecclesiastical polemical dispute. Allix continued to defend persecuted Protestants. His book
Remarks upon the ecclesiastical history of the ancient churches of the Albigenses
(1692) was a defence of the Reformation; in it, he argued that the pre-Refor-
mation Waldenses and Albigenses had preserved Christian truth from apostolic
times. In 1697, Allix was invited by the king to write a history of the councils of the
French church – expected to fill seven volumes – but this never materialised. In
his will, Allix stated that he had endeavoured to serve England and its Church;
and he expressed gratitude for a royal pension, although much of his wealth
remained in France so Allix was unable to fulfil all of his final financial obliga-
tions towards his wife and children at his death in London on 3 March 1717.[5]

3.   Peter Allix, *The judgement of the ancient Jewish church against
      the Unitarians in the controversy upon the holy Trinity and
      divinity of our Blessed Saviour* (1699)

3.1   Bull (1685), Nye (1695), Allix (1699)

The Christian doctrine of the Trinity was deeply controversial in early modern
England, especially in the 1690s. The emergence in the seventeenth to eighteenth
centuries of subordinationist Christologies, and the attendant disputes, has been

---

3 Proselyte converts from Catholicism did not have to be re-ordained. Dunan-Page: 2006, 37–38.
4 See, for instance, Farooq: 2013, 171.
5 Allix was the first to notice, in the later seventeenth century, since its earlier acquisition and
  arrival in Paris in 1602, that the fifth century *Codex Ephraemi Rescriptus*, one of the 'four great
  uncials' (the oldest biblical manuscripts in Greek that include both Old and New Testaments)
  was a palimpsest: a manuscript whose older (biblical) text had been erased and overwritten by
  another (Ephrem the Syrian). Allix seemingly made no use of this discovery. Lyon: 1959, 260–
  261.

explained in various ways. One scholar highlights the impact of external factors: shifting conceptions of language, politics, and philosophy in wider society; and of internal factors: "the fading of trinitarian imagination, fear of practical pneumatology, problems connected with exegesis, the development of what could be labelled 'over-familiarity' in talk about God, and the corrosive power of ridicule". Another scholar traces the controversy to James II's Declaration for Liberty of Conscience (1687) which fuelled the growth of anti-Trinitarian publications, and to splits within 'orthodoxy' (ante-Nicene Platonised subordinationist, and post-Nicene nominalist scholastic, trinities) that non-Trinitarians exploited.[6] That this became a "disciplinary crisis" was evident at the level of national institutions: "the controversy featured interventions from an unprecedented array of public authorities–Crown, Parliament, university, episcopate, and convocation–all claiming the preeminent custody of orthodoxy in an institutional landscape profoundly unsettled by revolutionary upheaval."[7] The individual human dimension must not be lost in this: Thomas Aitkenhead, an Edinburgh medical student, was, in 1697, the last person in the British Isles to be executed for expressing his religious views; among which, "he rejected the mystery of the Trinity as unworthy of refutation".[8]

AJC breathes this world of controversy. In chapter one of AJC, Allix reports that, about sixty years prior, a Latin tract had been written by a Socinian (unnamed) against the traditional view, argued by Georg Vechner (1590–1647): that *logos* 'word' in the Gospel of John has the same sense as in the Targums ("Chaldee paraphrases") from before Christ's time; in consequence, "it is to be understood of a Person properly so called in the blessed Trinity".[9] Faustus Socinus (1539–1604) had not accepted that *logos* referred to a pre-existent person distinct from the Father. Rather, Jesus Christ was the *logos* who interpreted God, but as he was miraculously born and a defied man, he was legitimately worshipped. However, a more radical movement had arisen since the mid-sixteenth century: the Unitarians, for whom God is identical with one and only one divine self, argued that Jesus Christ was a human religious leader, making the worship of him idolatrous. With this understanding, Unitarians claimed, monotheistic Jews were more likely

---

6 Respectively: Dixon: 2003, 208–219, and Levitin: 2015, 523. Cf. Lim: 2012.

7 Sirota: 2013, 26.

8 Proceedings against Thomas Aikenhead for Blasphemy. Howell: 1816, 917–920. Coffey: 2000, 200. The Blasphemy Act (1698) was precipitated, in part, by the publication of John Toland's *Christianity Not Mysterious* (1696). Rarely applied, its penalties (fines and imprisonment) were removed for Unitarians in *The Doctrine of the Trinity Act* (1813). Deemed obsolete, the whole Act was repealed in 1967.

9 Allix: 1821, 1–2. In this study, references are to the accessible facsimile of the second edition (Oxford, 1821), which incorporated the author's corrections, rather than to the first edition (London, 1699). Hebrew and Greek words are transliterated, and conventional modern spellings are adopted.

to convert to Christianity, unencumbered by the doctrine of the Trinity. After all, in the *Dialogue with Trypho* by Justin Martyr (c. 100–c. 165) the Jewish interlocutor says that the Jews had never held to the divinity of the Messiah, so nor would they hold to the belief in a divine Trinity. These claims struck at the heart of orthodoxy. Allix thus begins AJC:

> If the doctrines of the ever blessed Trinity, and of the promised Messias being very God, had been altogether unknown to the Jews before Jesus Christ began to preach the Gospel, it would be a great prejudice against the Christian religion.[10]

Two recent works had gained Allix's attention. George Bull, later bishop of St David's, published the *Defensio fidei Nicaenae. A defence of the Nicene Creed: out of the extant writings of the Catholick doctors, who flourished during the three first centuries of the Christian Church* (1685, ET 1725), in which he argued against Socinians and Unitarians.[11] Bull quoted from Jewish sources (e.g. Wisdom of Solomon, Philo of Alexandria, Targums, Kabbala) to show that the Jews had believed in a pre-existent logos identifiable with the God of Israel and spiritual phenomena mentioned in the Old Testament; that the Trinity was embedded in 'pre-Christian' texts; and that there were ancient Jewish precedents for Platonic language. Nye responded with *The judgment of the fathers concerning the doctrine of the Trinity; opposed to Dr. G. Bull's Defence of the Nicene faith* (1695).[12] The value of the Jewish sources, and Bull's arguments, were disputed in favour of the claim that Justin Martyr was the first to believe in the Trinity, as much as 140 years after Christ. It was also claimed that the Jewish texts appealed to were composed later than the early preaching of the Gospel; indeed, they were either Christian forgeries or the doctrine had been inserted into them by Christians. Even then, they did not agree with Trinitarian but with Jewish (hence Socinian) theological ideas. As for the idea of the Trinity itself, Scriptural ideas (e.g. word, angel, wisdom) had been mixed by Justin Martyr with aspects of Platonic philosophy (e.g. nature, substance) to make it acceptable to pagan audiences. In short, the doctrine of the Trinity was a later and foreign imposition of early Christianity.

---

10 Allix: 1821, 1.
11 Unitarianism was commonly called Socinianism well into the eighteenth century, the latter being a catch-all for anti-Trinitarianism. Early English Unitarians were Henry Hedworth (1626–1705) and John Biddle (1615–1662). Stephen Nye (1648–1719) was the first to use 'Unitarian' in a published title. It was Allix who 'outed' Nye as the author of *The brief history of the Unitarians* (1687). Dixon: 2003, 171. On the origins and impact of Socinianism, see Mortimer: 2010; and on Unitarianism, see Tuggy: 2016.
12 Allix: 1821, 2–3, refers to "Mr. N" as its author; its content is similar to Nye's works. Nye contested this, attributing the work to a 'Thomas Smalbroke', who is, however, "otherwise invisible". Levitin: 2015, 526 n474.

3.2   Strategy and content

It is to these claims, with their major ramifications for orthodoxy, that Allix responded with AJC. This was not Allix's first foray into Trinitarian disputes. He had earlier written *A Defence of the Brief history of the Unitarians, against Dr. Sherlock's answer in his Vindication of the Holy Trinity* (1691); Sherlock's work had hindered rather than aided the cause against the Socinians. Allix's recent works in this area were *Animadversions on Mr Hills Book* (1695) and *The fathers vindicated, by a Presbyter of the Church of England* (1697). Allix designed AJC (1699) so as to answer the latest Unitarian polemic, with a view to defending Bull's orthodoxy, and Trinitarianism in general. The following table summarises its contents:

Chapters	Section	Subjects
1	Preface	Plan of book
2–7	Sources	Traditional explanations of OT shared by Jews and Christians
		Authority of ancient Jewish sources
8–22	Beliefs	Jewish belief in the Trinity
		Word [*logos*] as a person and divine
		Word as God or the Angel of the Lord
		Messiah as the Word, the Son of God, Jehovah
		Christian and later Jewish belief in the Trinity and divine Messiah
23–27	Objections	Jews did not get the Trinity from Plato
		Responses to modern Jews and Unitarians
Appendix		Dissertation on the redeeming Angel in Genesis 48

The main sections treated the criticisms levelled against Bull: the unity of Jewish and Christian tradition against the claim of Christian innovation; the antiquity and authority of the Jewish sources against the claim of later Christian forgery and corruption; and the demonstration that those sources contain proofs of the Trinity and a divine Messiah against the claim of Christian doctrinal imposition. The philosophical Philo, in whose 'pre-Christian' Jewish writings the *logos* is prominent, he having derived his ideas from Moses, not the Greeks – a standard trope of Hellenistic Jewish (and later patristic apologetic) literature – was crucial to Allix's response. It was absurd, Allix argued, to suppose that the Jews would have continued to use texts such as the Targums if they had been corrupted by philosophical (Platonic) ideas.[13] The final sections deal with remaining ob-

---

13 Allix: 1821, ch. 23. Cf. Levitin: 2015, 531.

jections. The work is completed with a dissertation on a specific text, Genesis 48:15–16 (discussed below).

3.3   Allix's knowledge of Jewish literature

It is natural to ask the question: what made Allix's approach distinctive, and more than just a restatement of what Bull had argued? The answer is straightforward: his superior knowledge of Jewish literature, ancient and medieval, which made Allix well placed to deal with the criticisms of the orthodox standpoint. In AJC, Allix quotes from a wide range of Jewish sources. They include, from the ancient period, the Old Testament, the Apocrypha, Philo, Josephus, the Targums, the Talmud, and Midrashim; and authors and texts from the medieval period, among which the better known are Sa'adya Ga'on, Maimonides, Rashi, Ibn Ezra, and the Kabbalistic mystical texts *Yezirah* and *Zohar*.[14] Ever since Allix's works were published, it has been recognised that Allix possessed an impressive knowledge of Jewish literature. It was this that Allix brought to bear in his defence of Jesus Christ as a person of the divine Trinity and divine Messiah.

4.   Analysis

4.1   Christian Hebraism

The early Christians had largely known Biblical Hebrew texts in Greek translation – in what is now commonly referred to as the Septuagint (LXX). Most early Christian writers living in the Roman Empire continued to read and write in Greek; and subsequently in Latin as well. There were some Christian Hebraists in the sub-apostolic period (e. g. Origen, Jerome), as well as in the medieval period (e. g. Andrew of St Victor).[15] But by and large, Biblical and other Jewish literature in Hebrew came to be known in Latin or vernacular translations. The Renaissance and Reformation movements were watersheds in many ways: a return to the texts of antiquity in their original languages, including Biblical and other Jewish literature; the use by Christians of insights from rabbinic commentary based on Biblical Hebrew texts; the establishment of professorial chairs in Hebrew at European universities; and the study of Hebrew with practicing Jews.[16]

---

14 For a much fuller list, see Goldish: 1999, 147 n5.

15 See McKane: 1989, chs 1–2; Carleton Paget: 1996, 502–508; Kieffer: 1996, 663–681.

16 Cf. Goldish, 1999, 145–146. See Burnett: 2008; Burnett: 2012. European university and church institutions (and individuals) began to acquire Hebrew manuscripts. For example, the first

For Protestants, in particular, the turning to the Old Testament in its original Hebrew (and other Jewish literature), alongside the other ancient versions (i.e. Aramaic, Greek, Latin, Syriac), was allied to the doctrine of *Sola Scriptura*, 'Scripture Alone'. This was deemed to be a part of the way, given the need for Christian reform and renewal, by which to rediscover the origins and purer founts of Christianity.[17] It is in this context that the work of Peter Allix should be viewed. Goldish has placed Allix in a list of early modern Christian Hebraists, ranked according to whether they could read:

1. the Talmud and rabbinic texts in Hebrew and Aramaic fluently;
2. Biblical Hebrew with facility, rabbinic texts with a little difficulty, and Jewish texts mainly in Hebrew or translation;
3. some Biblical Hebrew, but Jewish texts mainly in Latin or vernacular translation.

Allix is placed in the second rank.[18] In later study, Goldish writes: "Allix was, as his works amply demonstrate, one of the most well read and knowledgeable Hebraists in England at that time."[19] This is noteworthy. On the one hand, professorial chairs in Hebrew had been established in Cambridge and Oxford (1540 and 1546 respectively), with Anglo-Christian Hebraism reaching a peak during

---

catalogue of Oxford's Bodleian Library (1605), arranged by four faculties (theology, medicine, law, arts), lists 58 books with titles in Hebrew script, in a collection comprising a few thousand entries in all (the first acquisitions were made in 1601). The Hebrew books were mostly from Venice, where Hebrew printing flourished. Some Hebrew titles are corrected in Latin by Thomas Bodley, whose interest was not only antiquarian but religious and political. In his autobiography, Bodley describes his early education in Geneva as a 12 year old refugee, whose family had fled persecution under Queen Mary: 'through my Fathers cost and care, sufficiently instructed to become an Auditour of Chevalerius in Hebrew, of Berealdus in Greeke, of Calvin and Beza in Divinity, and of some other Professours in that University; (which was then newly erected) besides my domesticall teachers, in the house of Philibertus Saracenus, a famous Physitian in that City, with whom I was boarded: where Robertus Constantinus, that made the Greek Lexicon, read Homer unto me.' Bodley mentions his interest, in founding the library, in 'the learned and modern tongues, as in sundry other sorts of scholasticall literature'. Bodley: 2006, 38, 52. Jayne: 1956, 68; Roth: 1962–67.

17 Saebo: 2008 is an informative starting-point. An influential Huguenot Hebraist was Louis Cappel (1585–1658), who taught at Saumur, where Allix studied. See Burnett: 2008, 789–792. Among the notable Christian Hebraists of earlier generations in the Reformed tradition were the Italian Jewish convert Immanuel Tremellius (1510–1580) and the Huguenot Isaac Casaubon (1559–1614), on whom see, respectively, Austin: 2007, and Grafton and Weinberg: 2011.

18 Goldish: 1998, 18: (1) Johannes Buxtorf the Elder and the Younger, Petrus Cunaeus, John Lightfoot, John Selden, Christian Knorr von Rosenroth, and Gerardus and Isaac Vossius; (2) Hugo Grotius, Hugh Broughton, Francis Mercurius van Helmont, Peter Allix, and many others; (3) Isaac Newton, John Milton, Henry More, and Gottfried Wilhelm von Leibniz.

19 Goldish: 1999, 147.

the Civil War of the mid-seventeenth century. But on the other hand, exposure to Hebrew had been limited, given the exclusion of Jews from 1290 due to the Edict of Expulsion (under Edward I) until the mid-seventeenth century; most studied Hebrew with written aids, not with practicing Jews.[20] Thus, the arrival in England of Peter Allix, a Huguenot Hebraist, benefited the ecclesiastical and educational institutions directly. His was a fine example of the way in which the Huguenot diaspora was a bonus for the host nation. This sets in relief the remarks of Larminie: "As he was a high profile refugee, his flight prompted an instruction from Versailles on 9 February 1686 to Bonrepaux, the French envoy in London, to offer him a pension of 3000 or 4000 livres if he would convert and return."[21] Allix did neither.

4.2   Doctrinal polemics in late seventeenth century England

Allix gained his theological bearings from three periods or developments in the history of Christianity. The first period, the early Church, witnessed Christianity emerging organically out of its originally Jewish setting, with doctrines formulated on the basis of the teachings of Jesus Christ and his apostles. Various views arose concerning the Trinity, with many judged to be heretical, while also being catalysts for creedal formulations. The second period, the Reformation, was when heresies among Catholic scholars (due to excessive rationalism or mysticism) were criticised by Socinians, whose subsequent influence marked the beginning of the third period. The errors of Socinus, from the perspective of orthodoxy, had paved the way for the Unitarians, whose claims were injuring the orthodoxy of the Church of England. Allix thus decided to respond to a controversy that had emerged "in this kingdom".[22] Allix's outlook may be seen in the following tabular format:

Jewish-Christianity	Modern Judaism
Protestantism	Modern Catholicism (Socinus)
Church of England (Huguenot)	Unitarianism

The first column identifies, according to Allix, the bearers of orthodoxy, and the second column the opponents whose writings introduced errors; although they

---

20 In Holland, by comparison, there was freer exchange between Christians and Jews. See Katchen: 1984; Berg and Wall: 1988. There was, nevertheless, a growth in Christian and Jewish interaction across Europe in the seventeenth century. For instance, Coudert: 2004, 300–301 presents a tabular appendix on European links at Sulzbach, Bavaria, a centre of Christian Hebraism; it includes a column on England that lists Newton and More (see n18 above).
21 Larminie: 2004.
22 Allix: 1821, xii.

intermingle frequently in AJC. With what apologetic approach, and by what authority, did Allix position himself in this way? Allix ascribed tell-tale hallmarks to his opponents: they contradict each other and/or falsely accuse the orthodox of corrupting texts.[23] Allix based his own doctrine on Scripture and the Christian tradition that could be shown to derive from it. On the latter point, Allix was not radical, as some Protestants could be, in their attitude towards tradition, even if his viewpoint was characteristically Protestant in outlook.[24] Indeed, an analogy may be drawn between his use of Christian tradition and his particular of Jewish tradition: distinguishing that which is in continuity with Scripture and that which is not. Allix was by no means alone in his Scriptural defence of Trinitarian orthodoxy. There were many keen critics of Unitarianism, such as Archbishop John Tillotson (1630–1694) and Bishop Edward Stillingfleet (1633–1699). That he was a French Protestant refugee, and a Christian Hebraist, serving in the Church of England, was due to his own life, education, and immediate circumstances. But therein lay his distinctive contribution.

4.3   Claiming primitive Jewish-Christianity

Ancient Judaism had become a major interest for Christians after the Reformation, for at least the reasons given above; it made Christian Hebraism important.[25] To awaken a sense of the original Jewishness of Christianity signified a return to the authentic and renewing roots of primitive Christianity. This was a hallmark of seventeenth century Christian literature as well, evident in the growth of the more historically-minded study of ancient Christianity, as well as in polemical rhetoric.[26] Even though 'Judaizing' was a charge made by Catholics and Protestants against each other, some groups (e.g. Socinians, Unitarians, anti-Trinitarians, Millenarians) welcomed the title, tracing themselves to the Nazarenes, the first Jewish Christians. Nye pointed out that Paul had been called a "ringleader of the sect [haireseōs] of the Nazarenes" (Acts 24:5). These were the ancestors of groups from the "first times", variously called "Ebionites, Mineans,

---

23 Allix: 1821, 237, 258, 259, 275, 287. Interestingly, Allix: 1821, 342 claims that just as there are wise and calm Catholic scholars, there are also some "Mahometans" (Muslims) who do not accuse Christians of corrupting their texts. This was an argument that could be used against Socinians, even if Muslims took on some of the Socinian criticisms of Christian orthodoxy.

24 Allix: 1821, 4, 5. Cf. Myllykoski: 2012, 23.

25 This included a turning to Millenarianism across Europe. See Berg and Wall: 1988; Capp: 1972; Popkin: 1994; Snobelen: 2001. On Allix, who opposed "the conception of a bright apocalyptic future which millenarians paint for Jews", seeing "millenarianism as a Judaizing error", see Goldish: 1998, 67–68; and Goldish: 1999, 154–161.

26 On the early modern emergence of the phrases 'Jewish Christian', 'Christian Jewish', and 'Jewish Christianity' in Toland's *Nazarenus* (1718), see Myllykoski: 2012.

Artemonites, Theodotians, Symmachians, Paulinists, Samosatenians, Photinians, and Monarchians".[27] Concerned not only with doctrine, attention to matters Jewish was characteristic of many groups, factions, and movements: the strict observance of the Sabbath by the 'Saturday Sabbatarians'; attempts to restore the practice of Biblical Law through the 'Barebones Parliament'; and in Scotland the avoidance of pork.[28]

Allix was well placed to interact with and, where necessary, challenge claims for primitiveness, due to his strong and often superior knowledge of Jewish literature. Allix argued that certain groups, factions, and movements had taken on doctrine from Jewish tradition without separating out the genuine from the "perfidious Pharisaic dross", a tradition that could be better used to confirm Trinitarian Christianity, against Unitarians (and a spiritual kingdom of Christ to come, against Millenarians), as was standard doctrine in the Church of England. Allix took the view that while some Jewish texts had absorbed anti-Christian rabbinic forgeries, the same texts preserved ideas in support of Trinitarian orthodoxy; but it required knowledge and skill to detect them.[29] Since, according to Allix, Trinitarians were in a healthier possession of the truth of primitive Jewish-Christianity, the Unitarians were not to be seen as authentically Jewish in the ancient sense. Moreover, they were not best placed, unlike Allix, to encourage the conversion of Jews to Christianity. It has been suggested, by Goldish, that at a time when aligning Christianity with ancient Judaism was not always seen as a liability, Allix was able to 'Judaize' more effectively in the service of traditional orthodoxy.[30]

4.4   Allix's use and assessment of Jewish tradition

Allix's use of Jewish literature must be placed in historical perspective. In the medieval period, the Spanish Dominican theologian and orientalist Raymond Martini (b. ca. 1220, d. ca. 1285–1290) wrote the encyclopaedic and influential work *The Dagger of Faith against Moors and Jews* (1278), in which he used Biblical, Classical, Christian, and rabbinic texts (and Islamic texts) to argue for the truth of Christianity against Jews (and Saracens, i.e. Arab Muslims). This was a key development in the medieval Christian understanding of Judaism. In the

---

27 Nye: 1687, 10.
28 Goldish: 1999, 145–146, 153–154. See also Katz: 2004.
29 Goldish: 1999, 146. This revived an argument of Martini (see below). Goldish: 1998, 65; 1999, 150.
30 Goldish: 1999, 161; cf. Shear 2011, 108. Allix seemingly had a role in the conversion of John Xeres, a North African Jewish merchant. Xeres: 1710. Katz: 1994, 202–203; and Ruderman: 2007, 128 n33.

twelfth to thirteenth centuries, scholars began to realise more than ever that if the Talmud (oral tradition, preserved as written commentary on the Torah) had an authoritative role in the interpretation of Scripture in Judaism, then both had to be used in defence of Christianity.[31] But Allix did not, as Martini had previously done, simply mine Jewish tradition for Christological proofs; and nor, as with Nye's attacks on Bull, did Allix question their value or authority.[32]

Rather, Allix turned Jewish tradition to his own advantage within an intra-Christian polemic. Divine oral tradition (i. e. Oral Torah) had stemmed from Mt Sinai, as was claimed in Judaism, but it had been corrupted by "later Rabbins": those who had rejected Christ. Importantly, for Allix, that Jewish tradition could be marshalled to show that many ancient Jews – the 'ancient Jewish Church' – had believed in the Trinity and a divine Messiah.[33] The New Testament shows Jesus and his apostles building on this in their preaching; otherwise, Allix argued, there would have been no conversions to Christianity among fellow Jews of their own day. By contrast, according to Allix, the Unitarians were in the position of having adopted beliefs from later anti-Christian Jewish opinion ("modern Jews"). Given this argument, Goldish has suggested that AJC, and Allix's other works, were the first instance of a polemical strategy originally designed for anti-Jewish polemic (e. g. Martini) being turned against Judaizing Christians within the Church. Allix was only able to achieve this through his expertise in Jewish literature.[34]

Allix's orthodox apologetic strategy was polemical, in its construction of, in effect, a historical lineage of doctrinal truth: the ancient synagogue, Christ and his apostles, the early Church, some ancient and medieval Jews, Protestants, and the Trinitarians of the Church of England. But there are also comments in AJC that imply a considerate recognition of much complexity in that history: an acknowledgement of disputes between Jews and Christians at Christianity's inception; and an awareness of the varied use of Jewish tradition in the history of Christianity. As for Jewish responses to the claims of Christianity, again Allix shows some considerateness. On the one hand, Jews have reacted to those claims with stubbornness, blindness, or spite. On the other hand, in their favour, Christ was rejected because his death did not conform to their messianic expectations; anyway, they were subsequently persecuted by Christians.[35] This mixed picture

---

31 On Martini, see the useful comments in Klepper: 2007; see also Dulles: 2005, 122–124.

32 For his brief commendation of Martini's use of the Targums, see Allix: 1821, 371.

33 Luther, Zwingli, Calvin, and More had occasionally used the phrases *ecclesia iudaeorum* 'the church of the Jews' and *ecclesia gentium* 'the church of the gentiles' to characterise the unity of the church of Jews and Gentiles. The phrase 'Jewish-Christian church' was first used in English literature by the Huguenot Pierre du Moulin (1568–1658) to describe faithful Jews persecuted during the Roman Empire, just as the Roman Church now persecuted the Protestant faithful. Myllykoski: 2012, 22–23.

34 Goldish: 1999, 150, 162. Ruderman: 2007, 128 n33. See also FRIEDMAN: 1994.

35 Allix: 1821, chs 19, 20, 24–26.

was the inevitable result of Allix's use of Jewish tradition as both 'friend and foe'. Indeed, it reflects the deep and long-standing 'family dispute' over Jewishness that lay at the origins of Christianity, which emerged out of a first century Jewish matrix, and which was then transplanted, with all of its complexity, into Christianity.[36]

4.5 Example: Genesis 48:15–16

In order to gain a sense of Allix's work, it will be useful to look at a specific example in a little more detail. AJC includes, at the end, "*A Dissertation concerning the Angel who is called the Redeemer,* Gen. xlviii", a full response by Allix to a brief conversation about its meaning that he had recently had with an unconvinced listener (addressed as "Sir", and not only with politesse but also with rigour and detail throughout).[37] This repays close attention because it illustrates Allix's aims and methods well. The Biblical passage, from Jacob's final blessing of Joseph's sons, Ephraim and Manasseh, reads as follows:

> (15) He [Jacob] blessed Joseph, and said, "The God [*elohim*] before whom my ancestors Abraham and Isaac walked, the God [*elohim*] who has been my shepherd all my life to this day, (16) the angel [*mal'ach*] who has redeemed [*ha-go'el*] me from all harm, bless the boys; and in them let my name be perpetuated, and the name of my ancestors Abraham and Isaac; and let them grow into a multitude on the earth." (Gen. 48:15–16 NRSV)

Allix recalls that his listener preferred to think that v. 16 does not refer to the *logos*, but to a created angel, a view supported by the authority of "some great names", especially Grotius (1583–1645). Allix opposes this by arguing that the angel is none other than the Son of God. After quoting three ancient versions (Hebrew, Greek, Latin), and noting that there are no major differences between them, Allix makes mention of the translation of Athias and Usque (i.e. the Ferrara Bible, 1553), a translation "of great authority with the Jews" unfamiliar with Hebrew. Another introductory avenue into matters Jewish and lexical are the comments made about *ga'al* and *go'el.* The latter has either the specific meaning of 'kinsman' (*agchisteus* Ruth 4:8 LXX), such that Jerome and others understood this angel to be the Messiah who would be born into the family of Jacob, or they have the regular meanings of 'rescue, ransom' (*lutroun* or *lutrotēs* in the LXX), as in the Spanish translation. However, Allix's concerns were not Jewish and lexical *per se.* Rather, this Biblical passage speaks of the

---

36 For discussions of anti-Christian Jewish and anti-Jewish Christian polemic – and much else in between – in antiquity, see Schäfer: 2007; and Carleton Paget: 2010. Cf. Myllykoski: 2012.
37 Allix: 1821, 349–371.

divinity of Jesus Christ, supported by Jewish literature, ancient and medieval, more broadly. To build his case, Allix poses three questions, and answers each in turn.

First: "Whether the ELOHIM spoken of, ver. 15, is the very YHWH whom the Jews acknowledge for their God?" Allix answers in the affirmative (citing Targums, and Gen. 48:3). He then points out that modern Jews are mistaken in seeing in v. 16 a reference to a "mere angel". They have missed the import of its language (i.e. to walk before God, v. 15); and they have wrongly used ancient Jewish tradition (Talmud), which held both that *Elohim, Jehovah*, and *Jehovah Elohim* were names of the uncreated angel ("which makes this Angel to be God") and that the title 'redeemer' is used of God alone. This provides Allix with a platform for Christian doctrine: vv. 15–16 do not refer to God the Father and God the Son (so Cyril of Alexandria) but only the Son (so John Chrysostom). This follows "all the ancient Christians" (Justin, Clement, Tertullian, Origen, Cyprian, etc.) who ascribed to the Son all the appearances of God: he was the 'Angel of Jehovah'. Genesis 48:15–16, then, is a prayer for the blessing of the *logos*. The ancient Christians made this identification "no more" than the Jews before them: ELOHIM is the *logos* (in Philo; Shekinah and Memra in the Targums; and in later Kabbalistic texts). God the Father, after all, remains unseen. Allix then criticises modern Catholics (Sanctius, Lorinus), who, in not taking this view, end up agreeing with modern Jews, rather than following "the authority of Christ" (John 1:18; 6:46) and the wisdom of "the primitive Christians".

Second: "Whether the GO'EL mentioned in ver. 16. is the same with that ELOHIM ver. 15. or differs from him as a creature doth from its Creator?" Allix argues that God (v. 15) is the redeemer (v. 16): they are one and the same. In defence of this, Allix makes various exegetical observations about Genesis 48:15–16, supported by other Biblical and Jewish texts. Lexically, no Hebrew conjunction 'and' separates God and the angel; both are preceded by the '*hē* demonstrative' (i.e. the definite article); and the verb 'bless' is singular, which signifies "one Person alone". Moreover, the attributes mentioned, especially that of redeemer, are proper to God alone. Furthermore, Jacob expected a blessing from God, not from an angel. Allix uses these observations to oppose modern Jews (Abarbanel, Alshich, Serrano), whose views lead to angel worship, risking idolatry; modern Catholics, who in praying to God but then saints and angels, risk the same; and some Reformed, who in not studying the passage carefully, have taken on erroneous opinions. Allix strengthens his answer with quotations from "the ancient synagogue", texts in which identifications were made between the angel and uncreated spiritual phenomena: Logos (Wis. 16:8, 12, Tg. Onk.; Philo *Leg. All.* 2) and Memra (Tg. Jon.). Jews after Christ (*Zohar*, Nachmanides, Recanati, Ben Asher, R. Menasseh ben Israel), who "did not immediately renounce the doctrine of their forefathers", also understood the angel to be uncreated spiritual phenomena in ways that identified them singularly and synonymously with God.

Third: "Whether the prayer contained in Jacob's blessing be made to God alone, or to the redeeming Angel together with him?" Allix answers that Jacob's words were a prayer to God *and* the angel, but that these addressed Christ. While it was God who fed Israel, and against whom Israel rebelled in the wilderness, this was Christ (1 Cor. 10), the Logos, and "not a mere angel", to whom worship is now offered (Eph. 1). Moreover, the attribute of shepherding (Gen. 48:15), which featured in Christ's preaching to his fellow Jews (John 10), made him "one with the Father". Furthermore, in Kabbalistic texts (Recanati), Genesis 48:15 and 49:24, which mention shepherding, are explained as the Shekinah or the Logos, which are elsewhere representative of God. Thus, Biblical and Jewish texts support the view that the prayer of Genesis 48:15–16 was offered to Christ as both God *and* the redeeming angel. These points are again made against modern Catholics (e. g. Bellarmine) who, by invoking saints and angels, in addition to God, risked idolatry; Socinians, who argue that the prayer was addressed to a "mere angel" just as Christ is prayed to for grace, but not as God; and Reformed Divines who, in taking the same view as Catholic Divines, dissent from both Jewish and Christian tradition alike.

Following these questions and answers, Allix treats two final objections. Against the tendency of modern Jews to understand the angel in Genesis 48 to be a created angel (i. e. Metatron, or Enoch translated to heaven), Allix observes that angelic names were formed from divine names, and were understood in Kabbalistic texts with respect to the ten *sephirot* 'emanations' from God. The angel Actariel, whose name derives from 'crown' (the first of the ten *sephirot*) was enthroned, and distinguished from the other ministering angels standing before the throne of God. As for Metatron, who discoursed with Moses and in whom God placed his name, this name not only expresses the same as *shadday* 'almighty' (Rashi) and Logos (Jerome) but in Kabbalistic texts this angel is the soul of the Messiah: "in our phrase" the pre-incarnate Logos. Indeed, Metatron has divine properties "incommunicable to a creature". Finally, regarding Revelation 1:4, which seems to refer to prayer to seven created angels before Jesus Christ is even mentioned, Allix builds an elaborate case that these angels represent the Holy Spirit alongside the Son, who, as the Messiah, has seven gifts from the Holy Spirit, and has seven horns that denote his empire. This is further supported by reference to Biblical, Jewish, and Christian texts. These points are directed, once more, against Catholic and Socinian scholars, after which Allix declares: "but it is time to give over".[38]

---

38 Allix: 1821, 371.

5.   Evaluation

5.1   Post-Scriptural Trinitarian discourse

Allix is clear that his case against the Unitarians is a Scriptural case. AJC was precipitated by disputes over the meaning of *logos* in John 1, but Allix soon branches out to discuss many texts in Scripture that pertain to his argument. This has a characteristically Protestant outlook in AJC: the doctrine of the Trinity and the divine Messiah, as a part of the "common faith of the Church", must be "a doctrine drawn from Scripture".[39] Thus, while AJC is a rich fabric – Biblical, Jewish and Christian texts in polemical dispute – Allix often focuses his attention on texts in Scripture. It is nevertheless obvious that Allix's language and conceptuality were indebted to post-Scriptural Trinitarian discourse, in which philosophical resources could be deployed to help 'express the inexpressible'. The belief that Jesus Christ was God incarnate, and the divine Messiah – in a Trinity of three persons with one divine nature – was the orthodox legacy of the early Church, as expressed in creeds and other early Christian literature, following sustained engagement with texts in Scripture. This is the legacy with which Allix identifies in AJC.[40] Allix's exegesis of Genesis 48:15–16 is, in this regard, comparable with early Church, and subsequent early modern, orthodox Trinitarian exegesis.[41] But what makes AJC distinctive is Allix's Christian Hebraism: the use of insights from Biblical and other Jewish literature in support of that discourse.

Some of his use of Hebrew opened him up to sharp criticism by his opponents. Nye, the target of AJC, accused Allix of tritheism, highlighting places in AJC where Allix translates the plural *elohim* as 'gods' (e. g. Gen. 1:1 "the Gods created"), since this was traditionally seen as a superlative singular ('God').[42] Nye proposed that in opposing one view (i. e. Unitarianism) Allix had fallen into its contrary view (i. e. tritheistic polytheism). However, Allix did not think that his approach in any way compromised the unity of God. That *elohim* was translated by the singular *theos* in Genesis 1:1 LXX had in fact obscured ancient Jewish belief in the plurality of God. That translation, Allix claims, following Jerome, the

---

39 Allix: 1821, 4.

40 As well as mentioning many Church Fathers in AJC, Allix: 1821, 250 alludes, for instance, to the clause, *filioque* 'and the Son' (i. e. signifying the double procession of the Spirit from the Father and the Son), added to the Nicene Creed in 589.

41 e. g. Justin Martyr *Dial.* 58; Clement *Paed.* 1.7; Cyprian *Test.* 2.5. About 150 years before Allix, but in continuity with early Christian tradition, Luther's exegesis of Gen. 48:15–16 is remarkably similar to Allix's. Luther: 1535–1545, in LW 8.161–168. Slotemaker: 2011, 240 places Luther's increasing attention on the Trinity in the context of the theological threats of "Jews, Turks, and anti-trinitarians *(Novi Ariani)*".

42 Nye: 1701, 4–14; Allix: 1821, 94, 96, 99. Dixon: 2003, 171.

"Talmudists" later excused: Ptolemy Philadephus, who authorised the translation, was not able to mistake the Jews as polytheists, like him.[43] After all, Allix
points out, in commenting on Genesis 1:1 LXX Philo mentions divine powers, an
indication of divine plurality which Allix finds elsewhere in Jewish tradition (e. g.
Targums, Kabbalists). Near the start of the chapter that had evidently appalled
Nye, Allix states: "the Jews generally have acknowledged, that the divine nature,
which is otherwise perfectly one, is distinguishable into certain properties, which
we call Persons".[44] Here Allix shows his indebtedness to the language and conceptuality of post-Scriptural Trinitarian tradition; but his particular claim was
that other Jewish literature supported this. In other words, Allix did not see
himself as stuck in the hole into which Nye argued he had incompetently fallen.
Indeed, Allix's role and status as a defender of orthodoxy was not in doubt among
near-contemporary Trinitarians.[45]

5.2   The use of Biblical and Jewish literature

It was certainly the case, as Allix states, that a strong pedigree of ancient Christian
forebears saw in passages such as Genesis 48:15–16 the pre-incarnate activity of
Jesus Christ. This was motivated in the early Church by the struggle against
subordinationist Christologies. The identification of not just theophanies but
what have more recently been called 'Christophanies' – appearances of the pre-
incarnate *logos* – confirmed for commentators the pre-existence of the Son of
God. Justin Martyr was an early exponent: the Angel of the Lord was the *logos*.[46]
Allix's concern to defend the unique divinity of Jesus Christ in this traditional
way led him to adopt, in an era of fierce ecclesiastical polemical dispute, a forceful
tone. Allix contrasts the vague "allusion" and "accommodation" of the Unitarians with his own "demonstration", "argument", and "proof".[47] Allix's treatment
of Genesis 48:15–16 for doctrinal purposes is indeed deft and taut. For instance,

---

43 Allix: 1821, 100, 107. Hayward: 1995, 29, 94–95.

44 Allix: 1821, 93; cf. 5.

45 Bishop Bull himself turned to Allix's AJC. Bull: 1714, 29, on Greek dependence on the Jews for
the notion of *logos*, mentions that "this Subject is thoroughly handled by the most learned Dr.
Allix". William Wotton (1666–1727), a theologian and classicist, remembered for his pro-
digious language learning, later recommended "Allix's Reflections upon the Books of the Old
and New Testament". Wotton: 1734, 240. Cf. Ruderman: 2007, 91. On the "otherwise unim-
pressible [John Peter] Bernard" (d. 1750), who praised Allix grudgingly, see Levitin: 2015, 530
n502.

46 See n41. In the later Arian controversy, Augustine preferred to see the angel as a created
representative of God (as did the Socinians). In continuity with the early apologists (and the
Reformers), Allix's view has its recent exponents. Kidd: 1852; Hansen: 1965; Borland: 1978.

47 Allix: 1821, Preface, chs 1, 16–18; and 231, 340.

his use of Hebrew in his second question, on the identification of God and "the Angel" (i.e. uppercase, as in AV, NIV, NAB; cf. 'angel' in NRSV), illustrates his lexical skills. Allix was not swayed by the frequent objection that Jesus Christ might be seen as a created angel: *mal'ach* means 'messenger', which is an "office" rather than a "nature", so the word applied to the ministry of the Son of God. This is also another example of how Allix deployed post-Scriptural Trinitarian discourse to hold together the unity and the distinction in the language of Gen. 48.[48]

Allix's broader use of Jewish literature is, however, rightly open to objection. On Allix's translation of *elohim* as 'gods', Nye was understandably shocked that Allix had claimed that the Jewish commentator Isaac Abarbanel (1437–1508) had pretended with impudence that *elohim* is singular, given that the latter is patently within its range of Biblical meanings. As for his exegesis of Genesis 48:15–16, Allix invoked Philo to identify spiritual phenomena and the *logos*, and the *logos* as divine, but Philo's exegeses of this passage never identify God and the angel; indeed, their activities are always of a quite different kind.[49] The same problem arises in Allix's defence of the divinity of the Messiah. Allix claims that the ancient Jews expected the Messiah to be 'God'. Allix highlights texts in Scripture that either describe God or a royal deliverer with divine attributes, and he then quotes Jewish texts to show that the these texts were read either messianically or messianically in terms of spiritual phenomena.[50] Allix states:

> That they [ancient Jews] look upon the *Shekinah* as the Angel, the Redeemer, so all their ideas of the redemption and of their salvation have a necessary relation to that Redeemer who is *Jehovah*; so that all that is spoken in all the prophets, of the redemption by the Messias, must by necessary consequence be referred to them to *Jehovah's* being the Messias, or to the Messias, as being *Jehovah* indeed.[51]

Some of these claims are supported in ancient Jewish tradition (e.g. the angel as divine, *logos*, and the Shekinah; the Messiah as divine); and there is no doubt about the fusing of identities in Second Temple Jewish thought.[52] But they were neither all referred to a single Messiah, nor "all their ideas" to God alone by "a

---

48 Allix: 1821, 279. It would be mistaken to pass this off as merely pre-modern doctrinal exegesis. Whether or not concerned with Trinitarian orthodoxy, for religious or other reasons, modern exegetes continue to explore how God and the angel seem to be identified in such passages. Johnson: 1961, 29–32; Sarna: 1989, 328, 383–384; Dearman: 2002: 36–37; Rooker: 2003, 863–864; Heijne: 2010, 92–99; Boyarin: 2012, 166–167. Cf. Malone: 2015, 113, 124, and his concerns in 129–142. For Christian exegetes who, at least on Gen. 48:15–16, do not pursue this line, see Westermann: 1986, 190; Wenham: 1994, 465.

49 *Leg. All.* 3.177; *Conf.* 181; *Fug.* 67. On the variability in ancient Jewish interpretations, that there was "no unambiguous or homogenous interpretation of 'the angel of the Lord' and his identity in our sources", see Heijne: 2010, 377. Cf. Knohl: 2016.

50 Allix: 1821, 223ff, 241–242.

51 Allix: 1821, 224.

52 On messianic ideas in this period, see Collins: 2009; Boyarin: 2012; Novenson: 2012.

necessary relation" or "necessary consequence".[53] In other words, by using a Trinitarian interpretation of New Testament texts for the "necessary" meaning of other ancient Jewish texts, Allix elides by chains of association Christian orthodoxy with the more complex, and sometimes markedly different, claims of Jewish tradition. There were similar patterns of thought in ancient Jewish and Christian texts, but they did not all speak with one voice. Greater clarity on this would have indicated not only the shared ideas of Jewish and Christian antiquity, but also the distinctiveness of early Christianity. There were significant developments in Second Temple Jewish thought, but the early Christian community was "impelled to move much further", building, nevertheless, on "a process that had already begun".[54]

5.3   Patterns of divine activity and identity

The latter objection does not signify that Allix's erudite invocation of Jewish tradition was misplaced. The overplaying of Jewish tradition in AJC need not detract from a more modest version of Allix's claim: that patterns or types (*tupoi*) of belief about divine activity and identity in ancient Biblical and Jewish texts cradled the ideas and claims of later Christian orthodoxy. This is not surprising, given the originally Jewish setting of early Christianity, so much so that the relationship between the two religions may be better characterised as one of siblings, rather than mother and daughter, until as late as the 4th Century.[55] Passages such as Genesis 48:15–16 express realities that were read by Christians with a forward-looking perspective: they, along with other texts in Scripture, indicate important, widespread patterns of divine activity and identity. With a backward-looking perspective, the same texts were seen in the light of the activity of God in Jesus Christ. Messianic passages were approached similarly, as were others and their motifs (e. g. the prophet like Moses, the suffering servant, the Son of Man). This hermeneutic was encouraged by New Testament writers (e. g. Luke 24:27; 2 Cor. 3:14–18), and it led, in time, to Augustine's influential formulation about Scripture: "In the Old Testament, the New is concealed [*lateat*]; in the New the Old is revealed [*pateat*]" (*Quaest. Hept.* 2.73).[56] To the extent that Trinitarian doctrine was a natural outflow from shared origins, in which philosophical re-

---

53 For arguments based on association and inference, see Allix: 1821, 208–209, 212, 229, 230, 231. For examples of speculative claims, see Allix: 1821, 280, 282, 291.
54 Fuller: 1997, 507–508. Note, however, the salutary critique and comments of FRIEDMAN: 1994.
55 Sandgren: 2010; cf. Segal: 1977; Kugel: 1998.
56 Augustine: 419, 141. On Augustine's hermeneutics, see Wright: 2008. Cf. Hays: 2014.

sources could be deployed to help 'express the inexpressible', these patterns of divine activity and identity were integral to its formulation.[57]

Allix's approach to Scripture was Trinitarian. In continuity with patristic exegesis, which set the direction of travel of Christian interpretation in motion, the "fundamental question for understanding meaning was discerning the reference", in which "The 'idea' preceded the chosen mode of expression"; moreover, the "difference between 'literal' and 'allegorical' references was not absolute, but lay on a spectrum".[58] To the extent that Allix does this, in discerning the literal (historical) and the figurative (spiritual), AJC displays deep-seated Christian instincts.[59] Allix's keenness to rule out other readings of Genesis 48:15–16 (whether other Trinitarian or non-Trinitarian), in arguing that Jesus Christ is the sole 'referent', might give pause for thought. After all, it is important to distinguish the type and the anti-type (or, the shadow and its reality, the promise and its fulfilment). This was not entirely lost on Allix: he acknowledges that there was less clarity "under the Old Testament"; and that Christ intended his audience to realise his significance over time.[60] A rationale for this is expressed in the New Testament: the gradual disclosure of the mystery of the redemptive drama for the incorporation of the gentiles (e.g. Col. 1:26; Eph. 3:9). This also means that the exegesis of Scripture must not be overridden by the constraints of another age, in this case late seventeenth century doctrinal polemics: its riches are not confined to Trinitarian ontology.

But for rooting Christian belief in the Trinity and a divine Messiah in its ancient Jewish setting, AJC, which is an early modern work in so many respects, nevertheless anticipates what is nowadays normative in studies in Christian origins. The deployment in this area of major evidence since discovered (e.g. the Dead Sea Scrolls), and the general turning toward investigating the Jewishness of the early Christian movement and its subsequent developments, only confirms this. In this regard, to the extent that AJC has contemporary resonance suggests, in turn, that the oft-proclaimed contrast between pre-modern and modern theological discourses is unsustainable. Allix's AJC complicates this conventional modern narrative nicely, as it is a work that owes deeply to pre-modernity, is

---

57 Horbury: 2015, 350 states, on Boyarin's work (on Daniel, 1 Enoch, and 2 Esdras): "The result is a book as far in atmosphere as possible from the comparably engaging scholarly writings of Geza Vermes, for whom 'Jesus the Jew' became a divine Christ through Christian misunderstanding. For Boyarin, by contrast, Christian Christology continues a pre-Christian Jewish trend which can still be traced among Jews after the rise of Christianity."

58 Young: 1997, 120.

59 Viewed in their ancient setting, Trinitarian and Christological readings of the New Testament and Christian tradition were not unhistorical or uncritical, let alone anti-Jewish. Wright: 2014, 94–98; Kugel: 2010; and, again, Young: 1997, with de Lubac: 1998–2009. Cf. Reimer: 1998, with Rowe and Hays: 2007.

60 Allix: 1821, 280, and ch. 22.

situated squarely in early modernity, and yet it is somewhat remarkably at home in late modernity.

6.   Conclusions

Allix's book *Ancient Jewish Church* (AJC) was first and foremost a response to intra-Christian polemical debates in late seventeenth century England, by a Huguenot refugee who allied himself with the Trinitarian orthodoxy of the Church of England. Responding to criticisms levelled against Bishop George Bull's use of Jewish literature by the Unitarian Stephen Nye, Allix brought to bear his wide knowledge of Jewish literature, both ancient and medieval. Allix was a strong Christian Hebraist, as his contemporaries and others later recognised, a learned role encouraged by the return to the Scriptures and other literature in their original languages following the Renaissance and the Reformation. This gained a new and particular focus in controversies about the Trinity and the divinity of the Messiah in the 1690s, in which primitive Jewishness was claimed by both established Christian denominations and other groups to different doctrinal ends. Allix used Biblical and Jewish literature to argue that traditional Christian orthodoxy had a more genuine and greater antiquity than Unitarian claims to the contrary.

Allix's closing dissertation on Genesis 48:15–16 illustrates his aims and methods well. In it, Allix argued that Trinitarian orthodoxy is Scriptural, although his exegesis was also indebted to the language and conceptuality of post-Scriptural Trinitarian discourse, as his use of Hebrew likewise demonstrates. Allix's use of Biblical texts shows skill; but he also overplayed Jewish tradition. And yet, there are similar patterns or types of divine activity and identity in ancient Biblical, Jewish, and Christian texts. That Allix argued Jesus Christ is the pre-Incarnate 'referent' of such patterns made him a classically Trinitarian reader of Scripture. That he argued this is supported by Jewish tradition more broadly was due to his strong Christian Hebraism. These patterns of divine activity and identity in ancient Biblical and Jewish texts, assisted by philosophical language and conceptuality to 'express the inexpressible', made the Christian doctrine of the Trinity and divine Messiah a natural outflow from them. While it owes deeply to pre-modernity, and sits squarely in the early modern period of doctrinal controversy, Allix's AJC is, for this reason, somewhat, if not remarkably, at home among late modern analyses of the originally Jewish setting of early Christianity.

Bibliography

ALLIX, PETER (1699), The judgement of the ancient Jewish church against the Unitarians in the controversy upon the holy Trinity and divinity of our Blessed Saviour, London.

AUGUSTINE (419), Locutiones in Heptateuchum, in Zycha, J. (ed.), Aureli Augustini Quaestionum in Heptateuchum, lib. II (Quaest. de Exodo), CSEL 28/2, Vienna: F. Tempsky, 92–223.

AUSTIN, KENNETH (2007), From Judaism to Calvinism: the Life and Writings of Immanuel Tremellius (c. 1510–1580), Aldershot: Ashgate.

BERG, JOHANNES, van der, WALL, ERNERSTEIN, G. E. van der (eds.) (1988), Jewish-Christian Relations in the Seventeenth Century. Studies and Documents, Dordrecht: Kluwer.

BODLEY, THOMAS, SIR (2006), *The Autobiography of Sir Thomas Bodley. With an Introduction and Notes by William Clennell*, Oxford: Bodleian Library.

BORLAND, JAMES, A. (1999), Christ in the Old Testament, revised and expanded edn, Chicago, IL: Moody Press.

BOYARIN, DANIEL (2012), The Jewish Gospels: The Story of the Jewish Christ, New York: New Press.

BULL, GEORGE (1714), The divinity of our Lord Jesus Christ, proved to be the primitive and apostolick doctrine of the catholick church: with a curious remark on the validity of the Sibylline oracles, London.

BURNETT, STEPHEN G. (2008), Later Christian Hebraists, in Magne Saebo (ed.), Hebrew Bible/Old Testament: The History of Its Interpretation. Vol. 2: From the Renaissance to the Enlightenment, Göttingen: Vandenhoeck & Ruprecht, 785–801.

— (2012), Christian Hebraism in the Reformation Era (1500–1660): Authors, Books, and the Transmission of Jewish learning, Leiden: Brill.

CAPP, BERNARD (1972), The Millennium and Eschatology in England, Past and Present 57, 156–162.

CARLETON PAGET, JAMES, N. B. (1996), Christian Exegesis in the Alexandrian Tradition, in Magne Saebo, (ed.) Hebrew Bible/Old Testament: the History of Its Interpretation, Vol. 1. From the Beginnings to the Middle Ages (Until 1300), Göttingen: Vandenhoeck & Ruprecht, 477–542.

— (2010), Jews, Christians and Jewish Christians in Antiquity, Tübingen: Mohr Siebeck.

COFFEY, JOHN (2000), Persecution and Toleration in Protestant England, 1558–1698, Harlow: Longman.

— (2009), Messiah, in Sakenfeld, K. D. (ed.) The New Interpreter's Dictionary of the Bible, Nashville, TN: Abingdon Press, vol. 4. 59–66.

COUDERT, ALLISON, P. (2004), Five Seventeenth-Century Christian Hebraists, in Coudert, A. P., Shoulson, J. S. (eds.), Hebraica Veritas? Christian Hebraists and the Study of Judaism in Early Modern Europe, Philadelphia, PA: University of Pennsylvania Press, 286–308.

DEARMAN, ANDREW, J. (2002) Theophany, Anthropomorphism, and the Imago Dei: Some Observations about the Incarnation in the Light of the Old Testament, in Davis, S. T., Kendall, D., O'Collins, G. (eds.), The Incarnation: An Interdisciplinary Symposium on the Incarnation of the Son of God, Oxford: OUP, 31–46.

DIXON, PHILIP (2003), 'Nice and Hot Disputes': The Doctrine of the Trinity in the Seventeenth Century, London; New York: T&T Clark.

DULLES, AVERY, (2005), A History of Apologetics, 2nd edn, San Francisco, CA: Ignatius Press.

DUNAN-PAGE, A. (2006), The Religious Culture of the Huguenots, Aldershot, England; Burlington, VT: Ashgate.

FAROOQ, JENNIFER (2013), Preaching in Eighteenth Century London, Woodbridge: The Boydell Press.

FRIEDMAN, JEROME (1994), The Myth of Jewish Antiquity: New Christians and Christian-Hebraica in Early Modern Europe, in Popkin, R. H., Weiner, G. M. (eds.), Jewish Christians and Christian Jews. From the Renaissance to the Enlightenment, Dordrecht: Kluwer, 35–55.

FULLER, REGINALD, H. (1997), The Vestigia Trinitatis in the Old Testament, in Evans, C. A., Talmon, S. (eds.), The Quest for Context and Meaning. Studies in Biblical Intertextuality in Honor of James A. Sanders, Leiden: Brill, 499–508.

GOLDISH, MATT (1998), Judaism in the Theology of Sir Isaac Newton, Dordrecht: Kluwer.

— (1999), The battle for 'True' Jewish Christianity: Peter Allix's Polemics against the Unitarians and the Millenarians, in Force, J. E., Katz, S. (eds.), Everything Connects: In Conference with Richard H. Popkin: Essays in His Honor, Leiden: Brill, 143–162.

GRAFTON, ANTHONY / WEINBERG, JOANNA (2011), "I have always loved the holy tongue": Isaac Casaubon, the Jews, and a Forgotten Chapter in Renaissance Scholarship, Cambridge, MA: Belknap Press.

GROOTJES, ALBERT (2014), Claude Pajon (1626–1685) and the Academy of Saumur: the First Controversy Over Grace, Leiden: Brill.

HANSON, ANTHONY, T. (1965), Jesus Christ in the Old Testament, London: SPCK.

HAYS, RICHARD, B. (2014), Reading Backwards, London: SPCK.

HAYWARD, CHARLES, T. R. (1995), Saint Jerome's Hebrew Questions on Genesis, Translated with Introduction and Commentary, Oxford: Clarendon Press.

HEIJNE, CAMILLA, H. von (2010), The Messenger of the Lord in Early Jewish Interpretations of Genesis, Berlin; New York: de Gruyter.

HORBURY, WILLIAM (2015), Review of Boyarin: 2012, JTS 66/1, 349–353.

HOWELL, THOMAS, B. (ed.) (1816), A complete collection of state trials and proceedings for high treason and other crimes and misdemeanors from the earliest period to 1783, with notes and other illustrations, vol. 13, London.

JAYNE, SEARS, R. (1956), Library Catalogues of the English Renaissance, Berkeley, University of California Press.

JOHNSON, AUBREY, R. (1961), The One and the Many in the Israelite Conception of God, Cardiff: University of Wales Press.

KATCHEN, AARON, L. (1984), Christian Hebraists and Dutch Rabbis: Seventeenth Century Apologetics and the Study of Maimonides Mishneh Torah, Cambridge, MA; London: Harvard University Press.

KATZ, DAVID, S. (1994), The Jews in the History of England, 1485–1850, Oxford: Clarendon Press.

— (2004), God's Last Words: Reading the English Bible from the Reformation to Fundamentalism, New Haven, CT; London: Yale University Press.

KIDD, GEORGE, B. (1852), Christophaneia. The doctrine of the manifestations of the Son of God under the economy of the Old Testament, ed. Dobbin, O.T., London.

KIEFFER, RENÉ (1996), Jerome: His Exegesis and Hermeneutics, in Magne Saebo, (ed.) Hebrew Bible/Old Testament: the History of Its Interpretation, Vol. 1. From the Beginnings to the Middle Ages (Until 1300), Göttingen: Vandenhoeck & Ruprecht, 663–681.

KLEPPER, DEEANA, C. (2007), The Insights of Unbelievers: Nicholas of Lyra and Christian Reading of Jewish Text in the Later Middle Ages, Philadelphia, PA: University of Pennsylvania Press.

KNOHL, ISRAEL (2016), The Angel Yahoel and the Two Messiahs of the Apocalypse of Abraham, Estudios de Filología Neotestamentaria 11 (2016), 39–54.

KUGEL, JAMES, L. (1998), Traditions of the Bible: A Guide to the Bible As It Was at the Start of the Common Era, Cambridge, MA; London: Harvard University Press.

— (2010), Early Jewish Biblical Interpretation, in Collins, J. J., Harlow, D. C. (eds.), The Eerdmans Dictionary of Early Judaism, Grand Rapids, MI; Cambridge: Eerdmans. 121–141.

LARMINIE, VIVIENNE (2004), "Allix, Peter [Pierre] (1614–1717)", DNB, Oxford: OUP.

LEVITIN, DMITRI (2015), Ancient Wisdom in the Age of the New Science: Histories of Philosophy in England, c. 1640–1700, Cambridge: CUP.

LIM, PAUL, C.-H. (2012), Mystery Unveiled: The Crisis of the Trinity in Early Modern England, New York; Oxford: OUP.

LUBAC, HENRI de (1998–2009), Medieval Exegesis, 3 vols, Grand Rapids, MI; Eerdmans; Edinburgh: T&T Clark.

LUTHER, MARTIN (1535–1545), Lectures on Genesis, Chapters 45–50, in Pelikan, J. (ed.), (1966) Luther's Works (LW), Saint Louis, MO: Concordia Publishing House, vol. 8, 3–333.

LYON, ROBERT, W. (1959), A Re-examination of Codex Ephraemi Rescriptus, NTS 5/4, 260–272.

MALONE, ANDREW (2015), Knowing Jesus in the Old Testament? A Fresh Look at Christophanies, Nottingham: IVP.

MCKANE, WILLIAM (1989), Selected Christian Hebraists, Cambridge: CUP.

MORTIMER, SARAH (2010), Reason and Religion in the English Revolution, Cambridge: CUP.

MYLLYKOSKI, MATTI (2012), "Christian Jews" and "Jewish Christians": The Jewish Origins of Christianity in English Literature from Elizabeth I to Toland's Nazarenus, in Stanley, J. F. (ed.), The Rediscovery of Jewish Christianity: from Toland to Baur, Atlanta, GA: SBL, 3–41.

NOVENSON, MATTHEW (2012), Christ Among the Messiahs: Christ Language in Paul and Messiah Language in Ancient Judaism, Oxford: OUP.

NYE, STEPHEN (1687), A brief history of the Unitarians, called also Socinians in four letters, written to a friend, London.

— (1701), The doctrine of the Holy Trinity, and the manner of our Saviour's divinity; As they are held in the Catholic Church, and the Church of England, London.

POPKIN, RICHARD (1994), Christian Jews and Jewish Christians, in Popkin, R., Weiner, G. M. (eds.), Jewish Christians and Christian Jews. From the Renaissance to the Enlightenment, Dordrecht: Kluwer, 47–72.

REIMER, DAVID, J. (1998), Old Testament Christology, in J. Day (ed.) *King and Messiah in Israel and the Ancient Near East*, Sheffield: Sheffield Academic Press, 380–400.

ROOKER, MARK, F. (2003), "Theophany", in Alexander, T. D., Baker, D. W. (eds.), Dictionary of the Old Testament: Pentateuch, Downers Grove, IL; Leicester, IVP, 859–864.

ROTH, CECIL (1962–67), Sir Thomas Bodley – Hebraist, Bodleian Library Record 7, 242–251.

ROWE, CHRISTOPHER, K. and HAYS, RICHARD B. (2007), Biblical Studies, in Webster, C., Tanner, K., Torrance, I. (eds.), The Oxford Handbook of Systematic Theology, Oxford: OUP, 435–455.

RUDERMAN, DANIEL, B. (2007), Connecting the Covenants: Judaism and the Search for Christian Identity in 18th Century England, Philadelphia, PA: University of Pennsylvania Press.

SAEBO, MAGNE (ed.) (2008), Hebrew Bible/Old Testament: The History of Its Interpretation. Vol. 2: From the Renaissance to the Enlightenment, Göttingen: Vandenhoeck & Ruprecht.

SANDGREN, LEO, D. (2010), Vines Intertwined: A History of Jews and Christians from the Babylonian Exile to the Advent of Islam, Peabody, MA: Hendrickson.

SARNA, NAHUM, M. (1989), The JPS Torah Commentary: Genesis, Philadelphia, PA: The Jewish Publication Society.

SCHÄFER, PETER, (2007), Jesus in the Talmud, Princeton, NJ; Oxford: Princeton University Press.

SEGAL, ALAN, F. (1977), Two Powers in Heaven: Early Rabbinic Reports about Christianity and Gnosticism, Leiden: Brill.

SHEAR, ADAM (2011), William Whiston's Judeo-Christianity: Millenarianism and Christian Zionism in Early Enlightenment England, in Karp, J., Sutcliffe, A. (eds.), Philosemitism in History, Cambridge: CUP, 93–110.

SIROTA, BRENT, S. (2013), The Trinitarian Crisis in Church and State: Religious Controversy and the Making of the Postrevolutionary Church of England, 1687–1702, JBS 52, 26–54.

SLOTEMAKER, JOHN, T. (2011), The Trinitarian House of David: Martin Luther's Anti-Jewish Exegesis of 2 Samuel 23:1–7, HTR 104/2, 233–254.

SNOBELEN, S. (2001), "The Mystery of this Restitution of All Things": Isaac Newton on the Return of the Jews, in Force, J. E., Popkin, R. H. (eds.), Millenarianism and Messianism in Early Modern European Culture: Book 3: The Millenarian Turn: Millenarian Contexts of Science, Politics and Everyday Anglo-American Life in the Seventeen and Eighteenth Centuries, Dordrecht: Kluwer, 95–118.

TUGGY, DALE (2016), Unitarianism (Supplement to Trinity), Stanford Encyclopedia of Philosophy (online).

WENHAM, GORDON, J. (1994), Genesis 17–50, WBC 2; Dallas, TX: Word.

WESTERMANN, CLAUS (1986), Genesis 37–50. A Commentary, tr. J. J. Scullion, London: SPCK; Minneapolis, MN: Augsburg Publishing House.

WOTTON, WILLIAM (1734), Some thoughts concerning a proper Method of studying Divinity. (Art. XXI), The Present State of the Republick of Letters 14 (October), 233–240.

WRIGHT, CHRISTOPHER, J. H. (2014), Knowing Jesus Through the Old Testament, 2nd edn, Carlisle: Langham Partnership.

WRIGHT, DAVID, P. (2008), Augustine: His Exegesis and Hermeneutics, in Magne Saebo, (ed.) Hebrew Bible/Old Testament: the History of Its Interpretation, Vol. 1. From the Beginnings to the Middle Ages (Until 1300), Göttingen: Vandenhoeck & Ruprecht, 701–745.

XERES, JOHN (1710), An address to the Jews, by John Xeres: containing his reasons for leaving the Jewish, and embracing the Christian religion, London.

YOUNG, FRANCES, M. (1997), Biblical Exegesis and the Formation of Christian Culture, Cambridge: CUP.

Emidio Campi

Giovanni Diodati (1576–1649), translator of the Bible into Italian

As a child, I did not know who Diodati was. I am nonetheless certain that one of
the first books that I had in my hands was a beautiful volume, bound in black
leather, gilt-edged, and black-dotted on the edges to mark the contents. This
volume was a Diodati Bible. I believe that I even learned to read from that Bible. I
now know that some of its words, such as *eziandio, imperoché*, and *avvegnaché*,
are "Tuscanisms" from the sixteenth century. As a child, however, they seemed to
me to be picture words, stimulating my imagination. In saying this, I do not
suppose that I descended from extraordinary stock. Rather, I am convinced that
the same could be said for many, many other families of the Protestant population of Italy. So I have taken your invitation[1] as an honour bestowed on all
those Italian-speaking Protestants who, from 1607 to about 1950, have taken the
"Diodatina" so seriously that they chiselled it indelibly on their heart.

   The stronger the feelings for a particular person, the greater the temptation to
reconstruct history as we would like it to be. But if we really want to respect
Giovanni Diodati's memory and his Bible translation, we have to study the man
and his work critically and avoid sentimental hagiography and confessional bias.
In any case, we have the duty to see Diodati as he was and not as we, perhaps,
would like him to have been. Consequently we need to ask ourselves if his
translation is really of enough historical importance to justify a quadricentennial
celebration or if we are merely entertaining an obsession with a scion of noble
house. Let's pose the question bluntly: Was it really worth it for Diodati to spend
his youth, yes, his entire life (not to mention his wealth) on this project?

1 This article is a revision of a lecture sponsored by the *Association des Amis du Musée international de la Réforme et l'Église Vaudoise de Genève* and given 9 November 2007 on the
   occasion of the quadricentennial of Diodati's translation of the Bible into Italian in 1607. The
   English version was published in English in my volume *Shifting Patterns of Reformed Tradition*
   (Göttingen: Vandenhoeck & Ruprecht 2014), 241–257.

1.   Biography

From the life and work of Giovanni Diodati,[2]I would especially like to highlight
his passion for Bible translation and to underline those aspects of both his
thought and his actions that were directly linked to his essential activity of
translator. We know that Giovanni Diodati characterised himself as being "from
Lucca" *(nation lucchese)* but the legal basis of his claim was rather dubious. In
reality, his home town was Geneva where he was born of Lucca parents and where
spent his entire life, most of it as professor of theology at the Academy. By the
time he came along, his family already had a respectable place in Genevan society.
His father Carlo was a member of the Council of Two Hundred, and the Diodatis,
along with the Burlamacchis, Calandrinis, Minutolis, and Turrettinis, constituted
the kernel of the Lucca expatriates, composed of sixty families who were, in large
part, from the oldest and richest nobility of the little Tuscan republic.[3] In a few
years these who had fled religious persecution had, by putting to work the capital
that they had gathered before fleeing Italy, recuperated and even increased their
riches. They had given birth to an oligarchy that exercised an influence second to
none in the commercial, civil, and religious life of their adopted land. The singular position of pre-eminence of that coterie of Lucca families in Geneva earned
them the nickname of "the Italian Cabal", and so they have passed into history.[4]
All his life long Giovanni Diodati remained true to the character of his family and
social circle. The Lucca families were so integrated into the "city of refuge" as to
be completely identified with the commonweal. Yet they were, all the while,
jealous of ancestral traditions, as would be expected of one of the proudest
aristocracies. They remained open to Genevan culture and yet were utterly
convinced of the immense value of the Tuscan language. They sensed the duty to
preserve it by speaking it at home and by maintaining both an Italian church and
numerous contacts with their native land.

---

2 Eugène de Bude, *Vie de Jean Diodati, Théologien genevois (1576-1649)* (Lausanne: Bridel,
  1869) ; William A. McComish, *The Epigones: A Study of the Theology of the Genevan Academy
  at the Time of the Synod of Dort, with Special Reference to Giovanni Diodati* (Allison Park,
  Penn.: Pickwick Publications, 1989); Emidio Campi, "Cronologia della vita di Giovanni Diodati," in: *La Sacra Bibbia*, eds. Michele Ranchetti, Milka Ventura Avanzinelli, vol. 1 (Milan:
  Mondadori, 1999), 187–222; Emanuele Fiume, *Giovanni Diodati: Un italiano nella Ginevra
  della Riforma* (Rome: Società Biblica Britannica e Forestiera, 2007).
3 Arturo Pascal, *Da Lucca a Ginevra: Studi sull'emigrazione religiosa lucchese nel secolo xvi*
  (Pinerolo: Unitipografica Pinerolese, 1935); Marino Berengo, *Nobili e mercanti nella Lucca del
  Cinquecento* (Turin: Einaudi, 1974); Salvatore Caponetto, *La riforma protestante nell' Italia del
  Cinquecento* (Turin: Einaudi, 1989), 329–364.
4 John-Barthélémy-Gaïfre Galiffe, *Le Refuge italien de Genève aux xvie et xviie siècles* (Genève:
  Georg, 1881); Francesco Ruffini, "'La Cabale Italique' nella Ginevra del Seicento," *La Cultura*,
  10 (1931), 786–808.

As his parents wished, Giovanni Diodati did his theological studies at the Academy of Geneva. He studied under Théodore de Bèze, Pierre Chevalier, and Isaac Casaubon. He acquired on the one hand a solid knowledge of theology and on the other a passion for biblical philology that was also to assure the success of his future scientific endeavours. In 1597, his studies barely completed, he was entrusted with teaching Hebrew at the Academy. Two years later, when Théodore de Bèze, by then an octogenarian, definitively tendered his resignation, he was named professor of theology. Diodati related that he was ready to translate the Bible when he was scarcely sixteen years old. From our vantage point, we cannot find any evidence of how dearly it cost him to produce it. We only know that, in 1603, the translation was already finished, even if, as we shall better see later, it was not published until 1607.[5] In the following year, Diodati, encouraged by compliments given him, was already publishing a new edition of the New Testament.[6]

If we now wish to delve into the intellectual and spiritual world of Diodati, we must seek to understand, without denying its historical limitations, the indisputable merit of Reformed theology at Geneva during the seventeenth century. Diodati and his two colleagues Théodore Tronchin (1582–1657) and Benedetto Turrettini (1588–1631) were among the most eminent representatives of that theology.[7] What was the theological direction necessary to face the heavy responsibilities of the time, responsibilities that featured the offensive of the Counter-Reformation in particular? In the neighbouring Zurich of Johann Jakob Breitinger (1575–1645) and in other Reformed institutions of higher learning, such as the academies of Montauban and Saumur and the University of Leiden, there was a reliance on Ramism, that is to say, on the thought of the French philosopher Pierre de la Ramée (1512–1572) rather than on the Aristotelianism followed by Beza. At Heidelberg, which asserted itself as one of the greatest intellectual centres of Protestant Europe, there developed an analytical theology (the Heidelberg catechism being an eloquent confessional statement based on it) that was accompanied by grandiose aspirations of a universal science. Not far from the Palatinate, in the Duchy of Nassau, the Academy of Herborn counted among its professors the founder of modern encyclopaedism, Johann Heinrich

---

5 *La Bibbia: cioe, i libri del Vecchio e del Nuovo Testamento,* nuouamente traslatati in lingua italiana de Giovanni Diodati, di nation Lucchese ([Geneva : Jean de Tournes], 1607).

6 *Il Nuovo Testamento del Signor nostro Iesu Christo* ([Genève], 1608).

7 Emidio Campi and Carla Sodini, *Gli oriundi lucchesi di Ginevra e il cardinale Spinola: Una controversia religiosa alla vigilia dell' editto di Nantes* (Naples; Chicago: Sansoni/Newberry Library, 1988); Richard A. Muller, *Post-Reformation Reformed Dogmatics,* vol. 2 : *Holy Scripture: The Cognitive Foundation of Theology* (Grand Rapids, Mich.: Baker Book House, 1993); Jan Rohls, *Protestantische Theologie der Neuzeit,* 2 vols. (Tübingen: Mohr Siebeck, 1997), 1: 78–88.

Alsted (1588–1638), whose ardent millenarian expectations undergirded his thought.

In this spiritual climate, the new generation of Geneva theologians was in the grip of two contrasting aspirations: on one side, the jealous defence of tradition, and on the other, openness to the vast horizons of knowledge. Supported by the Company of Pastors, they chose a middle way: they took in upon themselves to guard with tenacity, but without bigotry, the heritage of the Calvinian reform. Beyond the narrow limits of the Genevan republic's territory, the fame that Diodati, Turrettini, and Tronchin enjoyed was indissolubly linked to their role as vigilant guardians of Reformed orthodoxy during the years preceding the convocation of the Synod of Dort (1618–1619) and in the three decades that followed. This was especially true in the case of Diodati for whom the tenacious preservation of the Calvin-Beza heritage constituted the goal and measure to which all activity referred, whether it was theological education, civic responsibilities, or even political choices. Moreover, it is not at all audacious to recall that this energetic re-appropriation of the thought of these two great masters developed over a long period of time. Contrary to Benedetto Turrettini, who died while still young, Diodati taught at the Academy forty-eight years. He was nominated in 1597 and ended his career in 1645.

One very important period of time in Diodati's life was his participation, along with Theodore Tronchin, in the Synod of Dort. This assembly, very representative of Europe's Reformed churches, debated, among other things, the thorny question of predestination.[8] It is not easy to judge what role was played by the Italian-Genevan theologian in determining the Synod's conclusions because we know that everything was not transcribed into the official records. The sources agree, however, that he played a prestigious role in the Assembly and that his influence grew over time to the point that he was called to take part in the exclusive commission charged with editing the final version of the Synod's work. The Assembly refrained from defining predestination in the supralapsarian sense that Diodati would have preferred but limited itself to thinking of it as following the fall of humankind in Adam. That is, it defined predestination in an infralapsarian way. They welcomed, nonetheless, the thesis of Diodati on the "perseverance of the saints", which, though already upheld by Calvin and present in the works of the Italian theologian Girolamo Zanchi, rose for the first time in a written Reformed confession. Thus, thanks to the contribution of Diodati, strict

---

8 Johannes Pieter van Dooren, "Dordrechter Synode," *Theologische Realenzyklopädie,* vol. 9 (Berlin: de Gruyter, 1982), 140–147; *Confessions et catéchismes de la foi réformée* ed. Olivier Fatio (Geneva: Labor et Fides, 1986); William A. McComish, *The Epigones,* 74–125; John V. Fesko, *Diversity Within the Reformed Tradition: Supra- and Infralapsarianism in Calvin, Dort, and Westminster* (Greenville, S. C.: Reformed Academic Press, 2001).

Calvinism prevailed over humanistic currents and gained recognition among all the Reformed churches.[9]

The champion of Dort had won a place of first rank in cosmopolitan Reformed culture at the beginning of the seventeenth century.[10] But also he was henceforth an eminent citizen of the small Genevan republic, and, as such, he was always more loaded than before with the responsibility of being its representative and of being the religion consultant for the Petit Conseil. For example, when in August of 1630 Geneva found itself in great difficulty as the result of a terrible famine, the authorities called on Diodati and sent him to Zurich with the task of acquiring wheat for Geneva's population.

In 1632, there occurred the tragic "Antoine case" that did irreparable damage to Diodati's reputation as did the Servetus case to Calvin's. The pastor Nicolas Antoine (1602–1632) from Briey in Lorraine led a life very little befitting his position as a minister of the gospel. He was arrested, prosecuted, and, since the savage customs of the time made religious observance a civil matter, condemned to die "for the crime of apostasy and defaming divine majesty". Some pastors called for a suspension of proceedings or at least a delay of punishment to hear the opinion of their sibling churches, but the request fell on deaf ears. In the end, the hard line prevailed. Diodati, who was harsh in his judgment on the pastor from Lorraine, upheld the sentence. On 20 April 1632, Nicolas Antoine was burned at the stake.

In spite of his diplomatic and political preoccupations, Diodati did not neglect what was dearest to his heart: the translation of the Bible. In 1631, a work that had occupied him for a number of years, finally saw the light of day: the versification of the Psalter. It was entitled *I sacri Salmi di Davide messi in rime volgari italiane da Giovanni Diodati*.[11] Once the work was done, he sought to put the metricized

---

9 It suffices here to note that the Church of Geneva and the Swiss Reformed churches remained tied to the Canons of Dort for more that a century. The Canons were abandoned definitively in 1725 along with the *Formula consensus ecclesiarum helveticarum* (1675), a confession of faith that was in line with the principles enunciated during the Netherlands assises. Abandoning the older confessions was the work of so-called "rational orthodoxy", a new theology of the Cartesian stamp, whose coryphaeus was someone else of Lucca origin, Jean-Alphonse Turrettini. See also Maria C. Pitassi, *De l'orthodoxie aux Lumières: Genève 1670–1737* (Genève: Labor et Fides, 1992), 16–20 and 51–55.

10 Diodati made contact with a number of his fellow participants at the historic Synod of Dort. Among these were: Johann Jakob Breitinger, the combative head pastor of Zurich and valiant defender of religious minorities; Johann Heinrich Alsted, the polymath professor at Herborn; Abraham Scultetus, the court preacher for the Elector of the Palatinate; Gisbert Voetius, one of the grand masters of Dutch Reformed theology; William Ames, the brilliant disciple of William Perkins and intransigent Puritan. Diodati came to be appreciated by these intellectuals, and he began to correspond with them in an ever more cordial manner. Some of those corresponding with him even visited him in Geneva.

11 The work went to press in 1631 and had two printings that year; one was published by the

psalms to music so they could be sung during worship services in Geneva as well as in the other Italian churches that were spread throughout Europe, from Zurich to London, from Lyons to the German port city of Emden. But he did not live to see his ardent desire realized. But a son of his, living in the Netherlands, would see to publishing a posthumous edition in 1664 under the title, *I sacri Salmi di Davide messi in rime volgari italiane da Giovanni Diodati, di nation Lucchese, et composti in musica da A.G.*[12]

In 1641, the second edition of Diodati's translation of the Bible into Italian was published by Pierre Chouet. This Bible was Diodati's life's work, and his name will remain indissolubly tied to it: *La Sacra Bibbia.*[13] Diodati made no startling changes in this new edtion, though he did make philological and stylistic corrections. It was a splendid folio edition, whereas the first edition was a quarto. This format made it suitable for study and for public worship; as well, it was suitable as a family Bible. Its frontispiece had a solemn look: the Bible was placed on the top of an imposing Baroque altar, the Holy Spirit hovering above it. The altar was set on two foundations, on each of which there was an image: the one, a sower, already used in the first edition; the other, an open book, undamaged though placed on a reef in the midst of a raging ocean. It is clear that these images point to the blessings conferred by Scripture and the solids merits of the Biblical message. This edition also contained the deuterocanonical books and metrical translation of the Psalms already published in 1631. Moreover, the text included brief chapter and book summaries, a vast commentary, and, in the margins, cross references.

This Bible's annotations responded to the readers' needs and received the approbation of contemporaries. Proof of this is the English Parliament's decision to have a translation made of them to facilitate its people's Bible reading. The translation was printed in 1643 with the title *Pious and Learned Annotations upon the Holy Bible.* The English edition, welcomed and warmly praised, was enlarged and went through three more editions, the last being in 1651.[14] To understand how Diodati's annotations echoed across Europe, it is worth noting

---

Genevan publisher Pierre Aubert, and the other sported the device of anchor and dolphin, as if it were the work of Venice's storied Aldine Press, founded by Aldus Manutius (1449–1515). It was printed again in 1636, and again in 1641, this time as part of Diodati's translation of the Bible.

12 Also in Haarlem there was published the following year a second edition of Diodati's New Testament: *Il Nuovo Testamento del Signor nostro Jesu Christo. Tradotto in Lingua Italiana da Giovanni Diodati, di nation Lucchese* (Haarlem: Jacob Albertz Libraire, 1664).

13 *La Sacra Bibbia, tradotta in lingua Italiana, e commentata da Giovanni Diodati di nation Lucchese. Seconda Edizione, migliorata, ed accresciuta. Con l'aggiunta de' Sacri salmi, messi in rime per lo medesimo* (Genève: Pietro Chovët, 1641).

14 *Pious and Learned Annotations upon the Holy Bible, Plainly Expounding the Most Difficult Places Thereof* (London: J. Flesher, 1651).

that they were translated not only into English but even German—and there certainly was no lack of such Bible study aids in German. As a matter of fact, Diodati's commentary is found in two editions of Luther's Bible published in 1668 and 1693 in Frankfurt-am-Main with the approval of the electors of the Palatinate and Brandenburg.[15]

More stormy was the fate of his French translation of the Bible, *La Sainte Bible interprétée par Jean Diodati*, printed in Geneva by Pierre Aubert in 1644. Sketching in broad strokes the fortunes of this work is not without significance, for it illuminates the complex personality of our translator and permits us to situate him better in the dominant theological climate in the Geneva church as well as in the Reformed Churches of France.[16]

A memorable controversy, philological as well as theological, had arisen between the Jesuit Pierre Coton (1564–1626) and the Company of Pastors in Geneva.[17] The Company of Pastors was preoccupied with this affair for almost ten years (1618–1628). From this controversy Diodati had drawn the conclusion that the best response to the Jesuits' trenchant critique was to revise the Bible version used since 1588 in Geneva and in the French Reformed Churches, i. e., the *Bible des pasteurs et professeurs de l'Église de Genève*. But his proposal was never accepted. In spite of this, he did not get discouraged but undertook this work of revision with commendable zeal, with only sickness stopping him. In two years he completed the French translation of the Old Testament and submitted it 21 January 1620 to the judgment of his colleagues in the Company, but they, rather than authorizing its publication, counselled him to consult with the national Synod of France. So the Lucca/Geneva theologian informed the Synod of his audacious project, a new translation of the Bible into French. He presented his request to the assembly meeting in Alès in November of that same year, only to meet with a flat refusal. Even in Geneva, Diodati's later attempts to promote his

---

15 Although by about 1600 there were Calvinist translations of the Bible, of which the so-called "Piscator-Bibel" is best known, German speaking Reformed congregations favoured Luther's rendering. To meet the readers' need, the Heidelberg theologian Paul Toussain (1572-1634), latinized Paulus Tossanus, published a Luther-Bible with annotations in the Reformed spirit (*Biblia: Das ist: Die gantze H. Schrifft Durch D. Martin Luther Verteutscht : In dieser newen Edition, in welcher D. Luthers version durchauss behalten worden, ist der Text, wo er etwas tunckel und schwer auss den besten Ausslegungen, die heutigs tags zu finden, am rande kürtzlich und deutlich erklärt ... Durch Paulum Tossanum*, Heidelberg; Frankfurt : G. Tampach, 1617). Two other editions of the "Toussain-Bible" were published in Basel in 1644 and 1665 containing additional annotations drawn from Diodati's commentary. There followed the two Frankfurt editions: Balthasar Christoph Wust , 1668; Johann David Zunner, 1693.

16 Brian M. Armstrong, "Geneva and the Theology and Politics of French Calvinism: The Embarrassment of the 1588 Edition of the Bible of the Pastors and Professors of Geneva," in *Calvinus ecclesiae Genevensis custos*, ed. Wilhelm H. Neuser(Frankfurt-am-Main: Peter Lang, 1984), 195–215 ; McComish, *The Epigones*, 175–184.

17 See also McComish, *The Epigones*, 127–145.

initiative were not viewed favourably, all the more because he had the audacity to publish his translation of the Book of Job without having received authorization. When, toward the end of 1634, he again requested authorization from the Company of Pastors, his colleagues bluntly called upon him not to continue, which then occasioned a conflict so violent that the city authorities were obliged to intervene. At the Small Council, Diodati's initiative received some consideration, for at the 25 May 1635 session of the Council, it was decided to name a commission to follow closely his translation work. But Diodati continued to act imprudently and to speak inopportunely, until finally he lost the sympathy of his Genevan colleagues as well as the French Reformed. In spite of this, in October of 1638, he succeeded in obtaining the authorization that he so desired, even though it was limited to the poetical books of the Old Testament. They were published at Geneva by Jean de Tournes with this title: *Les livres de Job, Psaumes, Proverbes, Ecclésiaste, Cantique des Cantiques. Expliques par brieves annotations par Iean Diodati.*

In the meantime, in order to persuade the obstinate pastors of Geneva, Diodati came up with a tactic truly worthy of a veritable descendent of Lucca merchants. He threw himself headlong into completing that second edition, mentioned above, of his Italian translation of the Bible in the hope that he might take advantage of the prestige that the *Sacra Bibbia* brought to his reputation as a translator so as to gain the consent necessary for the publication of his French translation to which he attached so much importance. At last his tenacity overcame the opposition of the Company of Pastors and on 13 November 1641 the Small Council decided to condescend to allow the publication of the entire French Bible. It was published three years later but without the commendation of the Geneva authorities and, therefore, without receiving public subsidies. So it was Diodati himself who had to absorb the cost of publication, to the veritable ruin of a family fortune that had been considerable.

These long lasting troubles linked to the question of a new French translation of the Bible go well beyond merely illustrating Diodati's pigheadedness and shed light on his unique position in the landscape of Protestant theology of his time. In many ways he was a man tied to Reformed orthodoxy, but he managed to maintain his position faithfully without, for all that, accepting, as did his contemporaries, the primacy of dogma over philological reasoning. Certainly, the Geneva pastors were not at all obtuse fanatics, devoid of Biblical science, but they did not move an inch in their obstinate defence of their Bible. This was because they saw in this translation the perfect way to reaffirm the *punctum protesantissimum*, salvation by faith, and they attributed to it an importance similar to that which the Catholics gave to their Vulgate. Their battle, rather than being fought on the field of hermeneutics, took the character of a crusade by the true religion against the false. In sum, they did not reach the point where they could emerge from the mindset of the century of confessionalism, nor did they take into account the problem of translation's autonomy so ardently upheld by our Italian-Genevan translator. From this angle, then, Diodati was much less orthodox than he appeared to be if we take into account only his behaviour at the Synod of Dort. We can, and therefore we must, speak of his undeniable orthodoxy but not of an unshakeable close mindedness like that to which most of his contemporaries abandoned themselves.

In 1645, Diodati tendered his resignation at the Academy for health reasons. It is plain that his decision rested not only on the physical exhaustion of someone not of robust health but also on the interminable struggles tied to the French translation of the Bible. These struggles had led to painful consequences, as much theological as human, within the Company of Pastors. But those who imagined that his retirement was an opportune time to rid themselves of the burdensome presence of a theologian almost seventy years old were quickly disabused of such a notion. During the last five years of his life, that senior citizen, encumbered by unhappiness and disillusionment, again rushed headlong into managing the most arduous political-religious questions.[18] This he did, not as "the Cato of Geneva" (this is Virgile Rossel's unhappy expression) but rather as one who consecrated his last energies to fulfill his mission as a pastor called to examine and to bring into Scripture's light the moral comportment of his fellow citizens.[19]

Diodati died on 3 October 1649. Philippe Mestrezat, who gave the funeral oration, rose to the occasion when he recounted Diodati's long and labour-filled life and his commitment, which demanded so much of him, to the *Schola genevensis*, the church, and the city of Geneva. Without abandoning himself to inflated estimations of the deceased's worth, which would have been un-Calvinist, he limited himself to the unusual weaving together of "an inexhaustible treasury of doctrine, devotion toward God, Christian charity, a memorable liberality of spirit, and extraordinary eloquence".[20]

2.   The Diodati Bible of 1607

In 1607, Giovanni Diodati published at his own expense in Geneva (neither place of publication nor publisher being on the title page) *La Bibbia. Cioè, i Libri del Vecchio e del Nuovo Testamento. Nuovamente traslatati in lingua Italiana, da*

---

18 He did not, for example, ignore the execution of Charles I of England.

19 Virgile Rossel, *Histoire littéraire de la Suisse romande des origines à nos jours* (Neuchâtel : Zahn, 1903), 245.

20 *Inexhaustus doctrinae thesaurus, pietas in Deum, charitas [...], memorabilis animi libertas, grandiloquentia summa:* Charles Borgeaud, *Histoire de l'Université de Genève*, vol. 1: *L'Académie de Calvin 1559–1798* (Genève : Georg, 1900), 337.

Giovanni Diodati, di nation Lucchese. It was a quarto edition, printed with a clear type and decorations; the first letter of chapters was an embellished woodcut. On the frontispiece was an engraving representing a sower with the motto, "His art in God". That same engraving and motto also appeared in the 1641 edition.

From a distance of four hundred years, it seems quite normal that someone with the requisite talent would translate, at his own expense if need be, the Biblical text. But let us not forget that Italy from 1546 to 1757 was in a situation that appears to us, with the wisdom of hindsight, paradoxical. The Catholic Church used and honoured the Latin Bible but forbad and actively opposed the Bible in the vernacular, as Gigliola Fragnito has demonstrated in her work *La Bibbia al rogo (The Bible at the Stake).*[21] As we know, on 8 April 1546 the Council of Trent made the Latin Bible (the Vulgate) the official version for preaching and exposition of the Biblical text; then, with the apostolic constitution *Dominici gregis custodiae* of 24 March 1564, Pius IV disallowed translations of the Bible into the vernacular.[22] This prohibition was abolished by Benedict XIV on 13 June 1757 by a decree that permitted the publishing and reading of the Bible in the vernacular, provided any such Bible was approved by the Holy See.[23] This long exclusion of the Bible precipitated a long decline in Italian life and religious culture, a decline that has only been reversed in the last few decades.

What is, however, less well known is that, despite that prohibition, attempts to publish the Bible in the vernacular languages were not lacking in Italy. In fact, Bible translation was as important in Italy as in other European countries.[24] Already, before the Council of Trent, several modest attempts took place. Without going back to Malermi's Bible of 1471, it is enough here to mention Antonio Brucioli's, published in Venice in 1532.[25] Brucioli's Bible was published

---

21 Gigliola Fragnito, La *Bibbia al rogo : La censura ecclesiastica e i volgarizzamenti della Scrittura (1471–1605)* (Bologna: Il Mulino, 1997).

22 *Enchiridion symbolorum*, Heinrich Denzinger, ed. (Fribourg-en-Brisgau: Herder, 1965), 1851–1861.

23 *Codicis Iuris Canonici Fontes*, Giustiniano Seredi, ed. (Rome: Typis polyglottis Vaticanis, 1935), 7:724.

24 *Il Fondo Guicciardini nella Biblioteca Nazionale Centrale di Firenze*, Aldo Landi, ed., vol. 2, *Bibbie* (Florence: Giunta regionale toscana, 1991); Edoardo Barbieri, *Le Bibbie italiane del Quattrocento e del Cinquecento: storia e bibliografia ragionata delle edizioni in lingua italiana dal 1471 al 1600*, 2 vol. (Milan: Editrice Bibliografica, 1991–1992); *La Bibbia in italiano tra Medioevo e Rinascimento – La Bible italienne au Moyen Âge et à la Renaissance*, Lino Leonardi, ed. (Florence: SISMEL, 1998).

25 Malermi's Bible: *Biblia volgarizzata* (Venice: Vindelinus de Spira, 1471). Brucioli's Bible: *La Biblia quale contiene i sacri libri [...]* (Venice: Lucantonio Giunti, 1532). For the life and work of Brucioli, that indefagitably prolific author from Florence, see Giorgio Spini, *Antonio Brucioli: tra Rinascimento e Riforma* (Florence: La nuova Italia, 1940); and Milka Ventura Avanzinelli, "Il 'luterano' Brucioli e il suo commento al libro della Genesi", in *Bollettino della Società di studi Valdesi*, 159 (1986), 19–33.

numerous times, right up to 1559 when it was put on the Index by Paul IV. As well, the Dominican Santi Marmochino published, also in Venice, a Bible translation.[26] Even though Brucioli claimed to have translated directly from the original Hebrew and Greek, he was spinning a yarn. While he did not admit it, for the Old Testament he translated from Santes Pagnini's Latin version, and for the New, from Erasmus'. Marmochino, for his part, reproduced Bruciol's version for the Old Testament, and that of his confrere Fra Zaccaria for the New.[27]

The Geneva Bible (*Bibbia duroniana*) deserves special note.[28] This large quarto volume was published in Geneva by Francesco Durone in 1562. An in-depth study of this translation shows diverse influences. For the Old Testament, this Bible depends in part on Santes Pagnini's version and in part on the Vatable Bible (also known as the 1543 Latin Bible of Zurich), while for the New Testament, it descended from an anonymous translation originating in Geneva. The Geneva Bible cannot be placed among the major Italian translations; besides, that was not its goal. But that Bible remains interesting and very important. For more than a half century, in fact, it nourished the devotional life of Italian exiles in Geneva and beyond the borders of the tiny republic of Lake Leman. Moreover, as did few other sources of the era, it went in the direction of a vast current of thought that hoped still to see the dawn of a renewal of "Italy's princes and republics", as states the long and passionate dedicatory preface.

When it is in the presence of the other early Italian translations of the Bible, the 1607 Diodati Bible, whose quadricentennial we celebrate, stands out. In this Bible, the translator did not indicate where he had made the translation, nor was there a place of publication on the title page. It was produced in a portable quarto format.

All these facts indicate that it had a very precise objective: to be an instrument both of edification and of battle. It had to serve the needs of the worshipping community of Italian exiles scattered throughout Europe and, at the same time, to promote the diffusion of evangelical ideas in Italy. I would say that if we wish to celebrate Diodati's work but do not acknowledge these two aspects of his work or highlight only the literary aspect, we take too many liberties with history. This would not even pay proper homage to the memory of post-Tridentine church hierarchies that vigorously opposed the Diodati Bible. In fact, we have the duty to acknowledge these hierarchies' motives and consistency, even if we are obligated to state that, in impeding the Bible's spread in the vernacular, they were wrong from every point of view, including that of Catholicism in time to come. We can

---

26 *La Bibia nuovamente tradotta dalla hebraica verita in lingua thoscana [...]* (Venice: Lucantonio Giunti [eredi], 1538).
27 *Il Nuovo Testamento tradotto in lingua toscana* (Venice: Luca Antonio Giunti, 1536).
28 *La Bibia, che si chiama il vecchio Testamento [...]*, ([Genève]: Francesco Durone, 1562).

only give the 1607 Diodati Bible the respect due it by taking note of the tragic time in which it was published and by marking how deadly serious were the motives that drove some people to fight others.

The Genevan in whose veins ran the blood of a native of Lucca had, as a young man, undertaken the translation of the Bible in the language that he sensed as his mother tongue. As I have already remarked, the undertaking was driven by two desires: to supply a clear and faithful translation of the Biblical text for the Italian church of Geneva and to promote the diffusion of evangelical ideas in Italy. An excellent Hebraist and good Hellenist, Diodati, taking into account the versions of Brucioli and the Geneva Bible, translated from the originals. A galley-proof was ready in 1603, and the young professor, then 27 years old, presented it on 18 November of that year to a session of the Company of Pastors to get permission to publish it.[29] From his correspondence we infer that consciousness of his limitations predominated rather than arrogance based on the satisfaction of having completed a great work. That was why he let time pass before his work saw the light of day. In the interval he appealed to friends and experienced acquaintances or to proven experts to purge the text of all error and to improve the style. During the summer of 1607, the translation prepared by Diodati was printed and entitled *La Bibbia. Cioè i libri del Vecchio e del Nuovo Testamento. Nuovamente traslatati in lingua Italiana, da Giovanni Diodati, di nation Lucchese.* The sentiments of the young translator were reflected exactly in a 13 July 1605 letter addressed to the statesman and historian Jacques-Auguste de Thou. Also found in that letter is Diodati's ardent desire "to open for our Italians the door to the knowledge of heavenly truth".[30] We shall have no difficulty in recognizing in this assertion an eloquent writ of accusation against the post-Tridentine Catholicism that absolutely forbad the translating and reading of Holy Scripture in the vernacular.

Should the Bible be banished from a country's life and culture, or, on the contrary, should it be accessible to all levels of society? This was the question that took on an urgency and actuality when, as we know, Pope Paul V put Venice under interdict, in April of 1606. The Republic reacted by expelling the Jesuits and by brilliantly contesting, through the good offices of Fra Paolo Sarpi, the doctrinal justification of the pope's action.[31] This was the gravest crisis that

---

29 *Registres de la* Compagnie *des pasteurs de Genève*, vol. 8, 1600–1603, Gabriella Cahier, Matteo Campagnolo, ed. (Geneva: Droz, 1986), 273.

30 E. de Budé, *Vie de Jean Diodati*, 169.

31 Corrado Vivanti, Introduction, in Paolo Sarpi, *Istoria del Concilio tridentino* (Turin: Einaudi, 1974); Gaetano Cozzi, *Paolo Sarpi tra* Venezia *e l'Europa* (Turin: Einaudi, 1978); David Wootton, *Paolo Sarpi: Between Renaissance and Enlightenment* (Cambridge: Cambridge University Press, 1983); Corrado Vivanti, *Paolo Sarpi* (Rome: Istituto poligrafico e Zecca dello

Catholicism would know in early modern Italy. Among the people feeding antipapal sentiments was the wily Sir Henry Wotton, English ambassador to the *Serenissima*, the Republic of Venice. He was not limiting himself to observing events or to taking advantage of the "right to worship", that is to say, the right to celebrate the rites of his own confession in his own residence, but, by means of his chaplain, William Bedell, he initiated missionary activity whose aim was to introduce the Reformation to Venice. To this end, he contacted Diodati whom he had gotten to know during a visit to Geneva and with whom he had remained in touch by letter. By giving enticing details of the religious life in the city of lagoons, he let Diodati hope for an abundant harvest for Protestantism. Wotton first asked him to help find someone capable of spreading the evangelical faith, but later went further by asking Diodati himself to get directly involved.

The theologian from Lucca/Geneva, who had for a long time noted attentively the contrast between the interests of *La Serenissima* and those of the Roman curia, was not at all indifferent to Sir Wotton's request but gave it considerable attention. Diodati consulted with experts in the matter and with friends before deciding. A Frenchman, Philippe Duplessis-Mornay (1549–1623), enlightened founder of the Saumur Academy, "the pope of the Huguenots", not only encouraged Diodati to undertake the mission but also furnished him with detailed instructions and even sent him a young French nobleman, David de Liques, to accompany him on the trip. About mid-August of 1608, they both left for Venice for the purpose of doing their part to develop the most favourable situation possible for Protestantism. It is interesting to note that Diodati, in order to hide his identity during this mission, chose the pseudonym "Giovanni Coreglia", a name that was not too far from the truth since Diodati's family originated in Coreglia, a village in the Lucca region.[32]

After his return to Geneva, Diodati composed an account of his stay in Venice, an account he entitled *Briève relation.* He subsequently sent it to Duplessis-Mornay and Wotton.[33] This report was a thorough account of the facts; in it, the author plainly wished to understand the complex reality of matters there. He perceived clearly a craven sentiment for rebellion against the Roman Church and a vague desire for a change in religious confession, but he realized no one truly wished a total break with Rome and no one dared to found an evangelical

Stato, 2000); and *Ripensando Paolo Sarpi: Atti del convegno internazionale di studi nel 450° anniversario della nascita di Paolo Sarpi*, ed. Corrado Pin, (Venice: Ateneo veneto, 2006).

32 Paul Barbey, "Le théologien genevois Jean Diodati projette de constituer une communauté réformée à Venise, "in *Genève et l'Italie: études publiées à l'occasion du 80ᵉ anniversaire de la Société Genevoise d'Études Italiennes*, under the direction of Angela Kahn-Laginestra (Geneva : Société Genevoise d'Études Italiennes, 1999), 419–429.

33 Jean Diodati, *Briève relation de mon voyage à Venise en septembre* 1608, published by Eugène de Budé in *La Semaine Religieuse* (Geneva: Impr. Bonnant, 1863).

Reformed Church. Diodati represented Fra Paolo Sarpi as "the big wheel in this holy matter". But Diodati also described Sarpi as hesitant to take a position openly either because Sarpi was circumspect and prudent by nature or because he considered the situation not ripe for action.

When Diodati left Venice at the end of October 1608, he was quite discouraged by this experience. He was nonetheless able to distribute a fair number of copies of his translation of the Bible, and he settled on a prudent and cautious strategy of support for the pro-Protestant patricians of Venice. And so came about the proposal not to act through preachers but rather to lead *La Serenissima* into the Reformed fold through embassies to Venice, namely, the embassies of England, the Reformed cantons of Switzerland, the Palatine Electorate, and the Netherlands. But the assassination of Henri IV of France on 14 May 1610 effectively extinguished the hope to see the Interdict controversy transformed into a reform of religion. If Sarpi wrote with sadness to Duplessis-Mornay from his place in Venice that "Hope died with the king's passing",[34] Diodati, for his part, realized that the plans that he had laid in Venice were inappropriate. All the same, he continued to watch with sympathy events in *La Serenissima* by maintaining contact by letter both with Paolo Sarpi and Fulgenzio Micanzio as well as with the English ambassador Henry Wotton and his successor Dudley-Carleton. It was not by accident that Diodati took it upon himself to translate and in Geneva to publish in 1621 Sarpi's *Historia del Concilio tridentino*. Diodati's French version of it, *l'Histoire du Concile de Trente*, became a determining factor in its vast distribution in Europe.[35]

Thus is the backdrop to the story of the 1607 Diodati Bible. With this work he intended to bring to fruition his grand design to make the Biblical text accessible to those Italian readers who could not read Latin. With this polished and readable translation, very respectful of the Hebrew and Greek originals, he hoped (even though this hope proved ephemeral) that the Venetians, inspired by reading Scripture, would not evade the exigencies of a serious commitment to reform. As did many Italians at the beginning of the seventeenth century, Diodati looked on the Venetian Republic as the champion of what remained of Italian liberty. He was convinced that, strengthened in its political independence by the Interdict affair, Venice would be able to renew itself spiritually and initiate the reformation of the Church. As we know, not only did the politics of *La Serenissima* take another course entirely but also the Diodati Bible itself would be put on the Index. Nonetheless, tenacious as a fictional hero, Diodati did not give up and thirty-four

---

34 E. de Budé, *Vie de Jean Diodati*, 78.
35 *Histoire du Concile de Trente: Traduite de l'italien de Pierre Soave [...] par Jean Diodati* (Geneva : Estienne Gamonet, 1621).

years later published at his own expense the second edition of his translation of the Bible.

During the seventeenth and eighteenth centuries, numerous reprints of the Diodati Bible or parts thereof appeared one after the other, none of which we can examine here. Nor can we pay much attention to the Diodati Bible's early eighteenth century revisions or adaptations (*racconciature*),[36] the first of which was published by the *Sprachmeister* Matthias von Erberg of Nuremberg and was entitled *La Sacro-Santa Biblia*.[37] So much does it wander and multiply mistakes in language that it is amazing that this revision continues to be read. A version a little more rigorously philological is that of a catechist of Leipzig, Johann David Müller: *La Sacra Bibbia*.[38] It was followed, a few years later, by Giorgio Walter's revision, *La Sacra Bibbia*.[39]

The nineteenth century saw published an abundance of new editions of the Diodati Bible, maybe even more than those of the eighteenth century. But, from then on, they were printed in Italy and England rather than Switzerland. It was the new British and Foreign Bible Society (founded 1804) that assured the distribution of the Diodati Bible. Thanks to Giorgio Spini et Luigi Santini's research (now classic in the field) we can henceforth have at our disposal ample reliable knowledge of the letters and collaborative efforts linked to the publication and distribution of the Diodati Bible by the British Bible Society.[40] Italian Protestants, for their part, did not remain inactive. The young publishing house, Claudiana (founded 1855) put into its publishing lineup of 1860 a new edition of the Diodati New Testament.[41] In 1868 it published a complete Diodati Bible, an edition christened "The American Bible" because the cost of printing it was covered by

---

36 Emidio Campi, "La Bible des Réfugiés: histoire de la diffusion de la Bible en langue italienne en Suisse entre le XVIe et le XVIIIe siècle", in *La Bible en Suisse: origines et histoire*, Urs Joerg, David M. Hoffmann, ed. (Basel: Schwabe, 1997), 241–254.

37 *La Sacro-Santa Biblia in lingua Italiana, cioè il vecchio e nuovo Testamento nella purità della Lingua volgare, moderna e corretta [...] da Mattia d'Erberg cultore delle sacre Lettere* (Nuremberg: Alle spese di quest'istesso Autore, 1711).

38 *La Sacra Bibbia [...] tradotta in lingua italiana da Giovanni Diodati [...] riveduta di nuovo sopra gli originali e corretta con ogni maggior accuratezza da Giovanni David Müller* (Leipzig: Born, 1744).

39 *La Sacra Bibbia [...] tradotta in lingua italiana da Giovanni Diodati, riveduta per Giorgio Walther* (Dresden-Leipzig: Walther, 1757).

40 See, for example, Giorgio Spini, "Le Società bibliche e l'Italia : un episodio ignorato del Risorgimento", in Spini, *Studi sull'Evangelismo italiano tra Otto e Novecento* (Turin: Claudiana, 1994), 49–86; Spini, "Ancora sulle Società bibliche e l'Italia del Risorgimento", *ibid*, 87–98; Luigi Santini, "I Protestanti a Livorno nel periodo mediceo-lorenese", in *I valdesi e l'Europa* (Torre Pellice: Società di Studi Valdesi, 1982), 351–387.

41 *Il Nuovo Testamento del nostro Signore e Salvatore Gesù Cristo, tradotto in lingua italiana da Giovanni Diodati* (Turin: Claudiana, 1860).

moneys collected in the United States.[42] On 20 September 1870, when Italian forces entered Rome through *Porta Pia* after three hours of artillery barrage, there was, behind the *bersaglieri*, a Waldensian colporteur with Diodati Bibles. The adventure of the *Diodatina*, as the Italians from then on called Diodati's translation, continued until 1924, when it was replaced by the *Riveduta* ("Revised").[43] Even so, Italian speaking Protestants used it into the 1950's.

3.   Final Remarks

In 1711, Matthias von Erberg, in his reader's preface to his unhappy revision of the Diodati Bible, affirmed: "If the European languages, invited to the wedding feast of their Bridegroom, can pride themselves on delicious and exquisite treats reserved for them from each verse of the Scriptures, only the Italian language (however rich compared to the others) could have cause to complain that she had nothing but *panem arctum et aquam brevem*;[44] the reason for this is the extreme rarity of the Word of God imprinted on their vernacular". This statement reflects a notion that was rather widespread among the educated in Protestant Europe of the time and that was repeated in the centuries that followed. One may easily see there, in the first place, something praiseworthy in Protestantism: its love for the Scriptures, its indefatigable zeal for exegesis, and the importance that it accords to the translation of the Bible into the vernacular. At the same time, von Erberg's statement was equivalent to eloquently laying a charge against a Catholicism that prevented people from gaining knowledge of and access to the Bible in their own language.

If we are forced to admit that Italy, because of the well known vicissitudes of its political and religious life, suffered from an "extreme rarity of the Word of God", we immediately see that his polemic, based on confessionalism, did not lead Matthias von Erberg to distinguish between the distribution and the translation of the Bible. Now, this is a fundamental distinction for someone who wishes to understand the place of Scriptures in that country. It is true that the almost total disappearance of Protestantism in Italy, to which we add the punctilious application of the Council of Trent's decrees on the Biblical text and on its translation

---

42 *La Sacra Bibbia, ossia l'Antico e il Nuovo Testamento, tradotti da Giovanni Diodati con referenze del medesimo* (Florence: Claudiana, 1868).

43 *La Sacra Bibbia, versione « Riveduta » di Giovanni Luzzi* (Rome: Società Biblica Britannica e Forestiera, 1924). The revision begun in 1908. V. Bani, Enrico Bosio, and Giovanni Luzzi were mainly responsible for the final work. The type-setting and plate-making were done in Italy, but the book was printed at the Oxford University Press.

44 Vulgate, Isaiah 30:20: "narrow bread and little water". RSV: "And though the Lord give you *the bread of adversity and the water of affliction*".

into vernacular languages, pushed the Bible into the background of Italian religious life and culture to the point of allowing the Bible to fall into a long decline from which it has, only today, started to raise itself. Nonetheless, the distribution and knowledge of the Scriptures are one thing, and their translation is another. And regarding the latter, the Italian language, vis-à-vis the other European languages, is not lacking. It is true that not one translation into the vernacular could circulate in Italy from 1564 to 1773 (officially, at least), but the idea of a Christian faith nourished and inspired by the Scriptures lived on and produced translations of great exegetical, literary, and spiritual value. And the most important of those translations was that of Diodati. The soil was poor; even so, the seed was sown in abundance. The splendour of the divine Word, though eclipsed, was not extinguished. Apart from this, it remained true that Reformed Italians, dispersed throughout Europe and more particularly those who had found refuge in Switzerland from the sixteenth to the seventeenth century made a contribution much larger than their numbers warranted. Their pure and unshakable faith in the efficacy of the Scriptures, a faith that kept up the hope of this *ecclesia peregrinorum*, "church of sojourners", permitted the Italian language to participate in the great adventure of the translation of the Bible into the vernacular.

Jon Balserak

Inventing the Prophet:
Vermigli, Melanchthon, and Calvin on the Extraordinary
Reformer

"The charism of prophecy," the fourth-century writer, Apollinarius, observed, "must exist in all the Church until the second coming: this is the view of St. Paul" (cited in Aquinas, ST 2a2ae. 171). Such assertions are legion. Given its importance to the church, therefore, she has spent much time and effort seeking to understand prophecy. What is it and what are its uses in the church and the world?[1]

1.   Defining prophecy up to ca. 1500

"Prophecy is divine revelation," Cassiodorus declared in the preface to his *Expositio Psalmorum* (PL 70: 12). A similar note is struck in Augustine's *Super Genesim ad Litteram* (PL 34: 458–61) and Gregory the Great's homilies on Ezekiel (1986, 50–64). Such remarks would be repeated ad nauseum throughout the Middle Ages, as the writings of Albertus Magnus (19: 2, 85, 637), Bonaventure (1891–1902, 9: 564), and Thomas Aquinas (ST II–II q171 a1)[2] testify. In point of fact, many medieval thinkers connected the prophet's knowledge with that of the angels, believing it was of the same character and depth. This can be seen, for instance, in William of Auxerre's *Summa Aurea* (1500, 2: fol. 53r). A similar accent on prophecy as knowledge appears throughout the fourteenth century, as the influential postilla of Nicholas of Lyra demonstrate (Prohemium to Psalms, 1483, n.p.).

This understanding comes—these scholars maintained—from a sound basis, namely, the meaning of the word prophet, *prophētēs*, which is noted by numerous authors from Eusebius (PG 22: 345) to Basil (PG 30: 284), Chrysostom (PG 56: 111), and Isidore of Seville (PL 82: 283). Many of these authors contend the essential meaning of the word is (something like) predictor of the future. But that

---

1 On prophecy see, *inter alia*, Paul Alphandéry (1932, 334–59), Marjorie Reeves (1969); Bernard McGinn (1985).
2 See the collected thought of Aquinas on prophecy (2006).

being said, in more thorough treatments of the topic, prophetic knowledge is regularly said to not merely be knowledge of the future but more specifically knowledge of what is *hidden*. It can relate to the past, the present, or the future. Here once again the work of Gregory the Great is extremely clear: "Prophecy has three tenses; the past, of course; the present and the future" (1986, 56). Similar thoughts abound; see, for instance, Theodoret (PG 80: 861), Aquinas (ST II–II q171 a3), Lanfranc of Bec (PL 181: 958–59), and Peter Lombard (PL 191: 1659).

The question of how this knowledge was obtained occupied many ancient and medieval thinkers. Men like Tertullian, in his *De anima*, discussed it in relation to dreams, ecstasy, and mania (a topic discussed by many non-Christian authors, such as Plato). Aquinas devotes a whole question to the topic of ecstasy (*de raptu*) (ST II–II q175). Here numerous ancillary questions were also addressed; questions such as: does the prophet actually descend into a kind of madness, such that he loses self-control? Does she receive a revelation which entails separation from her senses? These and numerous other queries were raised.

Behind many of these questions was the basic issue: how does one distinguish God's revelation to a prophet from the experience of demonic possession? (the assumption was, of course, that these were radically different things, and therefore should be distinguishable one from another). Of great authority on such matters were the thoughts of Augustine, who in his *Super Genesim ad Litteram* 12: 9 and 12: 10–27 (PL 34: 461–464) discussed the means by which God communicates prophetic knowledge to his prophets in terms of signs being manifested in the human spirit through likenesses of corporeal objects and light being given to the mind of the prophet so that the images can be understood. In such works. Augustine analyzes the role of the body and spirit in a divine intellectual vision. He considered, for instance, the revelation that was given which produced Daniel's visions, recorded in places like Daniel 7–12). Not to be outdone, Augustine's contemporary Jerome also treated such matters (PL 25: 1041).

Endeavoring to advance the discussion, Thomas Aquinas identified four ways the prophetic revelation happens: by the inflowing of intellectual light, by the emission of intellectual species, by the impression or ordination of forms in the imagination, and by the expression of sensible images (ST II–II q173 a3). A sophisticated line of approach on this basic question of process (how does revelation to the prophet happen) had developed thanks to Augustine, Jerome, and others, which related to a distinction between an "intellective" and an "imaginative" vision. Some prophets experience both, it was believed, while others only experience one or the other. Perhaps not surprisingly, a debate of sorts arose about which of these modes of reception was the superior one. Is experiencing both "more excellent than that which is only intellective?" (Aquinas, ST II–II q174 a2) Augustine had asserted that the prophet who enjoyed both intellective and imaginative vision was superior to the one who enjoyed only the intellective (PL

34: 461; see also Jerome, PL 28: 598). Meanwhile, Peter Lombard (PL 191: 58), *inter alia*, asserted that receiving an imaginative vision, that is essentially a vision that employed images, detracted from the purity of the Spirit's revelation of an intellective vision, and was thus inferior. Returning to Aquinas, we find that he qualified the views of Augustine in a manner which strongly suggests that he did not disagree with such an eminent Christian writer as Augustine. Nonetheless, Aquinas did seem to believe a bare contemplation of the truth, without the use of mediating corporeal images, was superior (ST II–II q174 a2). Aquinas continued his addressing of these issues in article 3 of question 174 (ST II–II q174 a3). Franciscans also participated in the discussion, with Bonaventure adding his own appraisal of the character of the prophetic vision, which he argued is threefold, *secundum sensum exteriorem, imaginationem et intellectum.* (1891–1902, 1: 281, arg 4).

Given the focus not only upon knowledge and the character of that knowledge but also upon distinguishing between the manner in which this knowledge is conveyed to the prophet by God, it may come as little surprise that various theologians occupied themselves with identifying great prophets and even *the* greatest prophet. This they determined by means of assessing the manner in which they received their divine revelation. Augustine mentions Daniel as a pre-eminent example of one in whom was embodied the highest qualities of a prophet, though he stopped short of calling Daniel *the* greatest, again in Augustine's *Super Genesim ad Litteram* (PL 34: 458–61). Peter Lombard, on the other hand, identified David as the greatest of all prophets; David prophesied "on a more exalted and distinguished level (*digniori atque excellentiori modo*)" (PL 191: 55). Others, such as Aquinas, called Moses the greatest prophet (ST II–II q174 a4).

Developed concurrently with the idea of prophecy as knowledge is that of prophecy as interpretation. The prophet is an interpreter; specifically an interpreter of the Scripture. Ambrosiaster, for example, states: "Prophets, however, are those who explain the scriptures" (1516, 2, fol. 208).

As theologians expanded this understanding, they moved in one or two ways. Some gave prominence to the aspect of exploring scriptural mysteries while others emphasized the idea of proclamation and practical application (see, for instance, Bruno (PL 153: 192); Rabanus (PL 112: 116), Lanfranc (PL 150: 199); Strabo (PL 114: 542) and Haymo (PL 117: 580); Pseudo-Jerome (PL 30: 788); Thomas Aquinas in his *Expositio in Epistolam Romanos* 12: 6 (1852–73, 13, 123); and William of St Thierry (PL 180: 673)). As they extrapolated further on the subject, theologians discussed the content of the prophet's proclamation. Some adopted the viewpoint of being content to focus primarily on doctrine while others saw it as consisting of moral instruction. Many writers, in fact, made an explicit distinction between the Old Testament prophet and the New Testament prophet, with the former being identified as a recipient of supernatural knowledge and the latter as interpreters.

The question of what, precisely, is prophetic about this work of interpreting, exhorting, preaching, and so forth that distinguishes it from the ordinary work of a Christian minister occupied medieval thinkers. Some argued that special enlightenment was given to the prophet so that he, or she, could understand the mysteries of Scripture. It was sometimes explained that this was what distinguished the "prophet" from "doctor" (both New Testament offices), the latter having to study in order to come to an understanding of the scriptures. This is found at least as early as Chrysostom (PG 61: 265) and later as well, as can be seen in the work of Nicholas of Lyra. When treating 1 Corinthians 12: 10, Lyra comments: "second prophets. These are those receiving revelations immediately from God (*accipientes a deo immediate revelationes*)" (1483, n.p.). How these truths of the Bible are revealed to him or her, whether the prophet must at least read the scriptures, whether they need to read the scriptures in the original languages, and a host of other queries do not appear to have been of great importance to the Middle Ages. Later we find humanist-trained exegetes insisting on the ability to read Hebrew and Greek as essential for understanding the Scripture. Martin Luther, in fact, in *An die Radherrn aller Stedte deutsches lands*, contended this is what distinguishes the prophet from the ordinary teacher (WA 15: 40). But such questions are not infrequently set aside, so far as I have been able to tell, in the Middle Ages.

One theologian who does discuss some of these deeper matters is Thomas Aquinas. He touches on it in his dealings with 1 Corinthians 14, in which he sets out what prophecy consists of. Prophecy, he explains, is "the sight of things far off, whether they be future contingents or beyond human reason" (1852–73, 13, 281). This sight requires four things, he explains. It is required that in the prophet's imagination is formed the bodily likeness of things which are shown (*quae ostenduntur*). Second, it requires that light be given to the prophet's intellect. Third, it requires courage to proclaim the things revealed. And fourth, it requires the working of miracles which lends credence to the prophecy (1852–73, 13, 281). Continuing, Aquinas explained that men and women can be called prophets in various ways, some of which do not require the prophet to possess all four of these qualities. One may, he says, be called a prophet if he possesses the intellectual light to explain imaginary visions made to someone else, adding "or for explaining the sayings of the prophets or the scriptures of the apostles" (1852–73, 13: 281). One could even, Aquinas contended, be called a prophet if he, or she, merely announces the statements of the prophets or explains them or, even, sings them in church.

Now, as implied in the above paragraph, some medieval theologians, many in fact, believed that *both kinds* of prophecy were legitimate (i.e. God ordained) forms of prophecy. "We understand prophecy in a two-fold manner, not only as predicting the future but also as revealing the Scriptures," said Rhabanus Maurus (PL 112: 116) in words that also appear almost verbatim in many other writings by individuals like Bruno Carthusianorum (PL 153: 102, 192, 197), Herveus Burgidolensis (PL 181: 944, 959), Lanfranc (PL 150:197), and Peter Lombard (PL 191: 1665). Not everyone agreed, however. William of Auxerre, for example, openly criticised the idea that scriptural interpretation was prophecy. While many believed that the interpreting of the scriptures occurred prophetically by means of the same Spirit who brought forth the Scriptures, William argued in his *Summa Aurea* (1500, 2: 55r) that such an argument was a paralogism; that is, fallacious reasoning that has the appearance of being valid.

According to Apollinarius, as we have seen, prophets should exist on earth until Christ's return. This was an extremely common view up through the Middle Ages and into the Early Modern era. Many during the Middle Ages believed that prophets still existed and defended their beliefs from the scriptures. Jerome, for instance, commented on Matthew 11: 13 ("The prophets and the law prophesied until John"), declaring: "This does not mean that there were no more prophets after John" (1977, 222). This sentiment was repeated throughout the Middle Ages. Likewise, Aquinas noted in his *Summa Theologica* that "at no time have persons possessing the spirit of prophecy been lacking, not indeed for the declaration of any new doctrine of faith (*non ... ad novam doctrinam fidei depromendam*) but for the directing of human acts" (ST II–II q. 174, a.6, ad3).

The last sentiment suggested that the work of the contemporary (i.e. post-apostolic) prophet is focused on the work of instruction and moral guidance. Sure enough Aquinas said the same in his *expositio* on the Gospel of Matthew: "It ought to be said that the prophets were sent for two reasons: to establish faith and to correct behavior: Prov. 29: 18: 'When prophecy fails, the people are scattered (*dissipabitur*).' To establish the faith, as is said in 1 Peter 1: 10: 'Concerning that salvation, the prophets ...'" (1951, 145). Thus, Aquinas explained that prophecy had initially served two purposes. But this has now changed. Now, he says, that "the faith is established (*iam fides fundata est*), since the promises have been fulfilled in Christ. Prophecy that aims to correct behavior (*mores*), however, has not ceased, nor will it ever cease" (1951, 145). Denis the Carthusian said essentially the same: "Prophecy also contains those things which have to do with the instruction of human behavior, such as 'break your bread with the hungry...' and Micah says 'he has shown you, man, what is good and what the Lord requires of you.'" (1558, 2). We see something similar elsewhere. Haymo's declaration championed the ordinary aspects of prophecy and other offices too. He explained that whereas there used to be evangelists, prophets and pastors, now the fact is that whoever tells someone the good news is an evangelist and whoever speaks to his hearers about the joys of the elect and the punishments of the reprobate "is a prophet (*propheta est*)" (PL 117: 720). Rabanus Maurus produced similar reflections, drawing one to one correspondences between the New Testament offices and their modern equivalents. According to him, the prophet becomes a presbyter, namely, one who interprets the scriptures (PL 112: 430); likewise, someone like Herveus Burgidolensis (PL 181: 1246).

Yet despite this fulsome concern for ordinary aspects of prophecy, the medieval church was more intrigued with the apocalyptic prophets who appeared from time to time. One thinks of the likes of Hildegard of Bingen, Joachim of Fiore, Francis of Assisi, Birgitta of Vadstena, Jan Hus. Their character varied considerably, though they often brought terrifying visions which they proclaimed to the people. A particularly impressive example appears in the *Compendio di Rivelazioni* (1996) of Savanarola.

2.   Continuation and Change in Early Modern Thinking on Prophecy

Moving into the Early Modern period, we discover change, which had surely been precipitated by a number of factors the character of which we will curtly glance at in just a moment.

Naturally, much continuation in thinking on prophecy can be seen during this era. Prophecy as supernatural (and often apocalyptic) knowledge continued to be a prominent position held during this period, as a glance at the work of individuals like Meister Theodorius, Melchior Hoffman or Thomas Müntzer confirms. Hoffman, for instance, produced an exposition of Daniel 12, *Das XII. Capitel des propheten Danielis ausgelegt, … christen nutzlich zu wissen,* and also his *Weissagung aus heiliger gotlicher geschrift* and *Prophetische Gesicht und Offenbarung* (1526), which described Europe as already in the last days. Hoffman divided the last days into two periods of three and a half years, and which predicted the precise date of Christ's second coming. A myriad of other examples could be cited. Such apocalypticism grew extremely intense in parts of Europe, such as France (Crouzet: 1990).

The church also continued to see prophecy as interpretation. Erasmus offers us a superb example of this. He set out this belief in a number of places, including his paraphrase of Romans 12: 6 (1518, 110) and his annotations on 1 Corinthians 14: 1 (1516, 477). Nor is Erasmus the only one. Plenty of others discussed prophecy in terms of scriptural interpretation, including Guilielmus Estius (1841, vol 1, 369), Johann Bugenhagen (1524, 13r), Johannes Brenz (1588, 723), Caspar Olevianus (1579, 614), and Francois Lambert of Avignon (1525, 8r).

But changes were coming. With the growth of cities during the later Middle Ages, discernible growth occurred in the religious expression of the populace. No longer were intense expressions of personal Christian devotion confined to monasteries. The rise of women visionaries, from medieval women like Hildegard of Bingen, Mechthild von Magdeburg, and Birgitta of Vadstena to the appearance later of Ursula Jost and Barbara Rebstock, the Maid of Lorraine prophecies, Maria de Santo Domingo, Teresa of Avila, Lucrecia de León, Margery Kempe, Eleanor Davies, and others illustrates this (see Voaden: 1999 and Caciola: 2003). Further change, associated with the European Renaissance, witnessed a rise in magic and the occult, as seen in the work of figures like Heinrich Cornelius Agrippa of Nettesheim, Marsilio Ficino, Giordano Bruno, and Paracelsus.

The Early Modern period witnessed the rise, among some, of an intense concern over the problem of "idolatry" in Christian worship. Men like Ulrich Zwingli, Martin Luther, Johannes Oecolampadius and others became profoundly troubled by the Roman Catholic Mass, and the numerous cultic exercises which were part and parcel of the Roman Church.

These concerns may have arisen for several reasons, including the development of novel conceptions of piety during the fifteenth century and the republication in the same period of patristic writings in which Zwingli, Oecolampadius, and others believed they found a simpler form of worship. Wherever they came from, the concerns prompted men and women to engage in iconoclastic activity in cities throughout continental Europe and the British Isles, smashing statues and images of Christ, the Virgin Mary, and various saints. They also led to people deciding to leave the Roman Catholic church and found churches in which they could worship God faithfully (these were, in their judgment, not new churches at all but were churches which sought to remain faithful to the truths and traditions initially established by the apostles, from which the "papists' had departed). This marked a momentous shift in western Christendom, which rocked the foundations of the church and of European society.

Those who led the way in this seismic upheaval often believed themselves to have been especially called by God for such a task. Sometimes they professed this openly about themselves but often they did not. Often, they were identified by others as possessing a special call from God. In this regard, Ulrich Zwingli identified Martin Luther as Elijah, one of the two witnesses—Elijah and Enoch—promised in Revelation 11: 3 (ZW 7: 218–22). We also find Heinrich Bullinger, in his *De officio prophetico*. declaring, when speaking of Ulrich Zwingli, that he is a "prophet" and that "God raised up this man to restore the glory of his church" (1532, 33r). Bullinger also identified a "company of prophets" in one of his sermons on Revelation (preached in the early 1530s and published in 1537), listing "Mirandola, Reuchlin, Erasmus, Luther, Zwingli, Oecolampadius, and Melanchthon" (1557, 148).

Corresponding to these assertions was new thinking on prophecy and the role of the prophet. Thinking on the topic of prophecy during the Early Modern period flourished and was infused with an innovativeness which brought about new ideas in relation to what prophecy was and what the prophet did. There had, of course, always throughout the history of the church been variety in thinking on prophecy. Jerome, for instance, chose, in an odd comment in his commentary on Matthew's Gospel, to divide prophecy into predestination, foreknowledge and denunciation (1977, 80). Other divisions appear in the writings of Peter Lombard (PL 191: 59), William of Auxerre (1500, 2: fol. 53v), Hugh of St Cher (1977, 32), and Thomas Aquinas (ST II–II q174 a1). Likewise, in *Etymologiae* VII, viii, 32, Isidore of Seville divided prophecy into (1) ecstasy; (2) vision; (3) dreams; (4) through a cloud; (5) a voice from heaven; (6) the receiving of an oracle; and (7) being filled with the Holy Spirit (PL 82: 283–87; esp 285–287). Likewise, discussion of the grades (*gradus*) (Aquinas: ST II–II q174 a3 and Denis: 1558, 3), modes (*modis*), and kinds (*genera*) of prophecy (William of Auxerre: 1500, 2: fol. 53r) clogged the Middle Ages. So, during the Early Modern era as well, variation and creativity in thinking on prophecy appeared. This seems particularly to have been true regarding the duties (*officia*) of the prophet.

Concerning thinking on prophetic *officia* and activities, one finds various views, sometimes quite interesting; even slightly bizarre. Both Conrad Pellican (1539, 141) and Rudolph Gwalther (1590, 208r), for instance, explained that part of what fulfilled one's duty as a prophet was the simple act of being taught. *Listening*, in other words, was a part of the prophet's calling, in their judgment. Peter Martyr Vermigli set out an equally intriguing, and fuller, list of duties: "We also see here four duties (*officia*) of prophets which are set forth: first, fighting falsehood and teaching truth; second, predicting the future; third, doing miracles; and finally, praying on behalf of those who are afflicted" (1566, 117b). Praying and miracle-working, in particular, both catch the eye as peculiar ideas to be associated with the prophet.

This innovation and creativity led to more sophisticated musings on the duties of the prophet by some of these theologians. Here we might stick with Vermigli a moment longer. Much of his analysis of prophecy was quite historical in its approach. For instance, he asserted that there is, with respect to prophecy, a discrimination of times (*discrimina temporum*) (1567, 112r). Elaborating, he noted that there were prophets before the law, "Abraham, Noah, Enoch and Adam," prophets during the time of the law, "such as Moses and others," and prophets during the apostolic era, "such as the prophecies of many holy men during the time of the primitive church" (1567, 112r). Such historical framing, which is also found in the thinking (on prophecy) of individuals like Martin Bucer (1527, 84v–85r and 1530, 113v–115v) and Wolfgang Musculus (1569, 106), is significant in the case of Vermigli, because of how he employed it.

Vermigli employed this historical framing as part of his assessment of redemptive history and the role prophets play in that history. What we find is the following: Vermigli's treatment of the standard Pauline passages followed fairly familiar lines of inquiry (discussing prediction of the future (1579, 82v, 106v, 205r–207r), the ordinary ministry of the word (*ad verbi ministerium*) (1579, 206v–207r), and so forth),[3] and gave the very clear sense that Vermigli did not believe that the New Testament prophetic office continued into the post-apostolic church. In fact, he stated that the prophetic office ceased following the church's primitive era (1579, 81r). As one examines his views as stated in the whole of his corpus more thoroughly, though, it becomes clear that he had more in mind when discoursing on this topic than might immediately be apparent. Accordingly, turning to Vermigli's Old Testament commentaries, we find him stating: "[i]n my judgment, it ought not to be denied that there are still prophets in the church" (1579, 81r). This idea may appear to contradict what he said elsewhere. But, he explained his views further and in a manner which alleviated the potential for contradiction within the Italian's thinking. We see this, for instance, in his treatment of 1 Samuel, when he explained:

> If the ordinary ministry at any time does not fulfill their duty, God raises up prophets extraordinarily (*extra ordinem*) in order to restore things to order (1567, 113r).

Here, Vermigli proposed an idea which is able to be held without contradicting his earlier statement about the end of prophecy. He seemed, in other words, to believe the prophetic office had, in fact, ceased within the church as an *ordinary* office—an office like that of pastor or deacon—but was still employed by God as an *extraordinary* calling.

Now, Vermigli's proposal may well be the product of an era in which the idea of extraordinary reformers had arisen time and time again, the notion ingraining itself in the thought and imagination of the men and women of the era. We know Vermigli believed Zwingli to be one such prophet-reformer, the latter's writings being influential in Vermigli's turn to Protestantism. Thus, the above-cited statement from Vermigli's 1 Samuel commentary offers a kind of theological explanation (and perhaps justification) for the rise of individuals like Zwingli, and a verification of the truthfulness of Protestantism—and a sophisticated explanation at that.

Wherever it came from, Vermigli's idea of extraordinary prophets was novel. To be sure, Thomas Aquinas and Denis the Carthusian spoke, as we saw earlier, of prophets as those who encouraged and labored for personal reform. But what Vermigli was proposing was different. His was a seismic doctrinal reformation of a church that had gone astray and, in the case of the Early Modern papacy, had

---

3 For more on Vermigli's views on prophecy, see Jon Balserak (2012).

been taken over by Satan himself, whereas Thomas and Denis appear to have had in mind much-less grandiose reformations focused on (personal) moral improvement. To be sure again, individuals who could justifiably have been identified as extraordinary prophets had been raised up by God in previous eras, hundreds of years before Luther or Zwingli. Here one could think of Joachim of Fiore, Francis of Assisi, or Birgitta of Vadstena and innumerable others. But what is unique about Vermigli's analysis is *not* that he was proposing that God had never done this before, but rather that he was explaining in a new and theologically-sophisticated way what God does for the good of his church from time to time.

Vermigli was not alone in being novel. Some of his contemporaries, such as Philip Melanchthon and John Calvin, also set out similar views. Melanchthon's assertion is less substantial, but nonetheless still important. He declared it, unsurprisingly, of Martin Luther, identifying Luther as a prophet produced to reform. Melanchthon did this in his discussion of New Testament prophets. As examples of those prophets mentioned by Paul in 1 Corinthians who, Melanchthon explained, are singularly gifted for the renewal of doctrine, he stated: "as Augustine was in his age and Luther is in ours" (CR 15: 1133–34).

Melanchthon's brevity might have impressed John Calvin, who loved brevity, but on this occasion Calvin was not able to emulate it. On this topic, Calvin was (like Vermigli) more verbose, employing language impressively similar to that employed by Vermigli. When lecturing on Jeremiah 32, Calvin explained that "when through either laziness or ignorance, the priests failed in the performing of their office, God raised up prophets in their place" (CO 39: 28). Calvin also made the same remark in comments on Amos 7: 10–13 (CO 43: 131–32). In fact, in comments on Micah 3: 11–12, Calvin used the same phrase that was employed by Vermigli.

> We said elsewhere that it happened through the laziness of the priests that prophets were added ... [because of the irresponsibility and corruption of the priests] ... it became necessary that prophets should be raised up as it were extraordinarily (*quasi extra ordinem*) (CO 43: 333–4).

Whether one of them influenced the other or either of them were aware of the language the other was using is not the point. The issue worth highlighting, so far as this chapter is concerned, is that these theologians were explaining the rise of post-apostolic prophets in a novel way when considered from the perspective of Christian history

This idea of extraordinary prophets being called forth by God to implement wholesale reformation of the Christian church was one which these Protestant theologians applied to the Old Testament prophets as well as to the prophet who had arisen in their own day. The Old Testament prophets stood in a kind of relationship with their Early Modern counterparts. Both groups (Elijah, Isaiah, and Jeremiah during the Old covenant era and Luther, Zwingli, and Oecolampadius in the Early Modern covenant era) were, according to this reading of history, called and divinely-equipped to right the ship of God's church. Both lived with divine scriptures which were being ignored and trampled on by their respective covenant communities: Isaiah and Jeremiah had the Books of Moses, Luther and Zwingli the whole Christian Bible. Both, then, were not so much adding new revelation (though of course Vermigli, Melanchthon, and Calvin all believed that the Old covenant prosecutors were producing new revelation) as imposing, with divine authority, the *true* reading of the scriptures upon the covenant communities whom they served.

Such a reading of the prophetic office was, indeed, novel and had a certain symmetry and beauty to it, despite raising some theological problems (such as why Isaiah's interpreting of the law counted as inspired scripture but not Zwingli's).

3.   Conclusion

The Reformation church had a 1500 year vault of reflections on prophecy and the prophetic office from which to draw. This resulted in some strong continuities with lines of thinking on prophecy that could be traced back to the earliest post-apostolic writings the church had produced. Yet, it also resulted in novelty, as members of the Reformed community thought creatively about their environment and about the theological emphases and practical applications being made by inspired teachers like Martin Luther, Johannes Oecolampadius, and Ulrich Zwingli. Vermigli, Melanchthon, and Calvin all worked within the confines of the medieval tradition on this question of the nature of prophecy, as they did when dealing with so many other theological loci. Yet, as I have attempted to show, they also worked to break new ground.

To be sure, prophets and prophetesses had arisen prior to the sixteenth century, who sought to reform the churches in which they were raised. It was, however, a mark of the theological and historical acumen of men like Melanchthon, Vermigli, and Calvin that they were the ones to rethink—via biblical categories—the function or duties (*officia*) of the prophet, against the backdrop of redemptive history and their own love for the Old Testament.

4. Bibliography

ALBERTUS MAGNUS. S.D.E. (1952), Alberti Magni . . . Opera Omnia. 19 vols. Münster i. W: Aschendorff.

ALPHANDÉRY, PAUL (1932), "Prophètes et ministère prophétique dans le Moyen Age latin." Revue d'Histoire et de Philosophie Religieuses, 12, 334–59.

AMBROSIASTER (1516), Divi Ambrosii episcope Mediolanensis omnia . . . Basel: A. Petri.

AQUINAS, THOMAS (1852–73), Sancti Thomae Aquinatis doctoris angelici Opera Omnia ... Parma: P. Fiaccadori.

— S. Thomae Aquinatis (1951), ... super Evangelium S. Matthaei Lectura, ed. P. Raphaelis Cai OP. Taurini: Marietti.

— St Thomas Aquinas (2006), Summa Theologiae, vol. 45 (2a2ae. 171–178) Prophecy and Other Charisms, tr. Roland Potter OP. Cambridge: Cambridge University Press.

BALSERAK, JON (2012), 'We need Teachers today, not Prophets;' Peter Martyr Vermigli's Exposition of Prophecy in Archiv für Reformationsgeschichte 103, 148–172.

BONAVENTURE (1891–1902), Opera Omnia S. Bonaventurae, 10 vols. Quaracchi: Saint Bonaventure College Press.

BRENZ, JOHANNES (1588), In Epistolam, quam apostolus Paulus ad Romanos scripsit, commentariorum libri tres. Tübingen: Georgius Gruppenbachius.

BUCER, MARTIN (1527), Epistola Epistola D. Pauli ad Ephesios, . . . Strasbourg: s.n.

— (1530), Enarrationes perpetuæ in Sacra Quatuor Evangelia, recognitæ nuper [et] locis compluribus auctæ . . . Argentorati: Georgius Ulricherus Andlanus.

BUGENHAGEN, JOHANNES (1524), Annotationes Ioan. Bugenhagii Pomerani in X. epistolas Pauli, scilicet, ad Ephesios, . . . Hebraeos. Strassburg: Apud Iohannem Hervagium.

BULLINGER, HEINRICH (1532), De prophetae officio, et quomodo digne administrari posit, oratio. Zurich: Froschouerus.

— (1534), In priorem d. Pauli ad Corinthios epistolam, Heinrychi Bullingeri commentaries. Zurich: Froschouer.

— (1538), De scripturae sanctae authoritate . . . perfection, deque Episcoporum, . . . Libri duo. Zurich: Froschouerus.

— (1557), In Apocalypsim conciones centum. Basel: Johannes Oporin.

— (1575), Heinrychi Bullingeri Jeremias fidelissimus et laboriosissimus Dei Propheta ... concionibus CLXX. Zurich: C. Froschouerus.

CACIOLA, NANCY (2003), Discerning Spirits: Divine and Demonic Possession in the Middle Ages. New York: Cornell University Press, 2003.

CALVIN, JOHN (1863–1900), Ioannis Calvini Opera Quae Supersunt Omnia, 59 vols. Ed. Wilhelm Baum, Eduard Cunitz, and Eduard Reuss, Corpus Reformatorum, 29–87. Brunswick: C. A. Schwetschke.

CROUZET, DENIS (1990), Les Guerriers de Dieu: La Violence au temps des troubles de religion (vers 1525–vers 1610). 2 vols. Seyssel: Champ Vallon.

DENIS THE CARTHUSIAN (1558), D. Dionysii Carthusiani insigne opus commentariorum in Psalmos omnes Davidicos, Cologne: apud Haeredes J. Quentelii & G. Calenium.

ERASMUS, DESIDERIUS (1516), Novum instrumentum. Basel: Johann Froben.

— (1518), In Epistolam Pauli Apostoli ad Romanos Paraphrasis (Basel: Johann, Froben.

ESTIUS, GUILIELMUS (1841), Estius in Omnes Canonicas Apostolorum Epistolas. Paris: Mogunriae.

FRANÇOIS LAMBERT OF AVIGNON (1525), Praefatio in In Primum Duodecim Prophetarum, nempe, Oseam . . . Strasbourg: Johan Hervagium.

GREGORY THE GREAT (1986), Homélies sur Ézéchiel. Latin text, introduction, tr., and notes by Charles Morel SJ. Paris: Les Éditions du Cerf.

GWALTHER, RUDOLPH (1566), In D. Pauli apostoli epistolam ad Romanos homiliae. Zurich: Froschauerus.

— (1577), In prophetas duodecimo, quos vocant minores, Rodolphi Gualtheri . . . homiliae. Zurich: Froschoverus.

— (1583), Isaias: in Isaiam prophetam Rodolphi Gvaltheri Tigurini homiliae CCCXXVII. Zurich: Froschouerus.

— (1590) In Epistolam D. Pauli Apostoli ad Corinthios Priorem. Zurich: Froschouerus.

HOFFMAN, MELCHIOR (1526), Das XII. Capitel des propheten Danielis ausgelegt, . . . christen nutzlich zu wissen. Stockholm: Königliche Druckerei.

HUGH OF ST CHER (1977), Théorie de la prophétie et philosophie de la connaissance aux environs de 1230: La Contribution d'Hugues de Saint-Cher (Ms. Douai 434, Question 481), ed. Jean-Pierre Torrell OP. Leuven: Spicilegium Sacrum Lovanense.

JEROME (1977), Commentaire sur Saint Matthieu. Latin text, introduction, tr., and notes by Émile Bonnard. Paris: Sources chrétiennes.

MCGINN, BERNARD (1985), The Calabrian Abbot: Joachim of Fiore in the History of Western Thought. New York: Macmillan Publishing Co.

MELANCHTHON, PHILIP (1540), Commentarii in epistolam Pauli ad Romanos hoc anno M.D.XL. recogniti & locupletati. Strasbourg: Apud Cratonem Mylium.

— (1834–60), Corpus Reformatorum: Philippi Melanthonis opera quae supersunt omnia. 28 vols., ed. Karl Bretschneider and Heinrich Bindseil. Halle: A. Schwetschke & Sons.

MUSCULUS, WOLFGANG (1569), In Epistolas Apostoli Pauli ad Galatas, et Ephesios Commentarii. Basel: Hervagius.

NICHOLAS OF LYRA (1483), Lyra Biblia Latina: Biblia Latina cum postillis Nicolai de Lyra et expositionibus Guillelmi Britonis in omnes prologos S. Hieronymi et additionibus Pauli Burgensis replicisque Matthiae Doering. Nuremberg: Anton Koberger.

OECOLAMPADIUS, IOHANNES (1526), In Epistolam B. Pauli Apost. Ad Rhomanos Adnontationes a Ioanne Oecolampadio Basileae praelectae, & denuo recognitae. Basel: Andr. Cratandrum.

OLEVIANUS, GASPAR (1579), In epistolam D. Pauli Apostoli ad Romanos notae, ex Gasparis Oleviani concionibus excerptae, & a Theodoro Beza editae . . . Geneva: Apud Eustathium Vignon.

PATROLOGIAE CURSUS COMPLETUS, SERIES GRAECA (1857–99), 161 vols., ed. Jacques Paul Migne. Paris: Garnier, vol. 30: Basil the Great, Enarratio in Isaiam Profetam; vol. 80: Cyril of Alexandria, In Ezekiel; vol. 22: Eusebius, Demonstratio Evangel. v Prol; vol. 56: John Chrysostom, Homiliae in Isaiae; vol. 80: Theodoretus of Cyrus, In Psalm. Praef.

PATROLOGIAE CURSUS COMPLETUS, SERIES LATINA (1844–1904), 221 vols. ed. Jacques Paul Migne. Paris: Garnier, vol. 34: Augustine, Super Gen. ad litt. Libri duodecim; vol 153: Bruno the Carthusian. Expositio In Epistolas Sancti Pauli; vol. 70: Cassiodorus.

In Psalterium Praefatio; vol. 117: Haymo of Halberstadt. In Divi Pauli Epistolas Expositio. and Enarratio In Duodecim Prophetas Minores; vol. 181: Herveus Burgidolensis. Commentaria In Epistolas Divi Pauli; vol. 82: Isidore of Seville. Etymologiarum Libri Viginti; vol 25: Jerome. Commentariorum in Amos Prophetam Libri Tres; vol. 28: Jerome. Prolog.I & II Para; vol. 150: Lanfranc of Bec. In Epistolam I ad Corinthios; vol. 191: Peter Lombard. Prologo super Psalmos; vol. 30: Pseudo-Jerome. Commentarius In Epistolas Sancti Pauli [Incertus]; vol 112: Rhabanus Maurus. Enarrationum In Epistolas Beati Pauli; vol. 114: Walafrid Strabo (Anselm of Loan). Glossa Ordinaria; vol. 180: William of St Thierry. Expositio in Epistolam Ad Romanos.

PELLICAN, CONRAD (1539), In omnes apostolicas epistolas, Pauli, Petri, Iacobi, Ioannis et Iudae D. Chuonradi Pellicani . . . Zurich: Officina Froschoviana.

— (1582), In Prophetas Maiores et Minores, ut vulgo vocantur, hoc est, in Isaiam, Ieremiam, . . . Commentarii Conradi Pellicani . . . Zurich: Christoph. Froschouerus.

REEVES, MARJORIE (1969), The Influence of Prophecy in the Later Middle Ages: A Study in Joachimism. Oxford: Oxford University Press.

SAVONAROLA, GIROLAMO (1996), Compendio di Rivelazioni; Trattato sul Governo della città di Firenze. Casale Monferrato: Piemme.

VERMIGLI, PETER MARTYR (1560), In Epistolam S. Pauli Apostoli ad Rom. D. Petri Martyris, Vermilii Florentini, . . . commentarii doctissimi, cum tractatione perutili rerum & locorum, qui ad eam epistolam pertinent. Basel: Petrum Pernam.

— (1566), Est regum libri Duo posteriores cum commentariis Petri Martyris Vermilii. Zurich: Froschouerus.

— (1567), In duos libros Samuelis prophetæ qui uulgo priores libros Regum appellantur D. Petri Martyris Vermilii . . . Commentarii doctissimi,, cum rerum & locorum plurimorum tractatione perutili. Zurich: Froschouerus.

— (1579), In Primum librum Mosis, qui vulgo Genesis dicitur, commentarii doctissimi D. Petri Martyris, Vermilii Florentini, . . . nunc denuo in lucem editi. Zurich: Froschoerus.

— (1579), In Selectissimam D. Pauli Apostoli Primum ad Corinthios Epistolam Commentarii. Zurich: Froschoerus.

VOADEN, ROSALYNN (1999), God's Word, Women's Voices: The Discernment of Spirits in the Writing of Late-Medieval Women Visionaries. Rochester, NY: Boydell & Brewer.

WILLIAM OF AUXERRE (1500), Summa Aurea in quattuor Libros Sententiarium. Frankfurt: Minerva.

WRIGHT, DAVID F. (2006), Why was Calvin So Severe a Critic of Nicodemism?, in: Calvinus Evangelii Propugnator: Calvin Champion of the Gospel; Papers Presented at the International Congress on Calvin Research, Seoul, 1998, David F. Wright/Tony N. S. Lane/Jon Balserak (ed.), Grand Rapids: CRC Product Services, 66–90.

ZWINGLI, ULRICH (1525), De Vera et Falsa Religione . . . Commentarius. Zurich: Froscherus.

— (1905–59), Sämtliche Werke, ed. Emil Egli, Georg Finsler, and Walther Köhler. Berlin: Schwetschke.

Stefan Lindholm

Reformed Scholastics Christology: A Preliminary Sketch

1. Introduction

The debate between Martin Luther and Huldrych Zwingli about Christ's presence in the Eucharist gave rise to a sustained Christological debate. This debate continued to exercise a considerable influence on Reformed and Lutheran theologians in the post-reformation period. In this article, I shall not endeavour to offer a complete discussion of what followed after the first reformers but confine myself to some samples of both the traditional features as well as some more constructive features of Reformed scholastic Christology. My focus will be on the scholastic element of Christology in Reformed thought, on a rather small selection of central scholastic Christological *loci* found in the Reformed theologians of the period. Still, with this narrow focus, it should be pointed out that the range and number of texts about Christology in Reformed scholastic tradition and their deeply integrated philosophical concepts are presently not fully researched. Much research needs to be done, both on the historic as well as the systematic and philosophical aspects of Reformed Scholastic Christology for us to get a more comprehensive understanding of it (See e.g. Lindholm, 2016; Muller, 2008; Cross, 2000; Zuidema, 2008; Willis, 1966; Trueman, 2002; Spencer, 2000). I offer this chapter as a primer to fellow students, new and old.[1]

In the second section, I begin by outlining some interpretative problems when approaching Christology in said period. Then, in the third section, I introduce and exemplify the use of two Reformed principles that permeate, not only Christology but Reformed theology as a whole. In the fourth section, I look at some ways in which the Reformed tackled problems concerning the heart of the Christological debate: the hypostatic union and the communication of properties. In the fifth section I discuss a Reformed variety of the communication of

---

1 In order to facilitate further study for readers, I have chosen to use the few English translations of Christological texts. I have used Heppe's translations but sometimes changed it where I found it necessary. All other translations are my own.

properties. I conclude with some remarks about the implications of Reformed Christology for systematic and Sacramental theology.

2.   Old Problem in New A Guise

At the end of the historical overview of "Classical Christology" in his *Jesus Christ in Modern Thought*, John Macquarrie briefly comments on the Christology of Calvin (who he presents as "by common consent the best of the reformation theologians"). He reports that not much happened in Christology during the post-reformation scholastic period since it "remained firmly committed to Chalcedonian Christology" (1990, 171). And the next chapter rather abruptly leaps forward in time, to the dawn of a "new era" starting with Immanuel Kant. But such historiography is slightly misleading. It is true that many any of the old issues from the patristic and medieval scholastic period were reiterated in the protestant Christological debate but they did so in a new guise and with a new focus. For there is more wiggle room in the Chalcedonian tradition of Christology than what Macquarrie seems to suppose. There are (at least) two major factors we need to consider when we approach Reformed Scholastic Christology. First, that Reformed Christology was propelled and to large degree shaped by its opposition to (some) Lutheran understandings of the communication of properties. The early 16th century Eucharistic debate between the Lutherans and the Reformed demonstrated that a Christological shift had occurred: from the unity of the person in two natures (the standard problem in patristic and scholastic Christology) to the relation of the natures of the person. Second, that Reformed Christology was not merely built up around its opposition to Lutheranism but also exemplified a particular reception of the medieval scholastic Christology. (I shall discuss this factor more explicitly in section five below.)

The Lutheran scholastic discussion of the communication of properties, was codified in Martin Chemnitz's *On the Two Natures of Christ* ([1571] 1971) and the Formula of Concord ([1577] 1921) which distinguished between "three genera" (*tria genera*) of communication.[2] First, there is the idiomatic genus (*genus idiomatum*), which occurs when one predicates properties or *idiomata* from the two natures to the whole person of Christ. Second, the apotelesmatic genus (*genus apotelesmaticum*) concerns the works or salvific or *theandric* actions of the God-man. Third, the majestic genus (*genus maiestaticum*) signify the divine prerogatives and gifts that the human nature was enriched with in the incarnational

---

2 The order of the genera differs in the Formula and Chemnitz's work. Here I follow Chemnitz' order.

economy.[3] The third genus was the most controversial – the Lutheran "Ubiquitarians" used it to justify the omnipresence (*ubiquitas*) of Christ's human nature. There was in fact more than one view of ubiquity within the Lutheran context. Johannes Brenz advocated an absolute ubiquity of the human nature of Christ (see Brandy, 1991; Haga, 2012; Garwrisch, 1980). Martin Chemnitz held a moderate view, implying that Christ could be present in as many places simultaneously as he willed according to his human nature (*multivolipreaesentia*). Chemnitz tended to restrict the multipresence of Christ's human nature to the Ecclesiastical and Eucharistic contexts since those were plainly supported by promises in Scripture. Whatever the differences in details between these two groups, the third genus became an important concept to both interpretations of ubiquity (See Lindholm, 2016, ch. 5; Hägglund, 1980).

Now, there is a long held belief that the Reformed and the Ubiquitarians differed only with regard to the majestic genus (E. g. Strong, 1907, III, 560–1). That assumption does not quite capture some important nuances in the debate. For instance, the apotelesmatic genus was not understood in the same way by the two groups of protestant scholastics. Many Lutherans had asserted that the idiomatic and the apotelesmatic genera would not be possible without the majestic genus. Thus, the majestic genus seemed to them a prerequisite for the two other genera. For if there were no communication between the two natures there would not be any sign or evidence of a real sharing of *idiomata* and operations in one *hypostasis*. The hypostatic union was thought to yield a communication between the natures as well. Martin Chemnitz states the Lutheran position:

> From [the hypostatic] union a certain communication results between the united natures and their attributes, not indeed a natural or essential communion but, because of the personal union, a communion like that between the soul and the animated body or between fire and heated iron. For the things which are proper to the natures become the property of the person on account of the union." (1971, 72).

Here we see that the first and the third genera are closely bound together. Likewise, some of the things falling under the concept of *apostelesmata* could also fall under the concept of the majestic genus. This mixing of genera seems to be rooted in a rather fluid distinction between supernatural gifts and powers on the one hand and uncreated or divine gifts and powers on the other. For instance, Christ's power to raise Lazarus from the dead does not necessarily require a communication of uncreated powers but could either be construed as a miraculous gift (akin to that of the holiest of prophets in the biblical story such as Moses and Elijah) or that such miraculous gifts are not proper gifts of miraculous

---

3 In the 17th century, the debate between the Gißen and Tübingen lutherans developed a kenotic model of Christology and came to distinguished a fourth kenotic genus (*genus kenoticum*)

powers but merely a strong and intimate faith in God's power to bring about supernatural events. As Turretin points out: "the power of making alive" "belongs to God alone" and "the life of God is nothing else than is very active essence, which cannot be communicated to a created nature." (Turretin, 1992–7, II, 327)

As I have just mentioned, the Reformed scholastics did not merely react to the above understanding of the *tria genera* but developed their own view(s) of a supernatural communication of gifts to the human nature. We will come back to that later on. For now, we will look at a basic distinction that undergirded the debate.

3.   Two Reformed Principles and their Christological Use

There are two (in)famous principles operative in Reformed theology: (i) "the finite cannot grasp the infinite" (*finitum non capax infintini*) and (ii) the so-called *extra calvinisticum* which became the phrase which expressed the idea that the "Logos was also outside the flesh" (*Logos etiam extra carnem*) (See relevant entries in Muller, 1985). Although they are not unique to Reformed Christology, they have given a special shape to it (See Willis, 1966). Reformed dogmaticians took it for granted that the two principles expressed a proper understanding of the Chalcedonian Creed, especially the "negative adverbs" which say that the person of Christ is to be: "recognized in two natures, without confusion, without change, without division, without separation" (Tanner, 1986, I, 86). Indeed, the principles seem to naturally undergird the rejection of confusion and change of the divine and the human natures in Christ. However, they may seem to sit less comfortably with the negation of division and separation of the two natures. For if what is finite cannot contain or grasp the infinite and if the divine infinite nature also remains "outside" human nature in the incarnation it seem like we would generate an unorthodox division and separation of the natures. This was certainly a Lutheran suspicion. The Reformed theologians answered unanimously that the union is not a proper union unless there is a *distinction* between the things united. For a distinction is not necessarily the same thing as separation and division. A union requires two distinct realities unless the union is to annul the proper differences. Moreover, because the Logos is infinite it can also assume the finite *without* having to limit itself or stop governing and ruling the universe. Thus, unless the divine and human nature of Christ retain their respective characteristics in their union there remains nothing to separate or divide.

Two further comments on the two principles are in order (See, Lindholm, 2016, 124–139 for details of this and the next paragraph). First the *extra calvinistcum* could be read as a derivation from the *non capax*. If the finite cannot contain or grasp the infinite, the infinite divine nature will by necessity not be limited to the human nature, it will also be "outside" it. However, this should not be interpreted as a negation of the special and hypostatic presence of the Logos in human nature. By asserting that the divine nature is "also outside the flesh" (*etiam extra carnem*) the Reformed scholastics wanted to say that the special presence of the Logos in human nature does not exhaust the mode of the Logos' being.

Second, all finite being is a form of universally restricted and received being. A finite being is expressed through its own essence in that its mode of being is received and dependent on God (whereas God's infinite essence is not restricted or received in this way). Therefore, the Reformed scholastics tended to ground the *non capax* in the distinction between Creator as non-dependent (*a se*) and creation as dependent, ultimately in the attributes of divine simplicity which are the opposites of the universal creaturely attributes of composition. Whatever is composite is changeable and exists contingently and cannot contain that which is simple, unchangeable and *per se* necessary. This metaphysical model of creation as universally compositional also has an epistemic consequence: a composite intellect cannot understand that which is simple according its own mode of being.

The two principles are found all across the Reformed scholastic theological spectrum, especially the *non capax* as it was integrated into their Aristotelian understanding of nature. A presupposition in many arguments is that the finite and infinite modes of being cannot be conflated without contradiction. All finite natures are determined or restricted by their own mode of being, while the divine infinite nature is not. The Ubiquitarians accepted a basic Aristotelian school of metaphysics (see, Sparn, 1976) but integrated it with Christology in a different way than the Reformed. They assumed that unless the two natures are everywhere co-present, they would not be properly united in the person of Christ. Therefore, they found ways to argue for an *illocal* mode of the human nature of Christ, which would make it possible for Christ as man to walk through closed doors and be present in the Eucharist in many places at the same time (Thus, Hollartz in Schmid, 1899, 298). The Reformed argued for the opposite position, that the human nature retained its local and circumscriptive characteristics also in its union with the Logos (Baur, 2007). They contended that the divine nature then somehow would be enclosed in the human nature of Christ and that the finitude of human nature would be destroyed or rendered a Docetic illusion (Beza, 1570, 513). Thus, Turretin expresses the Reformed objection to the Ubiquitarians:

> "Locality and illocality are contradictories which cannot belong to the same thing... For the hypostatic union does not take away the nature of the body, it does not abolish its local being and so cannot give it an illocal being because what leaves one part of the contradiction cannot at the same time ascribe to it the other" (Turretin, 1992–7, II, 332)

We may even find corollaries and applications of the *non capax* principle implicit in philosophical works. For instance, Johann Heinrich Alstead argues in his *Metaphysica* from a metaphysical principle to a Christological *ad absurdum* position against the Ubiquitarians:

> [Third Theorem.] Unless a thing remain itself it cannot be. The reason is that the mode [of being] is nothing other than [its] the determination or, as Scalinger puts it, prescription of a thing. Therefore, if the mode of a thing will not be implied it will undo the nature (1616, Appendix Theorema III, 283).[4]

Alstead then uses the Ubiquitarian position as a telling example of how to break such a metaphysical *fundamenta*. According to Alstead, they patently contradict this theorem when they claim that, "the body of Christ is in heaven according to the natural mode and in, with and under the bread according to the majestic mode". But a thing cannot have such diverse modes of being (i.e. finite and infinite) and remain itself (idem, 284).[5]

In this section I have given examples of some of the ways in which the two principles functioned in Reformed scholastic Christology. We will have reason to come back to them as we now start to treat other topics. I will now continue to discuss the central issues in the 16th and 17th Christological debates: the hypostatic union and the communication of properties.

4.   The Hypostatic Union and the Communication of Properties

There are obvious similarities between the medieval and the Reformed scholastic treatments of the hypostatic union and a range of related topics that they chose worthy of attention. But as I just pointed out, the Reformed scholastics worked in a different polemical context than their medieval forbearers. (See, Lindholm, 2016, ch. 4). The hypostatic union was often discussed in terms of the patristic *similes* like the glowing iron, the sun and the rays and, above all, the soul-body

---

4 "[Theorema] III. *Modus rei nisi res ipsa maneat, nequit esse.* Ratio: quia modus nihil est aliud quàm rei determinatio, &, ut Scaliger ait, praescriptio. Iccirco modus non implicabit, sed explicabit naturam."

5 "Quicunque igitur modi abolent & destruunt rem, non sunt tolerandi. Tales sunt hi modi Ubiquitariorum: Corpus Christi est in coelo *naturali modo,* in, cum & sub pane *modo maiestatico:* Deus est omnipraesens per *modum* οὐσίας, corpus Christi per *modum* ἐξουσίας. Vide *Sadeelem de verit. humanae naturae Christi.* Hi & consimiles modi destruunt res ipsas, quorum modi esse dicuntur. Modi autem veri, sive sint naturales, sive supernaturales, sunt qui in Metaphysicis habent fundamentum. Exempli gratiâ, hic est modus essendi in Metaphysicâ: *aliquid est vel absolutè, vel respectivè.* Hic modus accommodatur ad varias materias: ut principi infligitur vulnus vel absolutè, cùm vulnus est in ipso principis corpore, vel σχετικῶς, cùm laeditur proprinceps, eiúsve legatus. Patiente Ecclesiâ, patitur Christus, non ἐν ἑαυτῷ, sed relatè: quia passio illa refertur ad Christum." (*Metaphysica,* 284).

union and the relation between wholes and parts. Both the Lutheran and Reformed parties used such *similes* and tended to push their uses of them to fit their Christological viewpoint. The Reformed assumed that a metaphysical framework like the one I have sketched in the preceding section was necessary for a proper application and understanding of these *similes*. As with their patristic and medieval forbearers, the Reformed were acutely aware that *similes* drawn from creaturely unions could not properly explain the hypostatic union. It was *sui generis*. Much of their labour on details of the hypostatic union still involved comparing the unions drawn from creation that most closely resemble the hypostatic union although no single one individually or all of them collectively could provide an exact explanation of the hypostatic union (Zanchi, 1593, 197).[6] In doing this they juxtaposed the most proximate natural unions with the hypostatic unions in order to make a clear distinction. Guilherme Bucanus makes the striking remark that the soul-body union:

> ... is indeed a paradigm for the personal union [of Christ], but does not completely square with it. In a human a third nature emerges (which is called 'human nature') composed from the nature of the soul and the nature of the body. In Christ there is no construction of a single third nature out of divine and human; each remain pure and unconfused (1630, Loc. II, art. XV, 17; Heppe, 2000, 430).[7]

Accompanied with qualifications such as these, the soul-body union and other *similes* were allowed in order to illuminate aspects of the hypostatic union. Despite the rejection of literal composition in the quote, the Reformed were accustomed to talk of the hypostatic union in analogous compositional terms, which was also sanctioned by a long scholastic and patristic tradition (See, Cross, 2002, 27–136). Compositional, or parts-whole, predications are problematic and must be treated carefully. For instance, predication from one nature (or its properties) to the whole of Christ does not necessarily admit a transfer of properties to the other nature. That is the burden of proof that the Reformed had put on the Lutherans with regard to the third genus, whether a communication of majesty entails a transfer of properties between the natures. It was generally agreed among the Reformed scholastics that just as one cannot (unless by some figure of speech, *synchedoche*, or qualification) allow predicates of the soul to the whole also to be predicated of the body, one also cannot allow predicates of the divine nature to be predicated of the whole and at the same time to be predicated

---

6 "Modum vero, quo hae duae diversissimae naturae in una & eadem persona unitae sunt, non explicarunt quidem, sed satis tamen luculenter indicarunt."

7 "Cuius quidem paradigma est unio animæ & corporis, sed quod not per omnia quadrat. Nam in homine ex natura animæ, & ex natura corporis, furgit natura tertia ex duabus composita, quæ dicitur humana natura. Sed in Christo non sit constructio unius tertiæ naturæ, ex Divina & Humana, sed manet utraque pura & inconfusa."

of the human nature. Thus, special attention was here paid to the relations between parts and wholes. A characteristic formulation is found in Jerome Zanchi:

> What is composed of whatever parts has a natural imperfection since it is imperfect with regards to the whole. The divine nature is perfect. Therefore it should be denied that the person of the Word is composed from two natures as if [from] parts. Rather it should be agreed that [the Word] is composed from [the natures] as from numbers or by a numerical reason (1593, 224).[8]

A straightforward or literal composition of Logos and the two natures is thus denied since it would yield a third thing (as seen in the Bucanus quote above), a thing that in the final analysis is neither divine nor human and would amount to the heresy of monophyistism. Yet not every kind of composition is denied. In keeping with the Chalcedonian negative adjectives, Zanchi argues that the composition in Christ is not properly expressible in parts-whole discourse but from a *simile* of a numerical distinction, i. e. the distinction between the natures is not exactly like that between two parts of a whole but is still a numerical distinction between two realities or "things" (Cf. Aquinas, 1963–80, III, q. 2, ad. 4).

The Reformed theologians did not always bother to submit this sort of qualification in Christological parts-whole discourse to examination. For instance, Bartholomew Keckerman argues explicitly from the logical principle "Whatever is in a part in an unqualified way, is also in the whole in a limited way according to that part" (*Quicquid parti inest absolue, etiam toti insit limitate, secundum illam partem*) to the Christological case:

> Thus, since the person of Christ is a whole constituted from two natures as its parts, it therefore is necessary that also the properties and their characters which are from each [nature], are in the person of Christ – just as certainly parts are of and in the whole so that whatever is predicated of a part is of and in the whole. For example: The human nature is a part of the whole of the person of Christ and in the whole person. Therefore, whatever is in the human nature is also in the whole of the person, which has the human nature as part (1610, 317 ff.).[9]

---

8 "Quod enim est pars alicuius compositi, rationé habet imperfecti, & imperfecta res est respectu totius. Natura autem divina res est perfectissima. Negat igitur personam Verbi ex duabus naturis tamquam partibus esse compositiam: sed concedit esse compositiam ex illis tamquam ex numeris: seu ratione numeri." This numerical simile recurs in many of the scholastics and was picked up straight from Aquinas The composition is "from [ex] natures is not so called on account of parts, but by reason of number [*ratio numeri*], even as that in which two [things] concur may be said to be composed of them." (1963–80, ST III, q 2, a 4, ad 2.) ("dicendum quod illa compositio personae ex naturis non dicitur esse ratione partium, sed potius ratione numeri, sicut omne illud in quo duo conveniunt, potest dici ex eis composit.")

9 "Cum ergo persona Christi sit totum quid, constans ex duabus naturis, tanquam partibus; ideo necesse est proprietates quoque & indolem eam, quae omnibus inest, personae Christi inesse, ut nimirum, sicut partes sunt totius, & in toto, ita quoque partium praedicata sint totius & in

Despite Keckerman's explicit reliance on parts-whole discourse with reference to Logical canons, I do not think that this passage should be read as an *explanation* of the hypostatic union but as a way to respect and defend its uniqueness. What he does is to provide us rules with how (not) to predicate things about Christ drawing on a common principle in logic. In effect, his complaint is that the Ubiquitarians are not able to make the basic logical distinction between absolute and relative or limited predication (*distinguere inter praedicatatotorum absoluta & inter praedicata limitata*). For instance, we may say that the whole person was born of a virgin and omnipotent without any communication between the natures since the whole of Christ is the subject of all predications. Much of the debate issuing from the first reformers' Lord's Supper controversy concerned the proper understanding of abstract concrete predication on the one hand and real and verbal on the other. The Lutherans had contested that a predication from the natures to the person (the first genus) is merely verbal and not real since it does not take the reality of communication between the natures seriously enough (the third genus). Contrary to the Ubiquitarians, Keckerman argues, as did all his Reformed colleagues, that the kind of predication described above is a *real* and not merely verbal predication since it is a concrete predication signifying the *subject with two natures* and respecting their essential differences (see also, Heppe, 1952, 442–3).

The Reformed understanding of Christological parts-whole discourse is also connected to the two Reformed principles. They made basic distinction between *totus Christi* and *totum Christi* (The whole of Christ and the entire or everything that belongs to Christ). Armed with this distinction drawn from a long theological tradition,[10] the Reformed theologians argued against the Lutheran understanding of a real communication of properties (typically in a strong Brenzian form). They interpreted the Lutheran position to imply or state that that the divine nature was "contained" or "enclosed" in the human nature of Christ in the incarnation and that the human nature was extended in a limitless way (See Heppe, 2000, 418 f). Theirs was a failure to observe the *totus-totum* distinction and would lead to heretical conclusions like:

(1) The whole of Christ is omnipresent
(2) The whole of Christ includes the human nature [since it is inseparably united to the Logos]
(3) Therefore, the human nature is omnipresent

---

toto. Exempli gratia: Humana natura est pars totius personae Christi, & est in tota persona; ergo quicquid inest humanae naturae, id etiam inest toti personae, cuius pars est humana natura" (Here he refers to lib. 1. *Systematis logici, sectione* 1. cap. 22)

10 Its introduction to Reformed Christology is due to John Calvin who refers to Lombard's "trite" distinction but the distinction was established by John Damascene and Augustine (in his treatment of the *decensus ad inferno*) to which Calvin's colleagues refers frequently. See my (2016, 126 fn. 49)

The Reformed claimed that we may block such heretical inferences by making a proper distinction between the *totus Christi* and *totum Christi*. Thus, Jerome Zanchi argues (1593, 215):

(4) The whole of Christ (*totus Christi*) is omnipresent according to his eternal person

(5) But everything that belong to Christ (*totum Christi*) is not omnipresent, i. e. his human nature

(6) Therefore, Christ is not omnipresent according to his human nature

The force of such arguments depends on the success that a logico-grammatical distinction between person and nature can be achieved with the terms *totus* (masculine) signifying the person and *totum* (neuter) the natures and the person. Zanchi, in effect, claims that Ubiquitarians misunderstand the meaning to *totus* as it appears in proposition (1) by conflating it with *totum*. Therefore they draw the invalid inference from (1) to (3).

The *totus-totum* distinction seems to have had the same logical function for the Reformed scholastics as the so-called *qua*-locutions did for the medieval scholastics (see Cross, 2002, 181–205). The medievals debated the two standard analyses of Christological propositions like "This man is God" either as reduplicative statement "This man is God according to his divine nature" or a specificative statement "This man according to his divine nature is God". The Reformed used these sorts of distinctions (See Turretin, 1992–7, II, 321–332) in analysing the communication of properties but rather took the validity for granted than debating them. To the reformed the distinction between concrete (of the person in two natures) and abstract (of the natures and their properties) predication was of greater importance since abstract predication between the natures requires another kind of analysis than the received medieval forms. Not only were they now required to analyse propositions like "This man is God" but also "The human nature is omnipotent" and "humanity is divinity".

Interestingly, the Reformed were often insistent that Luther himself was not the cause of the confusion between concrete and abstract predication (E. g. Turretin, 1992–7, II, 332). Instead, Johannes Brenz became the object of their sustained criticism – not always by name and in an altogether fair way since they do not always make a proper distinction between the Chemnitizian multivolepresence and Brenz's absolute presence. Sadly, these differences were not made clear to the interlocutors, since it could have helped them to bring greater clarity to their discussion (See, Lindholm, 2016, 116).

Having looked at some central issues in the Reformed scholastic's treatment of the doctrine of the hypostatic union and the communication of properties we now turn to their view of the human nature of Christ and deepen our understanding of their own distinctive view of the communication of properties to the human nature.

5.   Christ's Human Nature and The Reformed Communication of Properties

The assumed nature was, according the Reformed, viewed as complete and fully human with regard to its essential properties and integral parts. Thus, the Leiden Synopsis states:

> "Indeed, [Christ] was a complete man, endowed with the natural and also essential properties, which are part of man in a necessary and inseparable way. Such properties belong to the whole human nature, namely that it is created and finite; or the properties belong to one part of [human nature,]" (*Synopsis*, Forthcoming, Disp 25, 12).

This was important since, as the Chalcedonian Creed had expressed it, the assumed nature should be like ours in every respect except sin. From John Damascene, mediated through the medieval scholastics, the Reformed were accustomed to speak of it as of an individual (*atomo*) (Cross, 2002, 23 and Zanchi, 1593, 123). In other words, the assumed nature is not a general human nature but a particularized human nature (Keckerman, 1610, 315). Turretin explicitly draws on the Aristotelian tradition and calls it a "first substance" (1992–7, 327 ff.), i.e. it is a particular existing nature with essential and accidental properties. As such it lacks none of the properties qualifying it for substancehood but it lacks the "metaphysical" property of existing through itself (*per se*) or subsistence. However, subsistence, as Turretin, argues, is neither a part of the essence of a nature nor an accidental property of a nature. Personhood is that for which (*terminus ad quem*) it exists. This does not leave the human nature of Christ "impersonal" (as modern critics of Chalcedon have sometimes concluded) but it becomes a person in a different way than other human natures, not having its own subsistence. The human nature *receives* personhood through another (*in alio*) in its perpetual union with the Logos: it is (in itself) *anhypostasis* but in the union *enhypostasis* (idem, 328)

These are fairly traditional theological opinions, concepts and distinctions, the details of which the medieval scholastics had worked out well and the Reformed were happy to emulate. However, there are other developments in the Reformed tradition. As we have seen, the Reformed emphatically rejected any teaching that destroys the finite and human element in Christ (on the basis of the *non capax* principle). But they were not content to merely reject Lutheran versions of a communication of infinite gifts to the human nature (and merely allow a communication of properties to the person of Christ). They allowed other types of communication. Turretin distinguishes between natural (or physical) and supernatural (or hyperphysical) on the one hand and majestic (or uncreated) modes of communication to the human nature of Christ on the other (1992–7, II, 332). The communication of natural properties is equivalent to saying that the human nature of Christ had a fully human make up. Turretin, and many Reformed theologians from this high scholastic period, seize the opportunity to elaborate on the physical weakness and psychic agony of the human nature. For instance, the Reformed often had a separate locus on the *descensus ad inferno* arguing strongly that descent does not mean that his soul moved into some inner place of the earth (contra some Lutherans and papists) but refers to the infernal torments in the state of humiliation of Christ (Heppe, 2000, 490–4) A quite standard Reformed understanding of the papist view of the suffering of Christ limits it to the bodily pains and do not include the sufferings of the soul. Although not entirely accurate on historical grounds, it provides a clue to their emphasis on the human nature and specially the suffering of the soul (Turretin, 1992–7, II, 353) The Reformed ascribed suffering to both the so-called lower and the higher parts of the soul, i. e. both the intellective and the appetitive parts, and thus could argue that Christ felt the spiritual agony of the wrath of God deeper than any other human.

A communication of supernatural properties does not contradict the natural properties of human nature since they are not uncreated (as the majestic properties are) but "finite extraordinary gifts" (*dona extraordinaria finita*) communicated to the human nature in the hypostatic union. The communication of supernatural properties is sometimes spoken of as "the grace of union" (*gratia unionis*) as the human nature is made to participate in the supernatural in an eminent way. Such properties are gifts from the Holy Spirit bequeathed to the human nature of Christ in order for Christ to perform the office of Mediator in both natures. The Holy Spirit was given to Christ's human nature "without measure" (Is. 11), resulting in Christ's impeccability and supernatural wisdom and knowledge. As expected, the Reformed scholastics are quick to assure us that "without measure" merely imply a communication of supernatural and finite gifts not infinite or uncreated gifts (See Heppe, 2000, 434–8 and cf. with Preus, 1972, 167). An unspoken assumption here is, of course, the commonplace medieval notion that supernatural grace does not destroy but perfects nature.

One of the most telling ways in which Christ's supernatural endowment comes forth is in what we may call the maximalist view of Christ's mind. This was the majority view of the medieval scholastics (Cross, 2002, 137–42; 1999 and Adams, 1999). For they claimed that Christ's human nature blissfully beheld the divine essence while being a pilgrim (*simul viator et comprehensor*). As a consequence, the range and depth of Christ's human knowledge is supernaturally maximalized – but not to the level of divine omniscience. Thus, they claimed, faith and hope were not virtues that the supernaturally enriched human nature of Christ needed while still in the state of a fellow pilgrim journeying toward God.

The Reformed scholastics tended not to accept this teaching without qualification and there are also some variations of opinion among them on the matter – although it never seemed to have caused any major debate. Some go along with the maximalist view of human nature like Jerome Zanchi who appropriates the scholastic view, saying that the vision of God of Christ's soul is full but not total or exhaustive (*Totam…sed non totaliter*). The reason he gives is familiar by now: the infinite cannot be comprehended by the finite in any way (*quia infinitum comprehenderi a finito nullo modo potest*) (1593, 366). The knowledge of Christ's soul was far above the knowledge of all other creatures, including the angels (1593, 373–4 and Muller, 1987–2003, I, 145–53). Hence, because Christ's soul is finite, the manner of apprehension of the supernatural gifts will not exalt it above its limitations, only to its maximum. As some leading medieval scholastics such as Thomas Aquinas and Henry of Genth (Cross, 2002, 138), Zanchi thought that Christ did not need the theological virtues of faith and hope since these were graces that assisted wayfarers not yet enjoying the beatific vision. With regards to faith he writes:

> Indeed, the soul of Christ does not see or know God with lesser clarity in his early existence, than the blessed souls in heaven. It is because of this most clear vision of God, the blessed souls in heaven are no more said to believe, or see God through faith but through sight…Therefore, if the blessed souls in heaven are no more said to believe, because they see God face to face, neither should the soul of Christ be said to have faith in so far as faith is a [habitual] gift, through which one believes what cannot be seen. [Christ's soul] sees God no less than the blessed souls (1593, 360–1).[11]

Zanchi adds that Christ's beatific knowledge is first in order and dignity (*ordine & dignitate prima est*) and given from conception (1593, 369). All saints "see" in the divine nature everything they need for their beatitude (though their sharing in divine omniscience can differ in degree) (1593, 367–8). Christ's soul also has this beatified knowledge of direct vision like the blessed souls in heaven, yet through the hypostatic union this grace was maximally conferred on Christ's soul as the Spirit is given to Christ beyond measure. Consequently, Zanchi thinks that Christ's soul knows everything actual – past, present and future – but not everything that God could have done (1593, 368).

---

11 "Certe anima Christi non minus clare vidit & nouit Deum in terries existens, quam nunc animae beatorum in cælo. Atqui propter hanc clarissimama Dei visionem, anminæ beatorum non amplius dicitur credere, aut Deum videre per fidem, sed per speciem [Ref. to 1st Cor. 13] Ergo si animæ beatorum in cælo non amplius dicuntur habere fidem: quia Deum à facie ad faciem vident: neq; etiam anima Christi diecenda est habuisse fidem, quatenus fides est donum, quo creduntur, quæ non videntur. Illa enim non minus videat Deum, quam animæ beatorum."

As I indicated, there were also more cautious voices within the Reformed community. For instance, Leonard Rissen, remarks that "not a few condemn Calvin, because he attributes faith to Christ. But that faith must not be denied *simpliciter* to Christ, [which] Scripture shows in more than one passage." (Heppe, 2000, 437).[12] Thus, presumably following the lead of Calvin, these theologians argued for a more developmental and limited view of the supernatural endowment, that not all the supernatural graces were given at once, or at least they were not developed at once. Instead, there is a succession of anointments of the Holy Spirit from conception to the public ministry of Christ (See Heppe, 2000, 448). This caution might be understood as a more or less conscious reaction to the medieval maximalist view. Having said that, we should perhaps add that it was probably also a consequence of their reception of Calvin's biblical Christology that did not always follow along the same terminological and conceptual patterns of the medieval scholastics. Doubtless such developments in the history of Reformed Christology was due to an increasing exegetical interest among the Reformed scholastics. Writers such as Vermigli, Zanchi and Keckerman did not always agree with Calvin but rarely did they make a show of their disagreement. Thus, it is interesting that by the time of Francis Turretin, he chooses not to argue against his colleagues but against the "papists" who have it that Christ was "at the same time a traveller and an attainer" (1992–7, II, 351). Being an attainer, Turretin says, signifies the state in which one enjoys the full vision of God and belongs to the saints while being a traveller signifies the state in which one has to rely on faith and not "sight". These are two opposite states, the attainer is at the goal and the traveller is on the road labouring and suffering. Christ had to suffer as a real human being for the redemption of humans and thus he had to "run the race set before him". For if Christ were already an attainer, the reality of the suffering would be endangered or rendered an illusion. We should be careful to note that Turretin did not attribute faith in an unqualified way to Christ although he says that faith is indeed attributable to Christ since Scripture does so (e. g. Heb. 2:17). But that faith is not a "fiduciary apprehension of the mercy of God" – since Christ is sinless, faith in God's mercy is not needed. "Rather", Turretin asserts, faith can be ascribed to Christ "as to substance of *knowledge and assent to a thing known* (i. e., to the doctrine revealed of God) and as to *trust*, which rests in the goodness of God providing everything necessary for us." (1992–7, II, 348. Emphasis mine).

Turretin here expresses a more limited and developmental view of the supernatural graces than the maximalist view does. A possible polemical reason for

---

12 Calvin had in fact gone quite far in emphasising that Jesus assumed weakness and defilement. (None, however, went so far as later theologians and affirmed an assumption of sin or sinfulness more than in terms of the consequences of the fall and the curse of God upon the human race.)

this is that he wants to make Christ's human suffering and finitude more vivid against two fronts: the Socinians and anti-trinitarians on the one hand and the "papists" and the Lutherans on the other. For against both fronts, Turretin tended to use traditional language and talk of the communication of habitual graces as a historic series of anointments, both in order to emphasise the humanness and the divinity or divine mission of Christ as Mediator. Such anointments were not given all at once, but began at conception and were "dispersed through intervals of time, as also through various objects." (idem.)

I shall also mention a particularly interesting advocate of the developmental view, the English puritan theologian, John Owen, whose so-called "Spirit Christology" highlights the humanness of Christ to a greater degree than his predecessors (See e.g. Crisp, 2011, ch. 5; Spence, 2007; Daniels, 2004). According to one interpretation of Owen, the only act of the Logos in the incarnation is the act of the assumption. All other (supernatural) acts are to be attributed to the Holy Spirit. Christ's incarnation and ministry thus depends just as the saints on the assistance of the Holy Spirit. Christ, according to this view, assumes not only our weakness but also our condition as humans dependent on God's work through the Spirit. It is clear, on this view, that no beatific vision needs to be communicated to the human mind of Christ in his earthly sojourn and, as Luke 2:40 and 52 reports, as a child Christ grew in wisdom. Thus, Christ's impeccability is not a consequence of the beatific vision but of the Spirit's work. This quick glance that we find in Owen more than in his predecessors that Christ's humanity is more like ours in every respect except sin since the divine assistance and dependence on God is emphasised and seems to do further justice to the whole of the biblical portrayal of Christ.

6.   Concluding Remarks

With these samples, I have merely scraped the surface of the richly embedded Christology of the Reformed scholastics. Much research remains to be done in order to do it full justice. In particular, the Reformed discussions about the human nature of Christ reveal a development that could be of use in contemporary systematic theology. In many ways one must applaud their attempts to negotiate the traditional, scholastic and confessional view of Christ with the humanness found in the biblical portrayal of Christ. I shall end this chapter with two evaluative remarks in order to indicate how we may understand and, perhaps, learn something from them.

I will take a page from the great 19th century Reformed dogmatician, Herman Bavinck, who argued that there is an essential similarity in the Roman Catholic and the Lutheran perspective on human nature. He claims that "both [the Roman

Catholics and the Lutherans] elevate human nature above the boundaries set for it and dissolve into mere appearance but the human development of Jesus and the state of his humiliation" (2002, 258). Thus, both "contain within them a docetic element. The purely human development [of Christ] does not come into its own." He writes that the Reformed:

> ...had fundamentally overcome the Greek-Roman and Lutheran commingling of the divine and the human, also in Christology [....] In that way Reformed theology secured space for a purely human development of Christ, for a successive communication of gifts, and for a real distinction between humiliation and exaltation ...not the substance [the underlying reality] but the subsistence [the particular being] of the Son assumed our nature (2002, 258-9).

The fundamental question here is what the boundaries of human nature are and at what point "elevation" becomes an *elimination* of human nature or, in Christological terms, Docetic. It is clearly a case of the *non capax* principle at work that we see here. For Bavinck, it was the Greek-Roman/Lutheran comingling that was the problem. It is interesting to note that at least some of the Reformed scholastics (that Bavinck so frequently consults in his *Reformed Dogmatics*) would tend to hold on to such a "comingling" view – as seen in the maximalist view of the human nature of Christ. In Bavinck's opinion, they would be in danger of Docetism. Is this a fair judgement? I shall leave it to the reader to answer this question.

I will, finally, briefly reflect on a particular Christological point, which has ramifications for systematic and sacramental theology. Some of the Reformed accepted a maximalist view of the human knowledge of Christ. Now, the medieval scholastics had in different ways also posited a paralleling supernatural enrichment to the *causal powers* of Christ's human nature, which ultimately is seen through their sacramental theology: the blessings effected in the participants of the Eucharist are caused by the supernaturally enriched human nature of Christ (Barnes, 2012). Why, then, did the Reformed scholastics only admit that the human intellect of Christ was supernaturally endowed; why could not also the human causal powers of Christ be equally enriched? Of course, they were not obliged to accept supernatural gifts attributed to Christ of that sort. Indeed, they naturally accepted a moral supremacy to the will of Christ as seen in the ascription of impeccability but they did not accept a power to bring about the effects of the Eucharist according to his human nature. The miracles of Christ were brought about through the power of the Spirit. So why, then, did Christ become incarnate if his humanness is rendered "inert" after the resurrection in the church's life? I shall not attempt to fully answer this loaded question but point out that the Reformed reception of the scholastic Christological tradition had another agenda. To put it very bluntly, the Reformed had no need for an elevated human nature that could work miracles in the way that medieval sacramental theological systems required. The Reformed scholastics tended to emphasise the power of the Holy Spirit in the supernatural ministry in the life of Christ (as well as in the sacramental life of the church). This is partly rooted in an understanding of the apotelesmatic genus which claims that the acts proper to the respective natures *co-operates* for one and the same salvific work and partly in a particular Trinitarian division of labour that constructively moulds belief in the western tradition that the acts of the trinity are undivided (See Wittman, 2013).

Furthermore, if we accept Bavinck's analysis, we should attribute to the Lutheran position a systemic or sacramental "need" of a supernaturally endowed causal power to the human nature of Christ. The Lutherans, as I pointed out in the second section, were not always clear on the difference between the second and the third genus and, as a consequence, the pneumatic element in Christology seems to be given very little room (or in danger of a causal over-determination, where endowed human nature and the Spirit are both sufficient causes for the same effect in the Eucharist.). In the Reformed tradition the Christological desiderata that Christ is to be "like us in every respect except sin" can, on the contrary, receive a non- or, perhaps, less reductive shape: Christ is, in his human nature, as we are, radically dependent on God's Holy Spirit, not because of sin but because it is his mission as the Mediator in both natures. This observation is congenial to the connection between Christ's actions and Sacramental grace (mediated through the power of the Holy Spirit). Implications such as these seem to be guiding Bavinck's retrospect (as seen in the quotations above) of the Reformed Christological heritage, but in order to do so he had to turn a blind eye to a significant part of his own tradition.

Bibliography

ADAMS, MARILYN M. (1999), What Sort of Human Nature? Medieval Philosophy and the Systematics of Christology, The Aquinas Lecture, 1999. Milwuakee: Marquette University Press.

ALSTEDT, HEINRICH. (1616), Metaphysica, Tribus Libris Tractata. Herbornae Nassoviorum.

AQUINAS, THOMAS. (1963–80), Summa Theologiae. Latin text and English translation. Various Translators. New York: McGraw-Hill Book Company.

BEZA, THEODORE. (1570). Ad Ioannis Brentii Argumenta Responsum. Geneva: Iohannis Crispini.

BARNES, COREY L. (2012), The Two Wills of Christ in Scholastic Theology: The Christology of Aquinas in Its Historical Context. Toronto: PIMS.

BAUR, JÖRG. (2007), "Ubiquität" in Oswald Bayer and Benjamin Gleede eds. Creator Est Creatura. Luthers Christologie Als Lehre von der Idiomenkommunikation. Berlin: De Gruyter, 186–301.

BAVINCK, HERMAN. (2002), Reformed Dogmatics, vol. 3: Sin and Salvation in Christ. Grand Rapids, MI: Baker.

BRANDY, CHRISTIAN. (1991), Die Späte Christologie des Johannes Brenz. Beitrage Zur Historische Theologie. Tübingen: Mohr & Siebeck.

BUCANUS, GUILHERME. (1630), Institutiones Theologicae....Geneva.

CHEMNITZ, MARTIN. (1971), The Two Natures of Christ. Translated by J.A.O. Preus. Saint Louis: Concordia Publishing House.

CROSS, RICHARD. (2002), The Metaphysics of the Incarnation. Oxford: Oxford University Press.

CROSS, RICHARD. (1999), "Incarnation, Indwelling, and the Vision of God: Henry of Ghent and Some Franciscans", Franciscan Studies, 57, 79–130.

CRISP, OLIVER D. (2011), Revisioning Christology: Theology in the Reformed Tradition. Farnham: Ashgate.

DANIELS, RICHARD. (2004), The Christology of John Owen. Grand Rapids, Reformation Heritage Books.

GAWRISCH, WILBERT R. (1980), "On Christology, Brenz and the Question of Ubiquity" in Arnold J. Koelpin ed., No Other Gospel: Essays in Commemoration of the400th Anniversary of the Formula of Concord 1580–1980. Milwaukee: Northwestern Publishing House.

HAGA, JOAR. (2012), Was There a Lutheran Metaphysics? The Interpretation Communication Idiomatum in Early Modern Lutheranism. Göttingen: Vandenhoech & Ruprecht.

HÄGGLUND, BENGT. (1980), "'Majestas Hominis Christi'.Wie Hat Martin Chemnitz die Christologie Luthers gedeutet?" Luther Jahrbuch 47, 71–88.

HEPPE, HEINRICH. (2000), Reformed Dogmatics. Translated by G.T: Thomson and revised and edited by Ernst Bizer. London: Wakeman Trust.

KECKERMAN, BARTHOLOMEW. (1610), Systema S.S. Theologiae Tribus Libris Adorantum. Hanoviae.

LINDHOLM, STEFAN. (2016), Jerome Zanchi (1516–90) and the Analysis of Reformed Scholastic Christology. Göttingen: Vandenhoeck & Ruprecht.

MULLER, RICHARD A. (1985), Dictionary of Latin and Greek Theological Terms. Principally Drawn from Protestant Scholasticism. Grand Rapids, MI: Baker Book House.

— (1988 [2nd ed. 2008]), Christ and the Decree: Christology and Predestination in Reformed Theology from Calvin to Perkins. Grand Rapids: Baker.

— (1987-2003), Post-Reformation Reformed Dogmatics. 4 vols. Grand Rapids: Baker Academic.

PREUS, ROBERT D. (1972), The Theology of Post-Reformation Lutheranism. St. Louis: Concordia.

SCHMID, HENRICH. (1899), The Doctrinal Theology of the Evangelical Lutheran Church. Translated by Charles Hay and Henry E. Jacobs. Minneapolis. Augsburg Publishing House.

WALTER SPARN. (1976), Wiederkehr der Metaphysik. Der Ontologische Frage in der Lutherische Theologie der Fruhen 17. Jh. Calwer Theologische Monographien. Stuttgart: Calwer Verlag.

SPENCE, ALAN. (2007), Incarnation and Inspiration: John Owen and the Coherence of Christology. London: T&T Clark.

SPENCER, STEPHEN R. (1988), "Reformed Scholasticism in Medieval Perspective: Thomas Aquinas and Francois Turretini on the Incarnation" (Ph.D. Dissertation, Michigan State University.

SYNOPSIS OF A PURER THEOLOGY. Latin Text and English Translation, vol. 2. (Forthcomming), Vol. Ed. Dolf te Velde and Translator Reimer A. Faber.London: Brill.

STRONG, AUGUSTUS. (1907), Systematic Theology: A Compendium Designed for the Use of Theological Students. Philadelphia : Griffith & Rowland Press.

TANNER, NORMAN P. (ed.) (1990), Decrees of the Ecumenical Councils. 2 vols. Washington, DC: Georgetown University Press.

TRIGLOT CONCORDIA: THE SYMBOLICAL BOOKS OF THE EVANGELICAL CHURCH LUTHERAN CHURCH. GERMAN ENGLISH-LATIN. (1921), Translated by F. Bente and W.H.T. Dau. Ohio: Concordia Publishing House.

TRUEMAN, CARL. (2002), The Claims of Truth: John Owen's Trinitarian Theology. Carlisle: Paternoster Publishing.

TURRETIN, FRANCIS. (1992-7), The Institutes of Elenctic Theology. Translated by G. M. Giger and edited by J. T. Denison. Phillipsburg, NJ: P. and R. Publishing.

WILLIS, DAVID. (1966), Calvin's Catholic Christology Calvin's Catholic Christology: The Function of the so-called "Extra" Dimension in Calvin's Theology. Leiden: Brill.

WITTMAN, TYLER R. (2013), "The End of the Incarnation: John Owen, Trinitarian Agency and Christology" International Journal of Systematic Theology Volume 15, Issue 3, pages 284–300.

ZANCHI, JEROME. (1593), De Incarnatione Filij Dei Libri Duo. Heidelberg.

ZUIDEMA, JASON. (2008), Peter Martyr Vermigli (1499–1562) and the Outward Instruments of Divine Grace. Vandenhoeck & Ruprecht.

Alan C. Clifford

Amyraldian Soteriology and Reformed–Lutheran *rapprochement*

A warm spirit of Protestant ecumenicity was evident during the National Synod of the Reformed Churches of France held at Charenton near Paris in 1631. As cited by English admirer of the Huguenots, John Quick (1636–1706)[1] in his *Synodicon in Gallia Reformata* (his translation of original French documents), Chapter XXII of the "Synodical Acts" is headed: "An Act in favour of the Lutheran brethren":

> This Synod declareth, That inasmuch as the Churches of the Confession of Augsburg do agree with the other Reformed Churches, in the principal and fundamental points of the True Religion, and that there is neither superstition nor idolatry in their worship, the faithful of the said Confession, who with a spirit of love and peaceableness do join themselves to the communion of our Churches in this Kingdom, may be, without any abjuration at all made by them, admitted unto the Lord's Table with us; and as sureties may present children unto Baptism, they promising the Consistory, that they will never solicit them, either directly or indirectly, to transgress the doctrine believed and professed in our Churches, but will be content to instruct and educate them in those points and Articles which are in common between us and them, and wherein both the Lutherans and we are unanimously agreed.[2]

This noble "Act" breathes the spirit of Moïse Amyraut (1596–1664) who served as a synod delegate for the Reformed Churches in the Province of Anjou. As simply stated by Quick, "Moses Amyraud [was] Pastor of the Church of Saumur, and Professor of Divinity in that University."[3] As we shall shortly see, Amyraut showed immense courage in the way he addressed King Louis XIII on behalf of the Synod. Brian Armstrong further believes that Amyraut "was probably responsible, at least in part"[4] for drafting the above expression of the Synod's decision to promote Reformed–Lutheran *rapprochement*. In fact, Amyraut later published two important treatises on the subject. Since, as Armstrong indicates,

---

1 See *DNB*: 1885–; Clifford: 2007a, 21–43.
2 Quick: 1692, vol. 2, 297.
3 ibid., 259.
4 Armstrong: 1969, 78.

1631 was "especially eventful"[5] for Amyraut and his future distinguished career, a 'Quick' look at his life provides some context for this chapter.

The briefest look at the circumstances of Presbyterian pastor John Quick's part in our story is also in order. His *Synodicon in Gallia Reformata* (1692) consists of a pair of fascinating folios. The work chiefly reports the proceedings of all the National Synods – twenty-nine in all – of the French Reformed Churches from the first held at Paris in 1559 to the last permitted by Louis XIV at Loudun in 1659. Besides an historical introduction, Quick included the *Confession of Faith* and *Discipline* of the Reformed Churches together with the *Edict of Nantes* (1598) and the *Edict of Fontainebleau* (1685) commonly known as the 'Revocation of the Edict of Nantes'. Pope Innocent XI's congratulatory letter to the French king is also included along with an account of the dreadful persecution of the immediate post–revocation period. The author's title-page claim – "A work never before extant in any language" – is noteworthy. A French edition was later published at the Hague in 1710 by Jean Aymon. Unlike Aymon, Quick had direct access to original manuscript material borrowed from Huguenot refugees which he then collated and translated. Aymon then re–translated Quick's work back into French – which explains his repetition of some of Quick's inaccuracies! The *Synodicon* remains therefore a primary English source for Huguenot information during the early modern period.

Quick's deep interest in the Huguenots did not end with the *Synodicon*. He also prepared for publication a selection of fifty brief (some quite lengthy) bi-ographies of eminent pastors, theologians and martyrs of the French Reformed churches, the *Icones Sacrae Gallicanae*. Deposited in Dr Williams' Library in London, they remain unpublished. "The Life of Mons[r]. Amyraut, Pastor and professor in the Church and University of Saumur" is the thirty–fifth biography. Interestingly, in the two major studies of Amyraut during the last fifty years by Dr Brian G. Armstrong[6] and Dr Frans Pieter van Stam,[7] this work was neglected. While Quick's *Synodicon* is frequently cited, his *Icones Sacrae Gallicanae* are ignored.[8] However, biographical information is cited from Pierre Bayle's *Dictionnaire historique et critique* (1696),[9] described by Armstrong as "an under-valued and under–used source containing much that is still important and not readily accessible elsewhere."[10] For information about Amyraut, Bayle states that his source was "the memoirs communicated by M. Amyraut the son," a source

---

5 ibid., 77.
6 See Armstrong: 1969.
7 See van Stam: 1988.
8 Quick: 1700.
9 See Bayle: 1734.
10 Armstrong: 1969, 300; Labrousse: 1983.

(not located) also used by Quick. However, the latter's biography includes more personal features than Bayle revealed in his *Dictionnaire*.

His ancestors coming originally from Alsace and later Orleans, Moïse Amyraut was born in September 1596 at Bourgueil in Anjou, a small town in the Loire Valley 40 km west of Tour. Having provided an education in the humanities, his father sent him to study law at the university of Poitiers. Proving himself a diligent student working daily for 14 hours, Moïse graduated Licentiate after a year. Travelling home via Saumur, he visited M. Bouchereau, pastor of the Reformed Church, who recognised the young man's extraordinary abilities and piety. Being introduced to the Governor of Saumur, the famous Huguenot soldier-statesman and scholar The Lord Philippe du Plessis-Mornay, young Moïse was encouraged to abandon law and study theology. At first reluctant, his father agreed with the advice given. Studying other works by Tully, Demosthenes and Aristotle, Moïse felt drawn to theology and the Christian ministry through reading John Calvin's *Institutes of the Christian Religion.* He was admitted to the Reformed Academy at Saumur, founded by Lord du Plessis–Mornay in 1599. Moïse thus came under the influence of the Scottish theologian John Cameron (c. 1580–1625) who served as Professor of Theology from 1618–21. Cameron had a profound influence on Moïse who became his most famous pupil. Succeeding the Dutch Francis Gomarus at Saumur, Cameron challenged the ultra–orthodox theology of Calvin's successor Theodore Beza. Restless and outspoken, he became known as "Bezae mastyx" or "Beza's scourge." Effectively signalling a return to the balanced biblicism of Calvin, Amyraut embraced and developed Cameron's 'authentic Calvinism,' a *via media* between Arminianism and Bezaism. Such was Amyraut's admiration for Cameron that he imitated his gestures and even spoke French with a Scottish accent![11]

Little information is available about Amyraut for the years 1618–26. However, in 1626, he was called to succeed his life–long friend and former fellow student Jean Daillé (1594–1670)[12] as pastor at Saumur. Having authored his first major publication *A Treatise Concerning Religions* (1631),[13] Amyraut was appointed as theology professor in the Academy that same year. He joined the learned Hebraist Louis Capell and fellow theologian Josué de la Place on the faculty. All three being disciples of Cameron, they exhibited a remarkable harmony "as is rarely to be met with in academic land" says Bayle.[14] Writing more quaintly, Quick states that "it was commonly said of them, that their three heads were covered with one bonnet, i. e. with one and the same nightcap."[15]

---

11 Bayle: 1734, 288–9.
12 See Bayle: 1734, vol. 2, 580 ff; Quick: 1700, 39; Clifford: 2009, 80–95.
13 Amyraut: 1631.
14 Bayle: 1734, vol. 2, 261.
15 Quick: 1700, 962.

Before we proceed, it is important to remember the religious and political context in which the Huguenots lived.[16] While they were a sizeable and significant minority, their liberties within Roman Catholic France were defined by the Edict of Nantes, granted during the reign of Henri IV in 1598. After decades of religious conflict, the Edict guaranteed a degree of religious freedom and other public privileges. However, due to constant intrigue by the Jesuits and other Roman Catholic conservatives, the position of the Huguenots still made them vulnerable. As 'second class citizens,' they enjoyed a fragile and frequently-violated peace. To practise the Reformed religion always demanded a combination of courage and wisdom. Throughout their public lives and ministries, the Huguenot pastors generally proved exemplary in this respect. As noted above, it was during the National Synod of Charenton (1631) that Amyraut made his initial mark. According to custom, the Reformed delegate from the previous National Synod of Castres (1626) presented the Reformed Churches' complaints and grievances over violations of the Edict of Nantes before King Louis XIII *on his knees.* Determined to honour the king yet maintain their privileges as servants of Christ, Amyraut insisted that he would address His Majesty *standing.* Thus commissioned by the Synod, so he did. In fact, so impressive was Amyraut's demeanour in the whole matter, his courage, manners and integrity won him the esteem of Cardinal Richelieu.

Amyraut is chiefly remembered for setting the cat among the pigeons over the theology of predestination. When a Roman Catholic nobleman – otherwise sympathetic to the Reformed Faith – expressed doubts about what he perceived to be Calvin's teaching, Amyraut responded with his first work on the subject. However, his *Brief Treatise on Predestination* (1634)[17] aroused the wrath of the Reformed world when he expounded a position on election, the extent of the atonement and 'universal grace' at odds with accepted wisdom. Starting what Bayle described as a "kind of civil war among the Protestant divines of France"[18] it soon became clear that Amyraut – heavily influenced by Calvin – was pursuing a very different theological agenda from 'orthodox' theologians like the 'French John Owen' Pierre du Moulin, but one that was not exposed to many of the *biblical* objections raised by many then and subsequently.

Before proceeding, I acknowledge that within Early Modern scholarship on Calvin and Beza there are a variety of opinions on the topics on which I comment below. I have set out my position on these topics elsewhere (see my *Atonement and Justification, Calvinus* and *Amyraut Affirmed*) and cannot repeat my ar-

---

16 See Treasure: 2013; Holt, ed.: 2002; Wakeman: 1959; Grant: 1934.
17 Amyraut: 1634; see Harding: 2014.
18 Bayle: 1734, 261.

guments here due to space considerations, but will be assuming the veracity of my position in what follows.

Calvin clearly roots his teaching in a dualistic conception of the divine will, as found in Deuteronomy 29: 29, "The secret things belong to the LORD our God, but those things which are revealed belong to us and to our children...":

> To me there appears no doubt that, by *antithesis*, there is a comparison here made between the doctrine openly set forth in the Law, and the hidden and incomprehensible counsel of God, concerning which it is not lawful to enquire. ... It is a remarkable passage, and especially deserving of our observation, for by it audacity and excessive curiosity are condemned, whilst pious minds are aroused to be zealous in seeking instruction.[19]

Calvin taught that Christ was offered as the Redeemer of the whole world according to God's 'revealed' conditional will albeit only received by elected believers according to God's 'hidden' absolute will. As he makes clear, this 'double-aspect' divine will is the key to the whole issue, notwithstanding the rationally-challenging paradox involved:

> ...while in Himself the will is one and undivided, to us it appears manifold, because, from the feebleness of our intellect, we cannot comprehend how, though after a different manner, He wills and wills not the very same thing. ... [However] our true wisdom is to embrace with meek docility, and without reservation, whatever the Holy Scriptures have delivered.[20]

Thus Calvin maintained the doctrines of universal atonement and divine election side by side. Faced by clear biblical evidence for both, he refused to tamper with the scriptural texts. Logic was not allowed to dictate one emphasis at the expense of the other. Typical of his numerous statements on the extent of the atonement, Calvin commented thus on Romans 5: 18: "Paul makes grace common to all, not because it in fact extends to all, but because it is offered to all. Although Christ suffered for the sins of the world, and is offered by the goodness of God without distinction to all men, yet not all receive him."[21]

Unhappy with this kind of dualism, Calvin's rationalistic successor Theodore Beza deleted the universal aspect of Calvin's scheme in favour of limited atonement, which in turn provoked the equally-rationalistic Jakob Arminius to delete the particular aspect of Calvin's scheme in favour of conditional election. Unimpressed by either of the two deviants, Amyraut was persuaded that Calvin's original position alone possessed biblical integrity. For him, the only option was Calvin's 'authentic Calvinism' (although Dr Richard Muller dismisses my

---

19 Calvin: 1852–, 410.
20 Calvin: 1962, 202–5.
21 Calvin: 1961, 117.

claim[22]). Amyraut also insisted that Calvin's view, with its unique 'mind and heart-set', had enormous pastoral and evangelistic advantages. Roger Nicole (while missing the point) admits that Calvin's comment on Romans 5: 18 "comes perhaps closest to providing support for Amyraut's thesis."[23]

Reinforced by Crossway's academic 'blockbuster,'[24] Dr Muller's case for closing down the 'Calvin *versus* Calvinism' debate remains unconvincing.[25] His denials that Calvin taught a 'double-aspect' will in God and that Amyraut followed Calvin are simply incorrect.[26] Scholasticism was *more* than 'method'.[27] It *did* involve a 'content disconnect' between Calvin and his successors. Indeed, the evidence for the shift away from his conspicuous teaching remains too compelling to be ignored.[28] Even Muller admits elsewhere that "Calvin's teaching was ... capable of being cited with significant effect by Moïse Amyraut against his Reformed opponents."[29] According to Dr van Stam, at a time when Bezan ultra-orthodoxy had replaced Calvin's balanced biblicism, "Amyraut...revealed the attraction which the theology of Calvin held for him. He demonstrated this preference in an array of books, in the process proving his familiarity with the writings of this reformer. ... Amyraut rediscovered Calvin, as it were, and was perhaps the Calvin-expert of the day. In any case, Amyraut fell under the spell of Calvin's theology."[30] Thus historian Philip Benedict – who incorrectly imagines the Canons of the Synod of Dort (1618–19) to represent a *higher* orthodoxy than is the case – recognises Amyraut's position in France accurately when he says that "the theologians of the Academy of Saumur ... consciously opposed Beza and appealed to Calvin instead. ... In effect they reversed the steps that had been taken in the passage from Calvin to Calvinism."[31]

Two years after the publication of his *Brief Treatise on Predestination,* Amyraut directly appealed to Calvin in his *Six Sermons:*[32] In the first sermon on Ezekiel 18: 23 ("Do I have any pleasure at all that the wicked should die?" says the Lord God, "and not that he should turn from his ways and live?") Amyraut specifically (and correctly) cites the reformer's view of the 'double-aspect' divine will: a revealed conditional will to save all and a secret absolute will to save the elect:

---

22 See Muller: 2014, 198.
23 Nicole: 1966, 83.
24 See Gibson & Gibson: 2013 and Clifford: 2015a.
25 See Muller: 2012, 279.
26 ibid., 124 and Clifford: 2015b.
27 See Muller: 2003, vol. 1, 35, 132.
28 See Clifford: 1990; Clifford: 1996; Clifford: 2004; Clifford: 2007a; Clifford: 2009; Clifford: 2011.
29 Muller: 2000, 62.
30 van Stam: 1988, 431.
31 Benedict: 2001, 227.
32 Amyraut: 1636. See Harmon: 2008, 85–6.

Now we must see how God wishes all to be converted…But we must remark that God puts on a twofold character: for he here wishes to be taken at his word. As I have already said, the Prophet does not here dispute with subtlety about his incomprehensible plans, but wishes to keep our attention close to God's word. Now what are the contents of this word? The law, the prophets, and the gospel. Now all are called to repentance, and the hope of salvation is promised them when they repent: this is true, since God rejects no returning sinner: he pardons all without exception; meanwhile, this will of God which he sets forth in his word does not prevent him from decreeing before the world was created what he would do with every individual…[33]

Amyraut adds: "It is incomparably better to keep to the interpretation that the incomparable Calvin gives of this passage, to whom principally, after God, the Church owes her reformation, not only in France, but in many other parts of Europe."[34]

Amyraut's impeccable *authentic* Calvinist orthodoxy did not shield him from the charge of the Arminianising heresy, even though he claimed an orthodoxy consistent with the Canons of Dort. He – with his fellow pastor Paul Testard of Blois who had also published a similarly "heretical" piece – was tried and acquitted at the National Synod of Alençon (1637). They justified themselves by declaring in 'Dortian' terms that:

Jesus Christ died for all men sufficiently, but for the elect only effectually: and that consequentially his intention was to die for all men in respect of the sufficiency of his satisfaction, but for the elect only in respect of its quickening and saving virtue and efficacy; which is to say, that Christ's will was that the sacrifice of his cross should be of an infinite price and value, and most abundantly sufficient to expiate the sins of the whole world; yet nevertheless the efficacy of his death appertains only unto the elect;… for this was the most free counsel and gracious purpose both of God the Father, in giving his Son for the salvation of mankind, and of the Lord Jesus Christ, in suffering the pains of death, that the efficacy thereof should particularly belong unto all the elect, and to them only…[35]

Returning home from the Synod of Alençon, all Saumur rejoiced at Amyraut's acquittal. The Academy flourished for many years with many students attending from all parts of France and beyond. Indeed, the Saumur Academy became the premier institution of its kind. Amyraut's personal reputation grew with the years, not least among the Roman Catholics. As we have noted, the King's chief minister Cardinal Richelieu greatly admired him.

Doctrinal debate over the doctrines of grace involved Amyraut in further controversy in the 1640s. When the English Arminian Samuel Hoard, Rector of

---

33 Calvin: 1850, 248.
34 Harmon: 2008, 85.
35 Quick: 1692, vol. 2, 354.

Morton in Essex published an attack on predestination,[36] the impact of the work was also felt in France. Just as the English 'proto-Amyraldian' John Davenant replied to Hoard, so did Amyraut. It is fascinating to discover that both authors did not refute Hoard from a *Bezan* perspective.[37] They were conscious of doing so as 'authentic Calvinists'.[38] Amyraut could not have been more explicit in calling his reply *A Defence of the Doctrine of Calvin*.[39] Calvin's 'double-aspect' divine will and consequent 'double-dimension' teaching on the atonement lies behind his comment on 2 Peter 3: 9 ("The Lord…is long-suffering towards us, not willing that any should perish but that all should come to repentance":)

> This is His wondrous love towards the human race, that He desires all men to be saved, and is prepared to bring even the perishing to safety…It could be asked here, if God does not want any to perish, why do so many in fact perish? My reply is that no mention is made here of the secret decree of God by which the wicked are doomed to their own ruin, but only of His loving–kindness as it is made known to us in the Gospel. There God stretches out His hand to all alike, but He only grasps those (in such a way as to lead to Himself) whom He has chosen before the foundation of the world.[40]

Amyraut remarks accordingly:

> The confidence that Calvin had in the goodness of his cause and the candour with which he has proceeded in the interpretation of Scripture have been so great, that he had no qualms about interpreting the words of St. Peter in this manner.[41]

Thus Armstrong states that in this work, "Amyraut clearly identifies his own teaching with that of Calvin. Of all his writings, this is the most important in demonstrating the distinctives of Amyraldianism as compared to the scholastic orientation of the orthodox."[42] The degree to which Amyraut had absorbed Calvin's thinking is frankly astounding, as Armstrong makes clear:

> Certainly one of the striking aspects of Amyraut's work is the complete familiarity he shows with Calvin's writings. In his writing he piles quotation upon quotation from Calvin, drawing from a great variety of Calvin's work. There are, for example, more than a dozen quotes from Calvin in the *Six Sermons* of 1636, some thirty–seven often lengthy quotes in the *Eschantillon de la doctrine de Calvin* of 1636, at least 103 extensive passages from Calvin in his *Defense de la doctrine de Calvin* of 1644, and frequent references from Calvin in each of the writings in which Amyraut was defending his own position. There is almost a complete identification with Calvin at times, especially in the

---

36 Hoard: 1633.
37 See Clifford: 2006.
38 See Davenant: 1641, 142.
39 Amyraut: 1641; Amyraut: 1644.
40 Calvin: 1963.
41 Amyraut: 1644, 125; Armstrong: 1969, 166.
42 Armstrong: 1969, 99–100.

Defense de la doctrine de Calvin in which he often switches back and forth from the first to the third person.[43]

Persisting in the same stance that produced the heresy trial at Alençon in 1637, it was inevitable that Amyraut's critics would try to make more trouble for him at the next National Synod at Charenton in 1644–5. As before, all attempts to discredit him proved fruitless.[44] However, the controversy was to rumble on for decades, not only in France but throughout Europe and beyond. Even today, ultra-orthodox blood pressure is often raised when anyone dares to defend and expound the tenets of Moïse Amyraut. Sadly, for most students of French church history, knowledge of Amyraut is confined to his theological notoriety.

What is striking is the way Amyraut maintained his Reformed convictions without compromise. Surrounded as the Reformed community in France was by a large and not always benign Roman Catholic majority, tensions were not always easy to handle, even during the 'golden years' (1629–61).[45] However, in the true spirit of the Gospel, Amyraut avoided the extremes of social hostility and a servile ecumenism. When approaches were made, he made it plain to the Jesuit Father Audebert that union with Rome was out of the question. In 1646, he courageously urged his Saumur congregation to have nothing to do with the Roman Catholic festival of Corpus Christi. On his death-bed in 1664, with several Catholics present, he affirmed with deep conviction his commitment to the "Holy Reformed religion" as the only way of salvation. The outrageous charge that Amyraut was "the gravedigger" of the French Reformed Church does not stand up to scrutiny.[46]

However, if union with Rome was out of the question, Amyraut and his brethren thought and felt very differently where the Lutherans were concerned, despite a not–insignificant difference over the Lord's Supper. Indeed, Amyraut demonstrated his concern in his treatise, *Moses Amyraldi de secessione ab ecclesia romana deque ratione pacis inter evangelicos in religionis negotio constituendae, disputatio* (Saumur, 1647). Following more than a decade of asserting his 'authentic Calvinist' soteriology, chapter 7[47] of this work exploits the ecumenical potential of his teaching. In view of the close similarity between Luther's and Calvin's actual stance on the issues, Amyraut considered his teaching would help facilitate closer ties with the Lutherans who might travel or reside in France (possibly as refugees in the wake of the Thirty Years War, 1618–48). Armstrong is right to observe that in his treatise, "Amyraut addressed himself to the predes-

43 Ibid., 187.
44 See Quick: 1692, vol. 2, 455.
45 See Prestwich: 1987, 175–95.
46 See Clifford: 2007a, 30, 32–3, 42; Clifford: 1996, 16.
47 See Amyraut: 1647, 156–91.

tination question, explaining it in his customary terms and hoping this explanation would remove the difficulty that Lutherans had with Reformed teaching on this point."[48]

Of course, from the Lutheran side, the big obstacle was their perception of the Reformed doctrine of limited atonement, chiefly occasioned by the proceedings of the Lutheran-Reformed Colloquy of Montbéliard (1586). During exchanges over the universal text 1 John 2: 2 with the eminent Lutheran divine Jacob Andreæ, Theodore Beza had insisted that "Christ did not die for the sins of the damned."[49] Besides expressing what was standard Lutheran thinking after the *Formula of Concord* (1580), Andreæ's reply may be regarded as 'proto–Amyraldian': "Those assigned to eternal destruction … are damned for this reason, because they refuse to embrace Jesus Christ with true faith, who suffered, was crucified and died no less for their sins, than for the sins of Peter, Paul and all the saints…"[50]

It is striking to conclude that Calvin would have agreed with Andreæ rather than Beza:

> True it is that the effect of [Christ's] death comes not to the whole world. Nevertheless, forasmuch as it is not in us to discern between the righteous and the sinners that go to destruction, but that Jesus Christ has suffered his death and passion as well for them as for us, therefore it behoves us to labour to bring every man to salvation, that the grace of our Lord Jesus Christ may be available to them.[51]

Calvin made the same basic point elsewhere:

> To bear the sins means to free those who have sinned from their guilt by his satisfaction. He says many meaning all, as in Rom. 5:15. It is of course certain that not all enjoy the fruits of Christ's death, but this happens because their unbelief hinders them.[52]

Furthermore, Andreæ's statement amounts to an echo of Luther's comment on 1 John 2: 2:

> It is certain that you are a part of the world. Do not let your heart deceive you by saying: "The Lord died for Peter and Paul; He rendered satisfaction for them, not for me." Therefore let every one who has sin be summoned here, for He has made the expiation for the sins of the whole world and bore the sins of the whole world.[53]

Although Calvin had his reasons for exegeting the text a little differently in his commentary, he approved of its unqualified use in Articles III and IV of the Sixth

---

48 Armstrong: 1969, 108.
49 Andreæ: 1613, 447; Gibson & Gibson: 2013, 512.
50 Andreæ: 1613. 447–8; Williams: 2013.
51 Calvin: 1993, 548; Rainbow: 1990, 172–3.
52 Calvin: 1963, 131.
53 Luther: 1963, vol. 30, 237.

Session of the Council of Trent: "Him God set forth to be a propitiation through faith in his blood for our sins, and not for ours only, but also for the sins of the whole world...But though he died for all, all do not receive the benefit of his death, but those only to whom the merit of his passion is communicated..." Calvin stated unambiguously: "The third and fourth heads I do not touch..."[54]

While Amyraut faced incessant criticism from his 'ultra–orthodox' brethren in France, his view reflected precedents not only in Calvin but also in Luther and Lutherans such as Andreæ. What is clear is that these theologians, all within the Augustinian predestinarian tradition, had no hesitation in affirming their view of an atonement at once universal in provision but particular in application. Notwithstanding detailed minor differences, they all shared the basic contours of what may be affirmed as Amyraut's 'authentic Calvinism'. In his remarks on the allegedly "illogical" Articles I–II and XI of the Lutheran *Formula of Concord*,[55] 'rationalist' Philip Schaff seemed incapable of appreciating that, rooted in the double-aspect divine will (as per Deut. 29: 29), a biblical *via media* between over-orthodox Bezaism and sub–orthodox Arminianism is demanded by the textual data and thus may be articulated accordingly, as Schaff – aware of Calvin's *via media* (later adopted by Amyraut) – seems unwittingly to concede:

> The *Formula of Concord* sanctioned a compromise between Augustinianism and universalism, or between the original Luther and the later Melanchthon, by teaching both the absolute inability of man and the universality of divine grace, without an attempt to solve these contradictory positions..[56]

That said, had not Luther affirmed this view in his *De Servo Arbitrio* (1525)? He distinguished between "the published offer of God's mercy [to the whole human race]" and "the dreadful hidden will of God, Who, according to His own counsel, ordains such persons as He wills to receive and partake of the mercy preached and offered."[57] Indeed, Schaff seems to lack clarity on the issue:

> The Lutheran system, then, to be consistent, must rectify itself, and develop either from Art. II. in the direction of Augustinianism and Calvinism, or from Art. XI. in the direction of Synergism and Arminianism."[58]

However, the stance is at least as old as Augustine himself. Indeed, the author of *De predestinatione Sanctorum* (429) had earlier declared in *De Civitate Dei* (413–26):

---

54 Calvin: 1851, vol. 3, 93, 109.
55 See Schaff: 1877a, 106–114; 165–173.
56 Schaff: 1877b, 593.
57 Luther: 1957, 169, 302.
58 Schaff: 1877c, 315.

For it is good for all men to hear [Christ's] voice and live, by passing to the life of godliness from the death of ungodliness. Of this death the Apostle Paul says, "Therefore all are dead, and He died for all, that they which live should not henceforth live unto themselves, but unto Him which died for them and rose again" (2 Cor. 5:14–15). Thus all, without one exception, were dead in sins, whether original or voluntary sins, sins of ignorance, or sins committed against knowledge; and for all the dead there died the only one person who lived, that is, who had no sin whatever, in order that they who live by the remission of their sins should live, not to themselves, but to Him who died for all, for our sins, and rose again for our justification...[59]

In his decisive thesis, Stephen A. Strehle provides the evidence for this 'proto-Amyraldian' Lutheran case with numerous citations.[60] Regarding Luther, he concludes:

Luther makes his position clear, stating that Christ has borne "all the sins of all men," "the sins of the whole world, from Adam to the very last person," "not some, but all the sins of the whole world, great or small, few or many." His death would even have sufficed to remove the sins of "many, many worlds." But these conclusions only naturally follow from the mission of Christ in Luther to abrogate the whole law, to swallow up all the enemies of His reign in His deity. If Christ had not borne the sins of the whole world, He would not have completely eliminated within the divine economy the hostile elements, and as a consequence could not be considered as Lord over all things.[61]

When he comes to Calvin's views, Dr Strehle makes this brief but important statement:

With the exception of some inappreciable differences, Martin Luther finds a faithful disciple of his theological system in the other great pillar of the Reformation, John Calvin. In accordance with the methodology of Luther, Calvin stands piously submissive to the revelation of God, often explicitly imitating the expressions of Scripture, avoiding pretentious explorations into divine mysteries.[62]

Not surprisingly, Strehle is highly critical of Theodore Beza, perhaps even more so than Brian Armstrong:

Though too much blame has often been cast upon the shoulders of only one person, Theodore de Beze, [yet] for the influx of Scholasticism into Protestantism, Beze certainly stands as a monumental figure in this transition, particularly because of his notable role as the successor of Calvin at Geneva... Beze's system became so detached from the text of Scripture that the theological chair at Geneva and other schools were eventually split in two, teaching theology and the Scriptures as separate subjects.[63]

---

59 Augustine: 1872, vol. 2, 354.
60 Strehle: 1980, 64 ff.
61 ibid., 71. Strehle sources all these citations.
62 ibid., 84.
63 ibid., 125–8.

Based on precedents for Amyraut's view of the gospel (including the doctrine of justification *vis-à-vis* Beza's 'over–orthodox' teaching[64]), one may argue that Calvin led the way in Amyraut's pro-Lutheran ecumenical aspirations. Besides his willingness to "cross even ten seas"[65] to join with Archbishop Thomas Cranmer in a Reformed ecumenical synod, Calvin had earlier in a letter to Heinrich Bullinger spoken warmly of Luther (albeit with some justified criticisms of "serious faults"):

> [How] eminent a man Luther is, and the excellent endowments wherewith he is gifted, with what strength of mind and resolute constancy, with how great skill, with what efficiency and power of doctrinal statement, he hath devoted his whole energy to overthrow the reign of Antichrist, and at the same time to diffuse far and near the doctrine of salvation. Often have I been wont to declare, that even although he were to call me a devil, I should still not the less hold him in such honour that I must acknowledge him to be an illustrious servant of God.[66]

Neither must one ignore Calvin's kind and sympathetic disposition towards Philip Melanchthon who rejected Luther's doctrine of the Lord's Supper in favour of Calvin's. As is equally well known, Melanchthon's spirit was broken by the incessant theological turmoil among the Lutherans following Luther's death (1546).[67] Sadly, due to his philosophical tendency,[68] he failed to appreciate Calvin's case for faith's humble acquiescence in the 'double-aspect' divine will. Yet, doubtless aware of Melanchthon's 'proto-Arminian' drift,[69] which he endeavoured to correct,[70] Calvin's grief at the news of his German brother's death (1560) is unmistakable:

> O Philip, who art now in the bosom of Christ, and in peace expectest us, how often fatigued by the combat, and reposing thy head on my breast, hast thou said to me, God grant me to die upon this heart! and I too have a thousand times wished that we had lived together. Thou wouldst have shown more courage for the battle, and they who triumphed over thy great goodness, which they styled weakness, would have been restrained within bounds which they would not have dared to pass.[71]

It is difficult to imagine that Amyraut was ignorant of this gentle, even tender as well as truly magnanimous side to Calvin. Beyond doubt, in the century following, Calvin's gracious ecumenism was perpetuated by Amyraut.

---

64 See Clifford: 2007b.
65 Calvin: 2009, vol. 5, 348.
66 ibid., vol. 4, 433.
67 See Fisher: 1904, 408.
68 See Strehle: 1980, 96.
69 ibid., 104–5.
70 Calvin: 2009, vol. 5, 348.
71 Calvin: 2009, vol. 6, 61; Calvin: 2009, vol. 2, 496.

While Amyraut had numerous supporters in France (not to forget Geneva[72]),
he was aware of a kindred spirit in England, the much better known Richard
Baxter (1615–91).[73] Indeed, for the vast majority of students of church history and
Christian biography, the Huguenot Amyraut is an unknown figure compared
with someone like his near–Puritan contemporary. To be brief, Baxter's extraordinary ministry in seventeenth-century Kidderminster is celebrated by an
appropriate local statue; his nationwide influence was diffused by such still–
gripping page turners as *The Saints' Everlasting Rest* and *Call to the Unconverted;*
and his lovely hymn "Ye holy angels bright" is still enjoyed by modern wor-
shippers. Neither must we ignore his colourful and dramatic life as recorded in
his autobiography with its exotic Latin title *Reliquiae Baxterianae.* Lastly, Baxter
made a further mark on English church history by his courageous stand before
the infamous Judge Jeffreys in 1685. Yet within a British historical context, Richard Baxter is generally regarded as the chief exponent of Amyraldianism. Even
though, at one time, Baxter's doctrinal distinctives became identified as
'Baxterianism,'[74] he tends to be styled as an 'Amyraldian.'[75]

By contrast, while Amyraut had an effective pastoral and academic ministry,
he was no French Baxter: he never quite turned Saumur upside down, and this
charming town in the Loire Valley exhibits no statue to commemorate him.
Although (as we have seen) he wrote a series of highly–significant theological
works, he wrote no devotional or evangelistic classic, neither is a little-known
hymn ever sung. Lastly, no *Reliquiae Amyraldianae* exists to perpetuate his
memory. Yet he had an enormous influence on England's most famous Puritan.
Indeed, it should be remembered that Baxter's posthumously published treatise
Universal Redemption (1694) was with–held from publication in the 1650s "partly
because many narrow minded brethren would have been offended with it" and
partly because it would have needlessly duplicated the work of Bishop Davenant,
Moise Amyraut and Jean Daillé.[76] Baxter's views occasioned an attack on his
position by Louis du Moulin,[77] Camden Professor of History at Oxford, and son
of Amyraut's French arch–critic Pierre du Moulin.[78] Baxter was singled out as
Amyraut's "only proselyte in England", an error he was not slow to correct.

While Baxter was convinced of his views long before he had heard of Amyraut,
yet, just as the 'Amyraldian' label was to 'stick', the French divine's name was to
be honoured in Baxter's writings (books and letters) for over forty years. Indeed,

---

72 See Grohman: 1971; Klauber (1994).
73 See Nuttall: 1965, 130.
74 See Edwards': 1699.
75 See Keeble: 1982, 27.
76 Baxter: 1696, I. 123.
77 See *DNB:* 1885–.
78 See Armstrong: 1969, 83 ff..

it peppers his output. A few examples are selected almost at random. In the *Universal Redemption of Mankind* (started in the 1640s but published in 1694) he tells us at the end of an incomplete chapter: "Here Amyraldus and Dallaeus coming forth stopt me."[79] In the *Saints' Everlasting Rest* (1650), Baxter refers to "judicious Amyraldus."[80] Writing to his "dearly beloved friends" at Kidderminster the same year, Baxter urged them "to beware of extremes in the controverted points of religion. When you avoid one error, take heed you run not into another ... The middle way which Camero, Ludov. Crocius, Amyraldus, Davenant, &c. go, I think, is nearest the Truth."[81] In the *Christian Directory*'s (1673) amazingly–exhaustive "poor man's library" book list, the works of Amyraut are recommended.[82] In his *Catholick Theologie* (1675), he asks his Arminian disputant, "Have you not read the plain words of Calvin, cited by Amyraldus in *Defens. Doct. Calvin?*"[83] Since Amyraut and Baxter shared their nuanced perception of the reformer, it is hardly surprising to read of Baxter's debt to 'the blessed Calvin':[84]

> I know no man, since the Apostles' days, whom I value and honour more than Calvin, and whose judgement in all things, one with another, I more esteem and come nearer to.[85]

Also unsurprisingly, only a year before he died in January 1664, Amyraut wrote to Baxter expressing his appreciation for his English brother's frequent references to him. Sadly, the letter was occasioned by the mischief-making Louis du Moulin who reported that Amyraut had slighted the English Nonconformists and Baxter in particular. On hearing of such falsehood, and indignant that he had been so misrepresented, Amyraut promptly wrote to counter the story. Among other items of interest in this Latin letter (including an apology for the loss of English he had acquired in London forty years earlier), the Christian bond between Amyraut and Baxter is clear: "Your piety speaks with outstanding learning and eloquence. Do not then, I pray thee, Reverend, believe anything of the kind; ... Farewell, most Reverend Doctor, ... our friend the Lord, who has redeemed us by His blood, deign to take special care of you as well as the Church of England."[86]

No less surprising is the deep ecumenical concern shared by Amyraut and Baxter. In this respect also, the two men may be regarded as disciples of Calvin. If

---

79 Baxter: 1694, 376.
80 Baxter: 1650, II, ii. 3.
81 Baxter: 1991, vol. 1, 53.
82 Baxter: 1673, Quest. CLXXIV.
83 Baxter: 1675, II. 50.
84 Baxter: 1658, 735.
85 Baxter: 1658, 559.
86 See Baxter: 1696, II. 442; Baxter: 1991, vol. 2, 34.

the former was a precursor of Protestant unity in France,[87] the latter was likewise in England. Of course, since in Roman Catholic France, the Reformed communion was the only legally–tolerated exception to Rome, Baxter faced a more problematic situation due to sectarian proliferation. Indeed, he was perpetually grieved at the sectarian tendencies of Puritanism. All things considered, while he rejoiced in fellowship with godly souls whatever their churchmanship, Baxter's zeal for saving sinners was matched by his zeal to unite saints. In language Amyraut would doubtless have endorsed, Baxter's paraphrase on Christ's prayer for unity (John 17: 21) perfectly sums up his numerous treatises on the subject:

> May all speak the same thing which they have heard from Thee by me, and may love what we love, and do our work and not their own: That by their concord in faith, love and practice the world may be won to Christianity, and not scandalized by their discord and fractions, or by forsaking the true unity, and combining for worldly interest on worldly terms.[88]

Amyraut would have rejoiced at Baxter's influence among the Lutherans as well as others throughout Europe. He was held in high regard by Philipp Spener, the founder of German Pietism and Court Preacher to the Elector of Saxony. His friend Petrus Christophorus Martinus wrote from Dresden in early July 1688,[89] expressing appreciation for Baxter's *Nunc aut numquam* (*Now or Never*, 1662) and *De quiete sanctorum* (*Saints' Rest*, 1650). He mentioned eight other works by Baxter greatly appreciated in translation by his countrymen. These included *Manuale pauperum* (*The Poor Man's Family Book*, 1674), a work held in high regard by Spener, whose famous and influential work *Pia desideria* (Frankfurt: 1675) closely resembles it.

Besides the attraction of Baxter's 'practical works' among the Lutheran Pietists, they would have appreciated the hints of his theological stance (usually confined to his 'polemical works'). His view of the Gospel would have dispelled Lutheran anxieties regarding Bezan–style high orthodoxy. In the next century, the same advantage helped promote the books of Baxter's most famous English 'disciple', the 'Baxterian Calvinist' Dr Philip Doddridge (1702–51).[90] Besides showing a keen interest in publishing John Quick's biographies of Amyraut and his brethren in the last year of his life,[91] the Northampton pastor and academy principal had specific 'Lutheran links'. His maternal grandfather John Bauman of Prague left his homeland in 1626 following the persecution of the Lutheran pastors during the Thirty Years War. Taking refuge in England, he eventually

---

87 See Stauffer: 1962.
88 Baxter: 1685.
89 See Baxter: 1991, vol. 2, 296.
90 See Clifford: 2002, 137.
91 ibid. 242–2.

became the master of the Free School at Kingston–upon–Thames. As a result of his grandfather's exile, Philip came into possession of a copy of Luther's Bible, dated 1526.[92] There was some fitting 'payback'. James Robertson, formerly pupil and assistant to Doddridge, and afterwards Professor of Hebrew in the University of Edinburgh, studied for a while at the University of Leiden in Holland. In December 1749, he wrote to his former tutor:

> The Abbot of Sternmetz, in Magdeburg, who is a man of great piety and of considerable character among the Lutherans, proposed some time ago to translate the *Family Expositor* into High Dutch; upon which the Lutheran clergy were alarmed, and dreadfully afraid of your introducing the leaven of Calvinism into the Lutheran churches, which obliged the good Abbot to translate your sermons on the *Nature and Efficacy of Grace*, as a proof of your moderation in these points; which I believe by this time had the desired effect. … Mr Valentine Arnoldi, Pastor of Herborn [in Nassau] intends to translate the *Rise and Progress* into the German language.[93]

The story could doubtless be extended into the nineteenth century. Giants like Scotsman Thomas Chalmers,[94] Welshman John Jones Talsarn[95] and Englishman J. C. Ryle[96] would head the list, as would another Welshman in the twentieth century, D. Martyn Lloyd–Jones.[97] Calvinists all, they shared an immense admiration for Luther, expressing also a quasi–Amyraldian view of the Gospel. That said, it is time to terminate our story. It is hopefully now clear that, despite the suspicions entertained in some sections of the Reformed constituency towards Amyraut and those who shared his soteriological outlook, the 'Amyraldian' stance is arguably closer to the mind and heart of the Reformation than many would dare to admit. For 'authentic Calvinists', Luther's courageous affirmation at the Diet of Worms, "My conscience is captive to the Word of God" was more than ever–quotable rhetoric. It became not only the basis of the Gospel of the Reformed Faith (despite differences over other matters), but a biblical benchmark for avoiding both sub–orthodox and ultra–orthodox soteriologies. Thus the Reformation quincentenary has hitherto–unrecognised potential to teach some fundamental lessons. As recipients of such a legacy, may we become worthy pupils.

---

92 ibid. 23.
93 ibid. 227; Doddridge: 1979, 317.
94 See Chalmers: 1849, vol. 2, 403, 406; W. Hanna: 1854, vol. 2, 773.
95 See Clifford: 2013, 217 ff.
96 See Ryle: 2014.
97 See Lynch: 2015.

Bibliography

AMYRAUT, MOÏSE (1631), Traitté des religions contre ceux qui les estiment toutes indifferentes, Saumur: Girard & de Lerpiniere.

— (1634), Brief Traitté de la predestination et de ses principales dependences, Saumur: Isaac Desbordes.

— (1636), Six Sermons de la Nature, Estendue, Necessité, Dispensation, et Efficace de l'Evangile, Saumur: Girard & de Lerpiniere.

— (1644), Defense de la doctrine de Calvin, Saumur: Isaac Desbordes.

— (1647), Moses Amyraldi de secessione ab ecclesia romana deque ratione pacis inter evangelicos in religionis negotio constituendae, disputatio, Saumur: Isaac Desbordes.

ANDREÆ, JACOBUS (1613), Acta Colloquij Montisbelligartensis, Wittenberg: Myliander.

ARMSTRONG, BRIAN G. (1969), Calvinism and the Amyraut Heresy: Protestant Scholasticism and Humanism in Seventeenth-Century France, Madison: University of Wisconsin Press.

AUGUSTINE, AURELIUS (1872), The City of God in Works, (tr.), M. Dods, Edinburgh: T. & T. Clarke.

BAXTER, RICHARD (1658), Saints' Everlasting Rest, London.

— (1673), A Christian Directory, London.

— (1675), Catholick Theologie, London.

— (1685), A Paraphrase on the New Testament, London.

— (1694), Universal Redemption of Mankind, London.

— (1696), Reliquiae Baxterianiae, London.

— (1991), N. H. Keeble, Geoffrey F. Nuttall, (eds.), Calendar of the Correspondence of Richard Baxter, Vol. 2, Oxford: Clarendon Press.

BAYLE, PIERRE (1734), the Dictionary Historical and Critical of Mr Peter Bayle, London.

BENEDICT, PHILIP (2001), The Faith and Fortunes of France's Huguenots, 1600–85, Aldershot: Ashgate.

CALVIN, JOHN (1850), Commentaries on the Book of the Prophet Ezekiel, Vol. 2, Edinburgh: Calvin Translation Society.

— (1851), 'Antidote to the Council of Trent' in Tracts, Vol. 3, Edinburgh: Calvin Translation Society.

— (1852–), The Harmony of the Pentateuch, Edinburgh: Calvin Translation Society.

— (1961), The Epistles of Paul The Apostle to the Romans and to the Thessalonians, Edinburgh: Oliver and Boyd.

— (1962), (tr.) H. Beveridge, Institutes of the Christian Religion, London: James Clarke.

— (1963), Calvin's Commentaries on The Epistle of Paul The Apostle to the Hebrews and The First and Second Epistles of St Peter, Edinburgh: Oliver and Boyd.

— (1993), Sermons on Job (London; facs. Edinburgh: The Banner of Truth Trust).

— (2009), John Calvin: Tracts and Letters (Bonnet edition), Vol. 5 (Edinburgh: The Banner of Truth Trust).

CHALMERS, THOMAS (1849), Institutes of Theology, Vol. 2, Edinburgh: Sutherland & Knox.

CLIFFORD, ALAN C. (1990), Atonement and Justification: English Evangelical Theology 1640–1790 – An Evaluation, Oxford: Clarendon Press.

— (1996), Calvinus: Authentic Calvinism – A Clarification, Norwich: Charenton Reformed Publishing.

— (2002), The Good Doctor: Philip Doddridge of Northampton – A Tercentenary Tribute, Norwich: Charenton Reformed Publishing.

— (2004), Amyraut Affirmed, Norwich: Charenton Reformed Publishing.

— (2006), 'Introduction' to John Davenant, A Dissertation on the Death of Christ, Weston Rhyn: Quinta Press.

— (2007a), 'A Quick Look at Amyraut' in Christ for the World: Affirming Amyraldianism, Norwich: Charenton Reformed Publishing.

— (2007b) 'Justification: The Calvin–Saumur perspective', Evangelical Quarterly (79.4).

— (2009), Calvin Celebrated: The Genevan Reformer & His Huguenot Sons, Norwich: Charenton Reformed Publishing.

— (2011), 'Calvin & Calvinism: Amyraut et al', in John Calvin 500: A Reformation Affirmation, Norwich: Charenton Reformed Publishing.

— (2013), John Jones Talsarn: Pregethwr Y Bobl/The People's Preacher, Norwich: Charenton Reformed Publishing.

— (2015a), 'Crossway on the Cross: An Authentic Calvinist Critique' of From Heaven He Came and Sought Her: Definite Atonement in Historical, Biblical,Theological and Pastoral Perspective, eds. David Gibson & Jonathan Gibson (Wheaton, Illinois: Crossway, 2013) at http://www.nrchurch.co.uk/pdf/Crossway%20Book%20Review.pdf

— (2015b), 'Mulling over Muller' at http://www.nrchurch.co.uk/pdf/Mulling%20over%20Muller.pdf.

DAVENANT, JOHN (1831), J. Allport (tr.), Animadversions written by the Right Rev. Father in God, John, Lord Bishop of Salisbury, upon a treatise intituled, God's Love to Mankind, London: Hamilton.

Dictionary of National Biography (1885–), Oxford: OUP.

DODDRIDGE, PHILIP (1979), Geoffrey F. Nuttall (ed.), Calendar of the Correspondence of Philip Doddridge, DD (1702–1751), London: HMSO.

EDWARDS, THOMAS (1699), The paraselene dismantled of her cloud, or, Baxterianism barefac'd, London.

FISHER, GEORGE, P (1904), History of the Christian Church, London: Hodder and Stoughton.

GIBSON, D; GIBSON, J. (2013), (eds.), From Heaven He came and Sought Her: Definite Atonement in Historical, Biblical, Theological and Pastoral Perspective, Wheaton, Illinois: Crossway.

GRANT, A. J. (1934), The Huguenots, London: Thornton Butterworth.

GROHMAN, DONALD D. (1971), 'The Genevan Reactions to the Saumur Doctrine of Hypothetical Universalism: 1635–1685', Unpublished DTh thesis, Toronto School of Theology.

HANNA, WILLIAM (1854), Memoirs of Thomas Chalmers , Vol. 2, Edinburgh: Thomas Constable.

HARDING, MATTHEW S. (2014), A critical analysis of Moise Amyraut's atonement theory based on a new and critical translation of a Brief Treatise on Predestination, Unpublished PhD thesis, South–Western Baptist Theological Seminary.

HARMON, MATTHEW, P (2008), Moyse Amyraut's Six Sermons, Unpublished MTh thesis, Westminster Theological Seminary.

HOLT, MACK P. (2002), (ed.), Renaissance and Reformation in France, Oxford: OUP.

HOARD, SAMUEL (1633), God's Love to Mankind, manifested by disproving his absolute Decree for their Damnation, London.

KEEBLE, NEIL H. (1982) Richard Baxter: Puritan Man of Letters, Oxford: Clarendon Press.

KLAUBER, MARTIN I. (1994), Between Reformed Scholasticism and Pan-Protestantism, Selinsgrove, London and Toronto: Associated University Presses.

LABROUSSE, ELISABETH (1983), Bayle, Oxford: OUP.

LUTHER, MARTIN (1957), The Bondage of the Will, J. I. Packer and O. R. Johnson (trs.), London: James Clarke.

— (1963), The Catholic Epistles in Works of Martin Luther, Vol. 30, St Louis: Concordia.

LYNCH, J. E. Hazlett (2015), Lamb Of God – Saviour Of The World: The Soteriology Of Rev. Dr David Martyn Lloyd–Jones, Bloomington: WestBow Press.

MULLER, RICHARD, A. (2000), The Unaccommodated Calvin, Oxford, OUP.

— (2003), Post Reformation Reformed Dogmatics, Grand Rapids, Michigan: Baker Book House.

— (2012), Calvin and the Reformed Tradition, Grand Rapids, Michigan: Baker Academic.

— (2014), 'Beyond Hypothetical Universalism: Moïse Amyraut (1596–1664) on Faith, Reason and Ethics' in Martin I. Klauber (ed.), The Theology of the French Reformed Churches from Henri IV to the Revocation of the Edict of Nantes, Grand Rapids, Michigan: Reformation Heritage Books.

NICOLE, ROGER (1986), Moyse Amyraut (1596–1664) and the Controversy on Universal Grace, Unpublished PhD thesis, Harvard University.

NUTTALL, GEOFFREY F. (1965), Richard Baxter, London: Thomas Nelson.

PRESTWICH, MENNA (1987), 'The Huguenots under Richelieu and Mazarin, 1629–61: A Golden Age?' in Irene Scouloudi (ed.), Huguenots in Britain and their French Background, 1550–1800, London: Macmillan.

QUICK, JOHN (1692), Synodicon in Gallia Reformata , Vol. 2, London.

— (1700), Icones Sacrae Gallicanae, DWL 6, 38–39 (35), London: Dr Williams's Library.

RAINBOW, JONATHAN (1990), The Will of God and the Cross, Allison Park, Pennsylvania: Pickwick Publications.

RYLE, JOHN C. (2014), Ryle on Redemption, Alan C. Clifford (ed.), Norwich: Charenton Reformed Publishing.

SCHAFF, PHILIP (1877a), The Creeds of the Evangelical Protestant Churches, London: Hodder and Stoughton.

— (1877b), http://biblehub.com/library/various/creeds_of_christendom_with_a_history_ and_critical_notes/_45_the_form_of.htm.

— (1877c), Christian Classics Ethereal Library, http://www.ccel.org/ccel/schaff/creeds1.- viii.vii.html.

STAUFFER, RICHARD (1962), Moïse Amyraut: Un Précurseur français de l'oecuménisme, Paris: Librarie protestante.

STREHLE, STEPHEN A. (1980), 'The Extent of the Atonement within the Theological Systems of the Sixteenth and seventeenth Centuries', Unpublished PhD dissertation, Dallas Theological Seminary.

TREASURE, GEOFFREY (2013), The Huguenots, New Haven: Yale University Press.

VAN STAM, F. P. (1988), The Controversy over the Theology of Saumur, 1635–1650: Disrupting Debates among the Huguenots in Complicated Circumstances, Amsterdam & Maarsen: APA–Holland University Press.

WAKEMAN, HENRY O. (1959), The Ascendancy of France, 1598–1715, London: Rivingtons.

WILLIAMS, GARRY J. (2013), 'Punishment God Cannot Twice Inflict' in From Heaven He Came and Sought Her, Wheaton, Illinois: Crossway.

Author Bios

Jordan J. Ballor, Dr. theol., PhD, is a senior research fellow at the Acton Institute for the Study of Religion & Liberty, where he also serves as director of publishing. He is the author of three books, including *Covenant, Causality, and Law: A Study in the Theology of Wolfgang Musculus* (Vandenhoeck & Ruprecht, 2012), and editor of many other works, including *Law and Religion: The Legal Teachings of the Catholic and Protestant Reformations* (Vandenhoeck & Ruprecht, 2014). He is also associate director of the Junius Institute for Digital Reformation Research at Calvin Theological Seminary in Grand Rapids, Michigan, USA, and a general editor of Sources in Early Modern Economics, Ethics, and Law (CLP Academic) and Abraham Kuyper Collected Works in Public Theology (Lexham Press).

Jon Balserak, PhD, is Senior Lecturer in Early Modern Religion at University of Bristol (UK) and also a Visiting Scholar at University of Illinois at Chicago (USA). He has published on the Renaissance and Reformation. His most recent publications include *John Calvin as Sixteenth Century Prophet* (OUP, 2014) and *Calvinism: A Very Short Introduction* (OUP, 2016).

Emidio Campi, Dr. Dr. h.c. is Professor Emeritus of Church History at the University of Zurich. He has written extensively on Peter Martyr Vermigli, the Swiss Reformation, and the wider dissemination of the early modern Reformed tradition. He has been Visiting Professor at various universities in the United States, Europe, Middle East, and South Korea. His most recent authored and edited books include *Consensus Tigurinus* (Theologischer Verlag, 2009), *La Battaglia delle vocali* (Dehoniane, 2013), *Shifting Patterns of Reformed Tradition* (Vandenhoeck & Ruprecht, 2014), *Companion to the Swiss Reformation* (Brill, 2016, with Amy Burnett). He is co-editor of the *Peter Martyr Vermigli Library, Reformed Historical Theology,* and *Reformierte Bekenntnisschriften.* He serves on the Editorial Board of *Zwingliana, Reformation & Renaissance Review, Bollettino Società di Studi Valdesi.* He is a member of several scholarly societies.

Alan Clifford, MLitt, PhD is Pastor of Norwich Reformed Church, UK. His thesis *Atonement and Justification* (on John Owen and John Wesley) was published by Oxford University Press in 1990. Among other works published by Charenton Reformed Publishing are *The Good Doctor* (2002), a biography of the Non-conformist pastor and theologian Philip Doddridge, and the life of the Welsh Calvinistic Methodist *John Jones Talsarn, The People's Preacher* (2013). Until recently, he served for many years as a consulting editor for *The Evangelical Quarterly.* Currently engaged in a study of Richard Baxter, his present contribution reflects his ongoing interest in Huguenot history and theology.

Dr Hywel Clifford is the Director of Biblical Studies, and the Tutor in Old Testament, at Ripon College Cuddesdon, Oxford, and a member of the University of Oxford's Faculty of Theology and Religion. Hywel is also a member of SBL, SOTS, and EABS. Hywel has published on Amos, Isaiah 40–55, and Philo of Alexandria. Hywel edited and contributed to *Companion to the Old Testament: Introduction, Interpretation, Application* (2016). Hywel's areas of interest are monotheism, early Greek philosophy, the history of biblical interpretation, and the archaeology of biblical lands.

Dr. Rebecca A. Giselbrecht, PhD, is Director of the Center for the Academic Study of Christian Spirituality and Mandated Teaching Staff at the University of Zurich, Switzerland; and Professor of the History of Christianity and Spirituality at Fuller Theological Seminary, Pasadena. Her recent publications include *Sacrality and Materiality: Locating Intersections*, V&R Publishing, *Hör nicht auf zu singen: Zeuginnen der Schweizer Reformation*, TVZ Zurich. Her current research explores secular and Christian methodology to develop a common language for spiritual formation; editing and translating a book of prayers and the letters of a sixteenth-century noblewomen from Alsace. She is on the editorial board of the Journal *Spiritus.*

Pierrick Hildebrand, MTh, is *PhD candidate and assistant at the Swiss Reformation Studies Institute* at the theological faculty of the University of Zurich (Switzerland). He is working on a dissertation on the historical-theological beginnings of Reformed covenant theology. Articles on Zwingli and Bullinger have already been or about to be published. He is also a contributing editor of *Heinrich Bullinger Werke* as well as of the *Documents of the Synod of Dordrecht 1618/19.*

Stefan Lindholm, PhD, is a pastor in the Lutheran Church of Sweden and has formerly worked at L'Abri Fellowship, in England and Sweden. He is editor for the peer-reviewed journal, *Theofilos* (NLA University College, Norway) and has lectured in theology and philosophy of religion at Johannelund Theological

Seminary, Linköping University and Stockholm School of Theology (Sweden). He is the author of *Jerome Zanchi (1516–90) and the Analysis of Reformed Scholastic Christology* (Vandenhoeck & Ruprecht).

Joe Mock, PhD, ministers at Ashfield Presbyterian Church, Sydney, Australia. He has published articles on Bullinger and Calvin.

Jim West, ThD, is *Lecturer in Reformation History and Biblical Studies* at Ming Hua Theological College. He also serves as the Pastor of Petros Baptist Church, Petros Tennessee, USA. He has published a *Commentary on the Bible* (Quartz Hill Publishing House) and across the spectrum of Biblical studies (with Equinox and Bloomsbury, among others), as well as translations of several of Huldrych Zwingli's works. Additionally, he serves on the Editorial Board of the *Copenhagen International Seminar Series* and the *Scandinavian Journal of the Old Testament*. He holds memberships in several professional academic societies.

Reformed Historical Theology (RHT)

V&R Academic
Verlagsgruppe Vandenhoeck & Ruprecht | V&R unipress

www.v-r.de

Reformed Historical Theology (RHT)

V&R Academic
Verlagsgruppe Vandenhoeck & Ruprecht | V&R unipress

www.v-r.de